Frommer's Po

Puerto Vallarta, Manzanillo & Guadalajara

8th Edition

by David Baird &
Shane Christensen

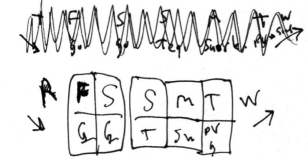

WILEY

John Wiley & Sons, Inc.

Published by:

JOHN WILEY & SONS, INC.

111 River St.

Hoboken, NJ 07030-5774

ISBN 978-1-118-09326-9 (paper); ISBN 978-1-118-16988-9 (ebk);
ISBN 978-1-118-16989-6 (ebk); ISBN 978-1-118-16990-2 (ebk)

Editor: Andrea Kahn
Production Editor: Eric T. Schroeder
Cartographer: Guy Ruggiero
Photo Editor: Richard Fox
Production by Wiley Indianapolis Composition Services
Front cover photo: Playa Mismaloya, south of Puerto Vallarta. ©Mexico /
Alamy Images

For information on our other products and services or to obtain technical support,
please contact our Customer Care Department within the U.S. at 877/762-2974,
outside the U.S. at 317/572-3993 or fax 317/572-4002.

Wiley also publishes its books in a variety of electronic formats. Some content that
appears in print may not be available in electronic formats.

Manufactured in the United States of America

5 4 3 2 1

CONTENTS

LIST OF MAPS

ABOUT THE AUTHORS

A writer, editor, and translator, **David Baird** has lived for several years in different parts of Mexico. Now based in Austin, Texas, he spends as much time in Mexico as possible.

A former resident of Mexico City, **Shane Christensen** has written various Frommer's guides to Mexico. He is also the author of *Frommer's Dubai* and *Frommer's Grand Canyon*. Though he's a California native, he considers himself Mexican at heart and returns to Mexico at every chance he gets.

HOW TO CONTACT US

In researching this book, we discovered many wonderful places—hotels, restaurants, shops, and more. We're sure you'll find others. Please tell us about them, so we can share the information with your fellow travelers in upcoming editions. If you were disappointed with a recommendation, we'd love to know that, too. Please write to:

Frommer's Portable Puerto Vallarta,
Manzanillo & Guadalajara, 8th Edition
John Wiley & Sons, Inc. • 111 River St. • Hoboken, NJ 07030-5774

ADVISORY & DISCLAIMER

Travel information can change quickly and unexpectedly, and we strongly advise you to confirm important details locally before traveling, including information on visas, health and safety, traffic and transport, accommodations, shopping, and eating out. We also encourage you to stay alert while traveling and to remain aware of your surroundings. Avoid civil disturbances, and keep a close eye on cameras, purses, wallets, and other valuables.

While we have endeavored to ensure that the information contained within this guide is accurate and up-to-date at the time of publication, we make no representations or warranties with respect to the accuracy or completeness of the contents of this work and specifically disclaim all warranties, including without limitation warranties of fitness for a particular purpose. We accept no responsibility or liability for any inaccuracy or errors or omissions, or for any inconvenience, loss, damage, costs, or expenses of any nature whatsoever incurred or suffered by anyone as a result of any advice or information contained in this guide.

The inclusion of a company, organization, or website in this guide as a service provider and/or potential source of further information does not mean that we endorse them or the information they provide. Be aware that information provided through some websites may be unreliable and can change without notice. Neither the publisher nor author shall be liable for any damages arising herefrom.

FROMMER'S STAR RATINGS, ICONS & ABBREVIATIONS

Every hotel, restaurant, and attraction listing in this guide has been ranked for quality, value, service, amenities, and special features using a **star-rating system.** In country, state, and regional guides, we also rate towns and regions to help you narrow down your choices and budget your time accordingly. Hotels and restaurants are rated on a scale of zero (recommended) to three stars (exceptional). Attractions, shopping, nightlife, towns, and regions are rated according to the following scale: zero stars (recommended), one star (highly recommended), two stars (very highly recommended), and three stars (must-see).

In addition to the star-rating system, we also use **seven feature icons** that point you to the great deals, in-the-know advice, and unique experiences that separate travelers from tourists. Throughout the book, look for:

special finds—those places only insiders know about

fun facts—details that make travelers more informed and their trips more fun

kids—best bets for kids and advice for the whole family

special moments—those experiences that memories are made of

overrated—places or experiences not worth your time or money

insider tips—great ways to save time and money

great values—where to get the best deals

The following abbreviations are used for credit cards:

AE	American Express	DISC	Discover	V	Visa
DC	Diners Club	MC	MasterCard		

TRAVEL RESOURCES AT FROMMERS.COM

Frommer's travel resources don't end with this guide. Frommer's website, **www.frommers.com**, has travel information on more than 4,000 destinations. We update features regularly, giving you access to the most current trip-planning information and the best airfare, lodging, and car-rental bargains. You can also listen to podcasts, connect with other Frommers.com members through our active-reader forums, share your travel photos, read blogs from guidebook editors and fellow travelers, and much more.

PLANNING YOUR TRIP TO MID-PACIFIC MEXICO

by Shane Christensen

Along the Pacific coast of Mexico, palm-studded jungles sweep down to meet the deep blue of the Pacific Ocean, providing a spectacular backdrop for the region's resort cities and smaller coastal villages. This lovely stretch of coastline, which extends from Puerto Vallarta down to Manzanillo, is known as the Mexican Riviera. Modern hotels, easy air access, and a growing array of activities and adventure-tourism attractions have transformed this region into one of Mexico's premier resort destinations. And for those who would like to explore the inland portion of the region, the bustling city of Guadalajara, home to some of Mexico's greatest artisans and mariachis, is only a few hours' drive away.

Travelers to Mexico should be aware of security concerns in certain parts of the country and take precautions to maximize their safety. For the most part, mid-Pacific Mexico is safe for travelers who steer clear of drugs and those who sell them, but visitors should still exercise caution in unfamiliar areas and remain aware of their surroundings at all times. For detailed information about safety concerns and precautions, see "Crime & Safety" (p. 24). Also visit the U.S. State Department's website, www.travel.state.gov, for up-to-date information on travel to Mexico.

For additional assistance in planning your trip and for on-the-ground resources in mid-Pacific Mexico, please see chapter 7, "Fast Facts."

THE REGION IN BRIEF

Puerto Vallarta, with its traditional Mexican architecture and gold-sand beaches bordered by jungle-covered mountains, is one of the most visited resort cities in Mexico. Although it has grown rapidly in recent years, Vallarta (as the locals refer to it) has managed to preserve its small-town charm. Just north of Puerto Vallarta is **Punta Mita,** home of the first Four Seasons resort in Latin America and a Jack Nicklaus golf course.

One of Mexico's most active commercial ports, **Manzanillo** is surprisingly relaxed, and also offers great fishing and golf. And along the **Costa Alegre,** between Puerto Vallarta and Manzanillo, pristine coves are home to unique luxury and value-priced resorts that cater to travelers seeking seclusion and privacy.

For a more traditional Mexican experience, head inland over the mountains to **Guadalajara,** Mexico's second-largest city and the birthplace of many of the country's traditions.

International airports at Puerto Vallarta, Manzanillo, and Guadalajara make getting to this region relatively easy; Guadalajara and Puerto Vallarta have the most frequent connections. Distances in the region are easily managed by car and the roads are in generally good condition. **Barra de Navidad,** for example, is so close to Manzanillo that it's easy to combine several days there with a stay in Manzanillo. Outside Puerto Vallarta, **Bucerías, Yelapa, San Sebastian,** and **Sayulita** all offer a change of pace and scenery. **Hotelito Desconocido** (p. 100) and **Las Alamandas** (p. 100) are both closer to Puerto Vallarta, while the remainder of the luxury coastal resorts between Manzanillo and Puerto Vallarta are nearer to Manzanillo. Flights to and from Puerto Vallarta are more frequent, however, and many people find that Puerto Vallarta provides the best access to the coastal area.

WHEN TO GO

Seasons

Mexico has two principal travel seasons: high and low. High season begins around December 20 and continues through Easter, although in some places high season can begin as early as mid-November. Low season begins the day after Easter and continues through mid-December; during low season, prices may drop 20% to 50%. In beach destinations, the prices may also increase during the months of July and August, the traditional national summer vacation period. Prices in inland cities, such as Guadalajara, seldom fluctuate from high to low season, but may rise dramatically during Easter and Christmas weeks.

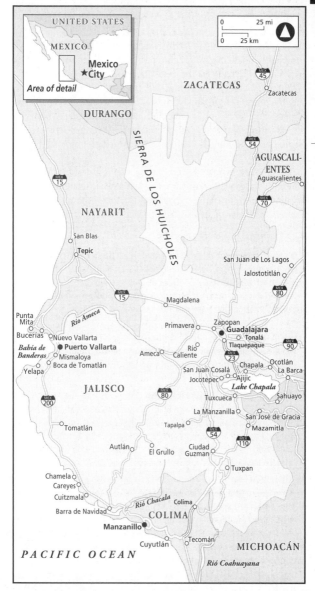

Climate

The region extending from Puerto Vallarta south all the way to Huatulco offers one of the world's most perfect winter climates— dry and balmy with temperatures ranging from the 80s during the day to the 60s at night. Here, you can swim year-round. High mountains shield Pacific beaches from *nortes* (northerns—freezing blasts out of Canada via the Texas Panhandle).

Summers are hot and sunny, with an increase in humidity during the rainy season, between May and October. Rains come almost every afternoon in June and July, and are usually brief but strong—just enough to cool off the air for evening activities. In September, heat and humidity are least comfortable and rains heaviest.

The climate in inland Guadalajara is mostly mild. During the winter, it's a good idea to carry a sweater when going out in the evenings. In summer, the city receives afternoon showers, although the rest of the day is usually hot and dry.

Calendar of Events

For an exhaustive list of events beyond those listed here, check http://events.frommers.com, where you'll find a searchable, up-to-the-minute roster of what's happening in cities all over the world.

During national holidays, Mexican banks and governmental offices— including immigration—are closed.

JANUARY

New Year's Day (Año Nuevo). National holiday. Parades, religious observances, parties, and fireworks welcome the New Year everywhere. January 1.

Three Kings' Day (Día de los Reyes). Commemorates the Three Kings' bringing of gifts to the Christ Child. Children receive gifts, and friends and families gather to share the *Rosca de Reyes,* a special cake. Inside the cake is a small doll representing the Christ Child; whoever receives the doll in his or her piece must host a tamales and atole party the next month. January 6.

FEBRUARY

Candlemas (Día de la Candelaria). Music, dances, processions, food, and other festivities lead up to a blessing of seed and candles, a ritual that mixes pre-Hispanic and European traditions marking the end of winter. All those who attended the Three Kings' Celebration reunite to share atole and tamales at a party hosted by the recipient of the doll found in the Rosca. February 2.

Día de la Constitución (Constitution Day), nationwide. This national holiday is in honor of the current Mexican constitution, signed in 1917 as a result of the revolutionary war of 1910. It's celebrated through small parades. February 5.

Carnaval. Carnaval takes place the 3 days preceding Ash Wednesday and the start of Lent.

Ash Wednesday. The start of Lent and time of abstinence. It's a day of reverence nationwide, but some towns honor it with folk dancing and fairs. Lent begins on February 22 in 2012 and February 13 in 2013.

MARCH

Benito Juárez's Birthday. This national holiday celebrating one of Mexico's most beloved leaders is observed through small hometown celebrations. March 21.

APRIL

Holy Week (Semana Santa). Celebrates the last week in the life of Christ, from Palm Sunday to Easter Sunday, with somber religious processions almost nightly, spoofings of Judas, reenactments of specific biblical events, and food and crafts fairs. Businesses close during this week of Mexican national vacations.

If you plan on traveling to or around Mexico during Holy Week, make your reservations early. Airline seats on flights in and out of the country are reserved months in advance. Buses to almost anywhere in Mexico will be full, so try arriving on the Wednesday or Thursday before Good Friday. Easter Sunday is quiet.

MAY

Labor Day (May Day). Nationwide parades; everything closes. May 1.

Holy Cross Day (Día de la Santa Cruz). Workers place a cross on top of unfinished buildings and celebrate with food, bands, folk dancing, and fireworks around the work site. May 3.

Cinco de Mayo. A national holiday that celebrates the defeat of the French in the Battle of Puebla. May 5.

Feast of San Isidro, nationwide. A blessing of seeds and work animals honors the patron saint of farmers. May 15.

Restaurant Week, Puerto Vallarta. In this resort city known as having the best restaurants in the country after Mexico City, some 40 participating restaurants offer fixed-price tasting menus for discounts of up to 50%. For more details, visit www.virtualvallarta.com/restaurantweek. Mid- to late May.

JUNE

Día de la Marina (Navy Day), various towns. All coastal towns celebrate the holiday, with naval parades and fireworks. June 1.

Corpus Christi. This day, celebrated nationwide, honors the Body of Christ (the Eucharist) with processions, Masses, and food. *Mulitas* (mules), handmade from dried cornhusks and painted, are traditionally sold outside all churches on that day to represent a prayer for fertility.

Dates vary, but celebrations take place on the Thursday following "Holy Trinity" Sunday.

National Ceramics Fair and Fiesta, Tlaquepaque. This pottery center outside Guadalajara hosts crafts demonstrations and contests, mariachis, dancers, and parades. June 14.

Día de San Pedro (St. Peter and St. Paul's Day). Celebrated wherever St. Peter is the patron saint, and honors anyone named Pedro or Peter. It's especially festive at San Pedro Tlaquepaque, near Guadalajara, with numerous mariachi bands, folk dancers, and parades with floats. In Mexcatitlan, Nayarit, shrimpers hold a regatta to celebrate the season opening. June 29.

AUGUST

Assumption of the Virgin Mary. This day is celebrated throughout the country with special Masses and, in some places, with processions. August 15 to August 17.

International Mariachi Festival, Guadalajara. Public mariachi concerts, with groups from around the world (even Japan!). Workshops and lectures are given on the history, culture, and music of the mariachi. Late August to early September.

SEPTEMBER

Independence Day. Celebrates Mexico's independence from Spain. A day of parades, picnics, and family reunions throughout the country. At 11pm on September 15, the president of Mexico gives the famous independence *grito* (shout) from the National Palace in Mexico City, which is duplicated by every *presidente municipal* (mayor) in every town plaza in Mexico. Guadalajara and Puerto Vallarta have great parties in the town plaza on the nights of September 15 and 16.

OCTOBER

Fiestas de Octubre (October Festivals), Guadalajara. This "most Mexican of cities" celebrates for a whole month with its mariachi music trademark. A bountiful display of popular culture and fine arts, and a spectacular spread of traditional foods, Mexican beers, and wines all add to the celebration. All month.

Día de la Raza ("Ethnicity Day," or Columbus Day). This day commemorates the fusion of the Spanish and Mexican peoples. October 12.

NOVEMBER

Day of the Dead. The Day of the Dead is actually 2 days, All Saints' Day (honoring saints and deceased children) and All Souls' Day (honoring deceased adults). Relatives gather at cemeteries carrying candles and food, and often spend the night beside the graves of loved ones. Weeks before, bakers begin producing bread shaped like mummies or round loaves decorated with bread "bones." Decorated sugar skulls emblazoned with glittery names are sold everywhere. Many days ahead, homes and churches erect special altars laden with Day of the Dead bread, fruit, flowers, candles, and favorite foods and photographs of saints and of the deceased. Children, dressed in costumes and masks, carry mock coffins and pumpkin lanterns through the streets at night, expecting people to drop money in them. November 1 and 2.

Gourmet Festival, Puerto Vallarta. In this culinary capital of Mexico, chefs from around the world join local restaurateurs to create special menus, as well as host wine and tequila tastings, cooking classes, gourmet food expos, and other special events. Dates vary; contact the Tourism Board (© **888/384-6822** in the U.S.; www.festivalgourmet.com) for a schedule. Mid-November.

Revolution Day. Commemorates the start of the Mexican Revolution in 1910 with parades, speeches, rodeos, and patriotic events. November 20.

DECEMBER

Puerto Vallarta Film Festival, Puerto Vallarta. Featuring a wide range of North American independent and Latin American productions, this elaborate event includes galas, art expos, and concerts, with celebrity attendees. Check local calendars or visit www.rivieranayarit.com for details. First week of December.

Feast of the Virgin of Guadalupe. Throughout the country, the patroness of Mexico is honored with religious processions, street fairs, dancing, fireworks, and Masses. It is one of Mexico's most moving and beautiful displays of traditional culture. The Virgin of Guadalupe appeared to a young man, Juan Diego, in December 1531, on a hill near Mexico City. He convinced the bishop that he had seen the apparition by revealing his cloak, upon which the Virgin was emblazoned. Children dress up as Juan Diego, wearing mustaches and red bandannas. December 12.

In Puerto Vallarta, the celebration begins on December 1 and extends through December 12, with traditional processions to the church for a brief misa (Mass) and blessing. Businesses, neighborhoods, associations, and groups make pilgrimages (called *peregrinaciones*) to the church, where they exchange offerings for a brief blessing by the priest. In the final days, the processions and festivities take place around the clock, with many of the processions featuring floats, mariachis, Aztec dancers, and fireworks. Hotels frequently invite guests to participate in the walk to the church. The central plaza is filled with street vendors and a festive atmosphere, and a major fireworks exhibition takes place on December 12 at 11pm.

Christmas *Posadas.* On each of the 9 nights before Christmas, it's customary to reenact the Holy Family's search for an inn, with door-to-door candlelit processions in cities and villages nationwide. Most business and community organizations host them in place of the northern tradition of a Christmas party. December 15 to December 24.

Christmas. Mexicans extend their celebration of this holiday throughout December, with festivities often lasting from 2 weeks before Christmas through New Year's. Many businesses close, and resorts and hotels fill up. December 24 and 25.

New Year's Eve. As in the rest of the world, New Year's Eve is celebrated with parties and fireworks.

ENTRY REQUIREMENTS
Passports

Citizens from most countries are required to present a valid passport to enter Mexico. As of March 1, 2010, all U.S. citizens, including children, have been required to present a valid passport or passport card for travel beyond the "border zone" into Mexico, with the "border zone" defined as an area within 20 to 30km (12–19 miles) of the United States. (See www.frommers.com/planning for information on how to obtain a passport.)

All U.S. and Canadian citizens traveling by air or sea to Mexico are required to present a valid passport or other valid travel document (see below) to enter or reenter the United States except if returning from a closed-loop cruise. In addition, all travelers, including U.S. and Canadian citizens, attempting to enter the United States by land or sea must have a valid passport or WHTI-compliant document.

Other valid travel documents (known as WHTI-compliant documents) include the new Passport Card and SENTRI, NEXUS, FAST, and the U.S. Coast Guard Mariner Document. Members of the U.S. Armed Forces on active duty traveling on orders are exempt from the passport requirement. U.S. citizens may apply for the limited-use, wallet-size **Passport Card,** available for a cost of about $40. The card is valid only for land and sea travel between the U.S. and Canada, Mexico, the Caribbean region, and Bermuda. As of March 1, 2010, the Mexican Immigration authorities accept the Passport Card for travel into Mexico by air. However, the card is **not** valid for international flights from the U.S. to countries other than Mexico, or to return to the U.S. from countries other than Mexico. This card is available only to U.S. citizens. For more details on application restrictions, see www.getyouhome.gov.

For U.S. citizens and permanent residents returning from Mexico, there is also the new *"Global Entry"* program for frequent travelers (www.globalentry.gov). U.S. Customs and Border Protection (CBP) offers this program for pre-approved, low-risk travelers. Participants' entry to the U.S. is expedited through the use of automated kiosks, available at various airports.

From our perspective, it's easiest just to travel with a valid passport. Safeguard your passport in an inconspicuous, inaccessible place, like a money belt, and keep a copy of the critical pages with your passport number in a separate place. If you lose your passport, visit the nearest consulate of your native country as soon as possible to obtain a replacement. See "Embassies & Consulates," p. 155, for consulate locations in Mexico.

Visas

Citizens from some countries will need a visa to enter Mexico. For detailed information regarding visas to Mexico, visit the website of the **National Immigration Institute** (https://embamex.sre.gob.mx/usa).

American and Canadian tourists are not required to have a visa or a tourist card for stays of 72 hours or less within the border zone (20–30km/12–19 miles from the U.S. border). For travel to Mexico beyond the border zone, all travelers from Australia, Canada, New Zealand, the U.K., and the U.S., as well as several other countries, can get their visas upon arrival. Many other countries require a pre-approved visa, although as of May 1, 2010, non-U.S. citizens with valid U.S. visas may enter Mexico with the U.S. visa, and do not have to obtain a Mexican visa. For the latest requirements, please refer to www.inm.gob.mx/EN/index.php.

Once in Mexico, all travelers must be in possession of a tourist card, also called Tourist Migration Form. This document is provided by airlines or by immigration authorities at the country's points of entry. Be careful not to lose this card, as you will be required to surrender it upon departure and you will be fined if you lose it.

Your tourist card is stamped on arrival. If traveling by bus or car, be sure you obtain such a card at the immigration module located at the border and have it stamped by immigration authorities at the border. If you do not receive a stamped tourist card at the border, you should, upon arrival at your destination within Mexico, go immediately to the closest National Institute of Immigration office and request a tourist card. Travelers who fail to have their tourist card stamped may be fined, detained, or expelled from the country.

An immigration official will determine the number of days you can remain in Mexico. Do not assume that you will be granted the full 180 days. An extension of your stay can be requested for a fee at the National Institute of Immigration of the Ministry of the Interior (www.inm.gob.mx) or its local offices.

If you plan to enter Mexico by car, please see "By Car" in "Getting There," p. 10, for required documents and other regulations.

Note on travel of minors: Mexican law requires that any individual under the age of 18 traveling to or from Mexico without both parents must carry notarized written permission from **each** parent or guardian who is not traveling with the child. This permission must include the name of the parent(s), the name of the child, the name of anyone traveling with the child, and the notarized signature(s) of the absent parent(s). The U.S. Department of State recommends that permission include travel dates, destinations, airlines, and a summary of the circumstances surrounding the travel. The child must be carrying the original letter (not a facsimile or scanned copy), proof of the parent/child relationship (usually a birth certificate or court document), and an original custody decree, if applicable. Contact the Mexican Embassy or closest Mexican Consulate for more information.

Tourism Tax

Mexican authorities impose a tourism tax (approx. $20) on all visitors to Mexico. This fee is normally included in airline ticket prices. Visitors arriving by road (car or bus) will be asked to pay this fee at any bank in Mexico (there is a bank representative at every port of entry). The bank will stamp your tourist card (an "FMT"). Visitors to the northern border zone (20–30km/12–19 miles from the U. S. border) and those entering Mexico by cruise ship are exempt.

For travelers entering Mexico by car at the border of Baja California, note that FMTs are issued only in Tijuana, Tecate, and Mexicali, as well as in Ensenada and Guerrero Negro. If you travel anywhere beyond the frontier zone without the FMT, you could be fined about $40. Permits for driving a foreign-plated car in Mexico are available only in selected towns such as Tijuana, Ensenada, Tecate, Mexicali, and La Paz.

Medical Requirements

No special vaccinations are required for entry into Mexico. For other medical requirements and health-related recommendations, see "Health," p. 21.

GETTING THERE
By Plane

Mexico has dozens of international and domestic airports throughout the country. Among the major airports along the mid-Pacific coast are Acapulco (ACA), Guadalajara (GDL), Manzanillo (ZLO), Mazatlán (MZT), and Puerto Vallarta (PVR). Many flights also connect through Mexico City (MEX). There is one major Mexican airline, Aeroméxico, and a handful of newer, low-cost carriers. For a list of the major international airlines with service to Mexico, see "Airline Websites," p. 162.

📎 Carrying Car Documents

If you bring a car into Mexico, you must carry your temporary car-importation permit, tourist permit, and your proof of Mexican car insurance in the car at all times (note that insurance is a requirement for all cars, not just rentals). The temporary car-importation permit papers are valid for 6 months to a year, while the tourist permit is usually issued for 30 days. When applying for the car-importation permit, it's a good idea to overestimate the time you'll spend in Mexico so if you have to (or want to) stay longer, you'll avoid the hassle of getting your papers extended. Whatever you do, don't overstay either permit. Doing so invites heavy fines, confiscation of your vehicle (which will not be returned), or both. Also remember that 6 months does not necessarily equal 180 days—be sure that you return before the earlier expiration date.

ARRIVING AT THE AIRPORT

Immigration and Customs clearance at Mexican airports is generally efficient. Expect longer lines during peak seasons, but you can usually pass through Immigration and Customs within a half-hour. For more on what to expect at Mexican Customs, see "Customs" (p. 154).

By Bus

Greyhound (*©* **800/231-2222;** www.greyhound.com) and its affiliates offer service from across the United States to the Mexican border, where passengers disembark, cross the border, and buy a ticket for travel into Mexico. Many border crossings have scheduled buses from the U.S. bus station to the Mexican bus station. We list bus arrival information in each applicable section of this book.

By Car

Driving is not the cheapest or safest way to get to Mexico. While driving is a convenient way to see the country, you may think twice about taking your own car south of the border once you've pondered the bureaucracy involved. One alternative is to rent a car once you arrive for touring a specific region. The mid-Pacific coast is a great place to do this. Rental cars in Mexico are generally clean and well maintained, although they are often smaller than rentals in the U.S., may have manual rather than automatic transmission, and are comparatively expensive due to pricey mandatory insurance. Discounts are often available for rentals of a week or longer, especially when you make arrangements in advance online or from the United States. Be careful about estimated online rates, which often fail to include the price of the mandatory insurance. (See "Car Rentals," p. 16, for more details.)

If, after reading the section that follows, you have additional questions or you want to confirm the current rules, call your nearest Mexican consulate or the **Mexican Government Tourist Office** (© 800/446-3942; www.visitmexico.com). Although travel-insurance companies are generally helpful, they may not have the most accurate information. To check on road conditions or to get help with any travel emergency while in Mexico, call the **Green Angels** (© 55/5250-8221, or 078 for emergencies; www. ontheroadin.com/travelinnformation/green_angels_of_mexico. htm), many of whom are English-speaking.

In addition, check with the **U.S. Department of State** (www. state.gov) for warnings about dangerous driving areas.

CAR DOCUMENTS

To drive your car into Mexico beyond 25km (16 miles), you'll need a **temporary car-importation permit,** which is granted after you provide a required list of documents (see below). The permit can be obtained after you cross the border into Mexico through **Banco del Ejército (Banjercito)** officials with Mexican Customs (*aduanas*), or at Mexican consulates in Austin, San Francisco, Phoenix, Albuquerque, Chicago, Houston, Dallas, Los Angeles, Sacramento, and San Bernardino. For more information, call © 877/210-9469 in the U.S. or visit www.banjercito.com.mx.

The following requirements for border crossing were accurate at press time:

o **Passport.**
o **Valid driver's license,** issued outside of Mexico.
o **Current, original car registration and a copy of the original car title.** If the registration or title is in more than one name and not all the named people are traveling with you, a notarized letter from the absent person(s) authorizing use of the vehicle for the trip is required; have it ready. The registration and your credit card (see below) must be in the same name. If the car is leased or rented, be sure to have a copy of the contract.
o **Original immigration documentation.** Likely your tourist card (see "Visas," p. 9).
o **Processing fee and posting of a bond.** You have three options for covering the car-importation fee: Pay $29 at the border, pay $39 in advance at a Mexican Consulate, or pre-pay $49 online at www.banjercito.com.mx. If you apply online, you'll need to wait about 2 weeks before you can go to the Banjercito office to obtain your permit. You will generally need a credit card

to make this payment. Mexican law also requires the posting of a bond at a Banjercito office to guarantee the export of the car from Mexico within a time period determined at the time of the application. For this purpose, American Express, Visa, or MasterCard credit card holders will be asked to provide credit card information; others will need to make a cash deposit of $200 to $400, depending on the make/model/year of the vehicle. In order to recover this bond or avoid credit card charges, travelers must go to any Mexican Customs office immediately before leaving Mexico.

If you receive your documentation at the border, Mexican officials will make two copies of everything and charge you for the copies.

For up-to-the-minute information, contact the *Módulo de Importación Temporal de Automóviles,* part of the Customs office in Nuevo Laredo (*Aduana Nuevo Laredo;* ✆ **867/712-2071**).

Important reminder: Someone else may drive, but the person (or relative of the person) whose name appears on the car-importation permit must *always* be in the car. (If stopped by police, a nonregistered family member driving without the registered driver must be prepared to prove familial relationship to the registered driver—no joke.) Violation of this rule subjects the car to impoundment and the driver to imprisonment, a fine, or both. You can drive a car with a foreign license plate only if you have a foreign (non-Mexican) driver's license.

MEXICAN AUTO INSURANCE (SEGUROS DE AUTO)

Liability auto insurance is legally required of all drivers in Mexico. U.S. insurance is not valid; to be insured in Mexico, you must purchase Mexican insurance. Any party involved in an accident who has no insurance may be sent to jail and have his or her car impounded until all claims are settled. U.S. companies that broker Mexican insurance are commonly found at the border crossing, and several quote daily rates.

You can also buy car insurance through **Sanborn's Mexico Insurance,** 2009 S. 10th, PO Box 52840, McAllen, TX 78505 (✆ **800/222-0158;** fax 800/222-0158 or 956/686-0732; www.sanbornsinsurance.com), for a daily, monthly, or yearly time period. The company has offices at all U.S. border crossings. Its policies cost the same as the competition's do, but you get legal coverage (attorney and bail bonds, if needed), roadside assistance, and for a premium, vandalism protection. You also get a detailed guide for your proposed route. Most of the Sanborn's border offices are open

Point-to-Point Driving Directions Online

You can get point-to-point driving directions in English for anywhere in Mexico from the website of the Secretary of Communica-
tion and Transport. The site will also calculate tolls, distance, and
travel time. Go to http://aplicaciones4.sct.gob.mx/sibuac_internet
and click on "Rutas punto a punto" in the left-hand column. Then
select the English version.

Monday through Friday; a few are staffed on Saturday and Sunday.
AAA auto club (www.aaa.com) also sells insurance.

RETURNING TO THE U.S. WITH YOUR CAR

You *must* return the car documents you obtained when you entered
Mexico when you cross back over the border with your car, or
within 180 days of your departure. (You can cross the border as
many times as you wish within the 180 days.) If the documents
aren't returned, serious fines are imposed (50 pesos for each day
you're late), your car may be impounded and confiscated, or you
may be jailed if you return to Mexico. You can only return the car
documents to a Banjercito official on duty at the Mexican *aduana*
building *before* you cross back into the United States. Some border
cities have Banjercito officials on duty 24 hours a day, but others
do not; some do not have Sunday hours. See www.mexbound.com/
mexican-vehicle-permits.php#hours for a list of office hours.

By Ship

Numerous cruise lines serve Mexico. Some (such as Carnival and
Royal Caribbean) cruise to Puerto Vallarta with likely stops in
Cabo San Lucas and Mazatlán. Others travel to Manzanillo,
Ixtapa/Zihuatanejo, and Acapulco. Several cruise-tour specialists
sometimes offer last-minute discounts on unsold cabins. One such
company is **CruisesOnly** (© **800/278-4737;** www.cruisesonly.
com).

GETTING AROUND
By Plane

Until recently, Mexico had two large private national carriers, but
Mexicana closed operations and filed for bankruptcy in 2010.
Now, only **Aeroméxico** remains (© **800/237-6399** in the U.S.,
or 01-800/021-4000 in Mexico; www.aeromexico.com), in addition
to several low-cost carriers. Aeroméxico offers extensive connections to the United States as well as within Mexico.

Low-cost carriers include **InterJet** (www.interjet.com.mx) and **Volaris** (www.volaris.com.mx). In each applicable section of this book, we mention regional carriers with all pertinent telephone numbers.

Because major airlines may book some regional carriers, check your ticket to see if your connecting flight is on a smaller carrier—they may use a different airport or a different counter.

Mexico charges an **airport tax** on all departures. Passengers leaving the country on international flights pay about $24 or the peso equivalent. It has become a common practice to include this departure tax in your ticket price. Taxes on each domestic departure within Mexico are around $17, unless you're on a connecting flight and have already paid at the start of the flight.

By Car

Many Mexican roads are not up to U.S., Canadian, and European standards of smoothness, hardness, width of curve, grade of hill, or safety markings. Driving at night is dangerous—the roads are rarely lit; trucks, carts, pedestrians, and bicycles usually have no lights; and you can hit potholes, animals, rocks, dead ends, or uncrossable bridges without warning.

The spirited style of Mexican driving sometimes requires keen vision and reflexes. Be prepared for new customs, as when a truck driver flips on his left turn signal when there's not a crossroad for many kilometers. He's probably telling you the road's clear ahead for you to pass.

GASOLINE There's one government-owned brand of gas and one gasoline station name throughout the country—**Pemex** (Petroleras Mexicanas). There are two types of gas in Mexico: *magna,* 87-octane unleaded gas, and *premio,* 93 octane. In Mexico, fuel and oil are sold by the liter, which is slightly more than a quart (1 gal. equals about 3.8L). Many franchise Pemex stations have restroom facilities and convenience stores—a great improvement over the old ones. Gas stations accept both credit and debit cards for gas purchases, and a small tip—5 to 10 pesos—is expected for the standard full-service.

TOLL ROADS Mexico charges relatively high tolls for its network of new toll roads, so they are less used. Generally, though, using toll roads cuts travel time. Older toll-free roads are generally in good condition, but travel times tend to be longer as these roads pass directly through small towns and villages.

BREAKDOWNS If your car breaks down on the road, help might already be on the way. Radio-equipped green repair trucks, run by uniformed English-speaking officers, patrol major highways during daylight hours (usually 8am–6pm). These **Angeles Verdes/ Green Angels** perform minor repairs and adjustments for free, but you pay for parts and materials. To contact them in Mexico, dial ☎ **078.** For more information, see www.sectur.gob.mx.

Your best guide to repair shops is the Yellow Pages. For repairs, look under *Automóviles y Camiones: Talleres de Reparación y Servicio;* auto-parts stores are under *Refacciones y Accesorios para Automóviles.* To find a mechanic on the road, look for the sign TALLER MECANICO. Places called *vulcanizadora* or *llantera* repair flat tires, and it is common to find them open 24 hours a day on the most traveled highways.

MINOR ACCIDENTS When possible, many Mexicans drive away from minor accidents, or try to make an immediate settlement, to avoid involving the police. If the police arrive while the involved persons are still at the scene, the cars will probably be confiscated and both parties will likely have to appear in court. Both parties may also be taken into custody until liability is determined. Foreigners who don't speak fluent Spanish are at a distinct disadvantage when trying to explain their version of the event. Three steps may help the foreigner who doesn't wish to do as the Mexicans do: If you were in your own car, notify your Mexican insurance company, whose job it is to intervene on your behalf. If you were in a rental car, notify the rental company immediately and ask how to contact the nearest adjuster. (You did buy insurance with the rental, right?) Finally, if all else fails, ask to contact the nearest **Green Angel** (☎ **55/5250-8221,** or 078 for emergencies; www.ontheroadin.com/travelinnformation/green_angels_of_ mexico.htm), who may be able to explain to officials that you are covered by insurance. See also "Mexican Auto Insurance *(Seguros de Auto),*" in "Getting There," earlier in this chapter.

CAR RENTALS You'll get the best price if you reserve a car on the Internet. Cars are easy to rent if you are 25 or older and have a major credit card, valid driver's license, and passport with you. Without a credit card, you must leave a cash deposit, usually a big one. One-way rentals are usually simple to arrange, but they are more costly.

Car rental costs are high in Mexico because cars are more expensive. The condition of rental cars has improved greatly over the years, and newer cars are increasingly common. You will pay the least for a manual car without air-conditioning. Prices may be considerably higher if you rent around a major holiday. Also double-check charges for insurance—some companies will increase the insurance rate after several days. Always ask for detailed information about all charges you will be responsible for. Also make sure the vehicle is in good shape and has been properly serviced before driving away.

Car-rental companies often charge a credit card in U.S. dollars.

DEDUCTIBLES Be careful—these vary greatly. Some are as high as $2,500, which comes out of your pocket immediately in case of damage.

INSURANCE Insurance is offered in two parts: **Collision and damage** insurance covers your car and others if the accident is your fault, and **personal accident** insurance covers you and anyone in your car. Note that insurance may be invalid if you have an accident while driving on an unpaved road. Although some international credit cards include as a benefit collision and damage coverage, they almost never include liability.

DAMAGE Inspect your car carefully and note every damaged or missing item, no matter how minute, on your rental agreement, or you may be charged.

By Taxi

Taxis are the preferred way to get around almost all of Mexico's resort areas. Fares for short trips within towns are generally preset by zone, and are quite reasonable compared with U.S. and European rates. For longer trips or excursions to nearby cities, taxis can generally be hired for around $15 to $20 per hour, or for a negotiated daily rate. A negotiated one-way price is usually much less than the cost of a rental car for a day, and a taxi travels much faster than a bus. For anyone who is uncomfortable driving in Mexico, this is a convenient, comfortable alternative. A bonus is that you have a Spanish-speaking person with you in case you run into trouble. Many taxi drivers speak at least some English. For safety reasons, *sitio* (radio) taxis should be used rather than *libre* taxis off the street. Your hotel can assist you with the arrangements.

By Bus

Mexican buses run frequently, are readily accessible, and can transport you almost anywhere you want to go. Taking the bus is common in Mexico, and the executive and first-class coaches can be as comfortable as business class on an airplane. Buses are often the only way to get from large cities to other nearby cities and small villages. Don't hesitate to ask questions if you're confused about anything, but note that little English is spoken in bus stations.

Dozens of Mexican companies operate large, air-conditioned, Greyhound-type (or better) buses between most cities. Classes are *segunda* (second), *primera* (first), and *ejecutiva* (deluxe), which goes by a variety of names. Deluxe buses often have fewer seats than regular buses, show movies, are air-conditioned, and make few stops. Many run express from point to point. They are well worth the few dollars more. In rural areas, buses are often of the school-bus variety, with lots of local color.

Whenever possible, it's best to buy your reserved-seat ticket, often using a computerized system, a day in advance on long-distance routes and especially before holidays.

For each relevant destination, we list bus arrival and contact information. The following website provides reservations and bookings for numerous providers throughout Mexico: www.ticketbus.com.mx/wtbkd/autobus.jsp.

MONEY & COSTS

The currency in Mexico is the peso. Paper currency comes in denominations of 20, 50, 100, 200, and 500 pesos. Coins come in denominations of 1, 2, 5, 10, and 20 pesos, and 20 and 50 **centavos** (100 centavos = 1 peso). The current exchange rate for the U.S. dollar, and the one used in this book, is approximately 12 pesos; at that rate, an item that costs 12 pesos would be equivalent to $1.

THE VALUE OF THE MEXICAN PESO VS. OTHER POPULAR CURRENCIES

Pesos	US$	Can$	UK £	Euro €	Aus$	NZ$
100	8.59	8.26	5.35	6.02	7.98	10.25

Frommer's lists exact prices in the local currency (unless rates are given in U.S. dollars). The currency conversions quoted above were correct at press time. However, rates fluctuate, so before departing consult a currency exchange website such as **www.oanda.com/convert/classic** to check up-to-the-minute rates.

In general, Mexico is considerably cheaper than most U.S. and European destinations, although prices vary significantly depending on the specific location. The most expensive destinations are those with the largest number of foreign visitors, such as Puerto Vallarta. The least expensive are those off the beaten path and in small rural villages. In the major cities, prices vary greatly depending on the neighborhood. As you might imagine, tourist zones tend to be much more expensive than local areas.

Many establishments that deal with tourists, especially in coastal resort areas, quote prices in U.S. dollars. To avoid confusion, they use the abbreviations "Dlls." for dollars and "M.N." (*moneda nacional,* or national currency) or "M.X.P." for Mexican Pesos. **Note:** Establishments that quote their prices primarily in U.S. dollars are listed in this guide with U.S. dollars.

Money Matters

The **universal currency sign ($)** is sometimes used to indicate pesos in Mexico. The use of this symbol in this book, however, denotes U.S. currency.

Getting change is a problem. Small-denomination bills and coins are hard to come by, so start collecting them early in your trip. Shopkeepers and taxi drivers everywhere always seem to be out of change and small bills; that's doubly true in markets. There seems to be an expectation that the customer should provide appropriate change, rather than the other way around.

Don't forget to have enough pesos to carry you over a weekend or Mexican holiday, when banks are closed. Because small bills and coins in pesos are hard to come by in Mexico, U.S. $1 bills are also useful to have on hand for tipping. *Note:* A tip of U.S. coins, which cannot be exchanged into Mexican currency, is of no value to the service provider.

Casas de cambio (exchange houses) are generally more convenient than banks for money exchange because they have more locations and longer hours; the rate of exchange may be the same as at a bank or slightly lower. Before leaving a bank or exchange-house window, count your change in front of the teller. In addition, most major hotels will change money for you.

Large airports have currency-exchange counters that often stay open whenever flights are operating. Though convenient, they generally do not offer the most favorable rates.

The bottom line on exchanging money: Ask first, and shop around. Banks generally pay the top rates.

Banks in Mexico have expanded and improved services. Except in the smallest towns, they tend to be open weekdays from 9am until 5pm, and often for at least a half-day on Saturday. In larger resorts and cities, they can generally accommodate the exchange of dollars (which used to stop at noon) anytime during business hours. Some, but not all, banks charge a 1% fee to exchange traveler's checks. But you can pay for most purchases directly with traveler's checks at the establishment's stated exchange rate. Don't even bother with personal checks drawn on a U.S. bank—the bank will wait for your check to clear, which can take weeks, before giving you your money.

Travelers to Mexico can easily withdraw money from ATMs (*cajeras*) in most major cities and resort areas. The U.S. Department of State recommends caution when you're using ATMs in

A Few Words About Prices

Many hotels in Mexico—except places that receive little foreign tourism—quote prices in U.S. dollars or in both dollars and pesos. Thus, currency fluctuations are unlikely to affect the prices most hotels charge.

Mexico, stating that they should only be used during business hours and in large protected facilities, but this pertains primarily to Mexico City, where crime remains a significant problem. In most resorts in Mexico, the use of ATMs is perfectly safe—just use the same precautions you would at any ATM. However, beware of using ATMs in dubious locations; there have been reports of people having their card numbers "skimmed" (a process through which information is copied and money stolen or cards fraudulently charged). The ATM exchange rate is generally more favorable than at *casas de cambio*. Most machines offer Spanish/English menus and dispense pesos, but some offer the option of withdrawing U.S. dollars.

In Mexico, Visa, MasterCard, and American Express are the most accepted cards. You'll be able to charge most hotel, restaurant, and store purchases, as well as almost all airline tickets, on your credit card. Most Pemex gas stations now accept credit card purchases for gasoline, though this option may not be available everywhere and often not at night—check before you pump. Generally you receive the favorable bank rate when paying by credit card. However, be aware that some establishments in Mexico add a 5% to 7% surcharge when you pay with a credit card. This is especially true when using American Express. Many times, advertised discounts will not apply if you pay with a credit card.

Beware of hidden credit card fees while traveling. Check with your credit or debit card issuer to see what fees, if any, will be charged for overseas transactions. Recent reform legislation in the U.S., for example, has curbed some exploitative lending practices. But many banks have responded by increasing fees in other areas, including fees for customers who use credit and debit cards while out of the country—even if those charges were made in U.S. dollars. Fees can amount to 3% or more of the purchase price. Check with your bank before departing to avoid any surprise charges on your statement.

For help with currency conversions, tip calculations, and more, download Frommer's convenient Travel Tools app for your mobile device. Go to http://frommers.com/go/mobile and click on the Travel Tools icon.

WHAT THINGS COST IN MEXICO	PESOS (US$ WHERE INDICATED)
Puerto Vallarta beachfront double room, expensive	US$250
Manzanillo beachfront double room, moderate	US$120
Guadalajara double room, moderate	US$110
Puerto Vallarta dinner for one, moderate	200–300
Manzanillo dinner for one, moderate	100–150
Guadalajara dinner for one, moderate	100–200
Tacos from market or street vendor	20–30
Puerto Vallarta canopy tour	US$75
Admission to most archaeological sites	50
Night dancing in Puerto Vallarta	US$40

HEALTH

For the latest information on health risks when traveling to Mexico, and what to do if you get sick, consult the **U.S. State Department**'s website (www.travel.state.gov), the **CDC**'s website (www. cdc.gov), or the website of the **World Health Organization** (www.who.int).

In most of Mexico's resort destinations, you can find health care that meets U.S. standards. Care in more remote areas is limited. Standards of medical training, patient care, and business practices vary greatly among medical facilities in beach resorts throughout Mexico. Puerto Vallarta has first-rate hospitals, for example, but smaller cities along the Pacific Coast often do not. In recent years, some U.S. citizens have complained that certain healthcare facilities in beach resorts have taken advantage of them by overcharging or providing unnecessary medical care. On the other hand, Mexican doctors often spend more time with patients than doctors do north of the border, and may be just as good for less cost.

Prescription medicine is broadly available at Mexico pharmacies, and many drugs that require a prescription in the U.S. can be obtained in Mexico simply by asking. However, be aware that you may still need a copy of your prescription or to obtain a prescription from a local doctor.

SUN/ELEMENTS/EXTREME WEATHER EXPOSURE

Mexico is synonymous with sunshine; much of the country is bathed in intense sunshine for much of the year. Avoid excessive exposure, especially in the Tropics where UV rays are more dangerous. The hottest months on the Pacific Coast are in summer (June–Aug), but the sun is intense throughout most of the year.

DIETARY RED FLAGS   Travelers' diarrhea—often accompanied by fever, nausea, and vomiting—used to attack many travelers to Mexico. (Some in the U.S. call this "Montezuma's revenge," but you won't hear it called that in Mexico.) Widespread improvements in infrastructure, sanitation, and education have greatly diminished this ailment, especially in well-developed resort areas. Most travelers make a habit of drinking only bottled water, which also helps to protect against unfamiliar bacteria. In resort areas, and generally throughout Mexico, only purified ice is used. If you do come down with this ailment, nothing beats Pepto Bismol, readily available in Mexico. Imodium is also available in Mexico and is used by many travelers for a quick fix. A good high-potency (or "therapeutic") vitamin supplement and even extra vitamin C can help; yogurt is good for healthy digestion.

Since dehydration can quickly become life-threatening, be careful to replace fluids and electrolytes (potassium, sodium, and the like) during a bout of diarrhea. Drink Pedialyte, a rehydration solution available at most Mexican pharmacies, or natural fruit juice, such as guava or apple (stay away from orange juice, which has laxative properties), with a pinch of salt added.

The U.S. Public Health Service recommends the following measures for preventing travelers' diarrhea: **Drink only purified water** (boiled water, canned or bottled beverages, beer, or wine). Choose food carefully. In general, avoid salads (except in first-class restaurants), uncooked vegetables, undercooked protein, and unpasteurized milk or milk products, including cheese. **Choose food that is freshly cooked and still hot.** Avoid eating food prepared by street vendors. In addition, something as simple as clean hands can go a long way toward preventing an upset stomach.

HIGH-ALTITUDE HAZARDS   Travelers to certain regions of Mexico occasionally experience **elevation sickness,** which results from the relative lack of oxygen and the decrease in barometric pressure that characterizes high elevations (more than 1,500m/5,000 ft.). Symptoms include shortness of breath, fatigue, headache, insomnia, and even nausea. At high elevations, it takes about 10 days to acquire the extra red blood corpuscles you need to adjust to the scarcity of oxygen. To help your body acclimate,

Over-the-Counter Drugs in Mexico

Antibiotics and other drugs that you'd need a prescription to buy in the States are often available over the counter in Mexican pharmacies. Mexican pharmacies also carry a limited selection of common over-the-counter cold, sinus, and allergy remedies. Contact lenses can be purchased without an exam or prescription, should you run out.

drink plenty of fluids, avoid alcohol, and don't overexert yourself during the first few days. If you have heart or lung trouble, consult your doctor before flying above 2,400m (7,872 ft.).

BUGS, BITES & OTHER WILDLIFE CONCERNS Mosquitoes and **gnats** are prevalent along the coast and in the Yucatán lowlands. *Repelente contra insectos* (insect repellent) is a must, and you can buy it in most pharmacies. If you'll be in these areas and are prone to bites, bring along a repellent that contains the active ingredient DEET. Another good remedy to keep the mosquitoes away is to mix citronella essential oil with basil, clove, and lavender essential oils. If you're sensitive to bites, pick up some antihistamine cream from a drugstore at home.

Most readers won't ever see an *alacrán* (scorpion). But if one stings you, go to a doctor immediately. The one lethal scorpion found in some parts of Mexico is the *Centruroides,* part of the *Buthidae* family, characterized by a thin body, thick tail, and triangular-shaped sternum. Most deaths from these scorpions happen within 24 hours of the sting as a result of respiratory or cardiovascular failure, with children and elderly people most at risk. Scorpions are not aggressive (they don't hunt for prey), but they may sting if touched, especially in their hiding places (which can include shoes). In Mexico, you can buy scorpion-toxin antidote at any drugstore. It is an injection, and it costs around $25. This is a good idea if you plan to camp in a remote area, where medical assistance can be several hours away. Note that not all scorpion bites are lethal, but a doctor's visit is recommended regardless.

TROPICAL ILLNESSES You shouldn't be overly concerned about tropical diseases if you stay on the normal tourist routes and don't eat street food. However, both dengue fever and cholera have appeared in Mexico in recent years. Talk to your doctor or to a medical specialist in tropical diseases about precautions you should take. You can protect yourself by taking some simple precautions: Watch what you eat and drink; don't swim in stagnant water (ponds, slow-moving rivers, or wells); and avoid mosquito bites by covering up, using repellent, and sleeping under netting.

CRIME & SAFETY

Mexico is one of the world's major tourism destinations and millions of visitors travel here safely each year. Yet drug-related violence and widespread media coverage of Mexico's security issues have had a severe impact on its tourism industry. Mexican drug-trafficking organizations have been engaged in brutal fights against each other for control of trafficking routes, and with the Mexican government, which has deployed military troops and federal police across the country. Much of the worst drug-related violence has occurred in the border region. In an April 2011 Travel Warning, the U.S. Department of State urged U.S. citizens to defer non-essential travel to the states of Michoacán and Tamaulipas, and to parts of Chihuahua (particularly Ciudad Juarez), Coahuila, Durango, Jalisco, San Luis Potosi, Sinaloa, Sonora, and Zacatecas. (In Jalisco, the main areas of concern are the regions bordering Zacatecas and Michoacán, several hours by car from Puerto Vallarta and Guadalajara.)

The Mexican government is working hard to protect visitors to all major tourist destinations, which do not experience anything like the levels of violence and crime reported in the border region and along major drug trafficking routes, mainly in the north. In most places, it's uncommon for foreign visitors to face anything worse than petty crime. The risk of pickpockets and petty theft rises considerably during the high tourist season in winter. Always use common sense and exercise caution when in unfamiliar areas. Leave valuables and irreplaceable items in a safe place, or don't bring them at all. Use hotel safes when available. Avoid driving alone, especially at night. You can generally trust a person whom you approach for help or directions, but be wary of anyone who approaches you offering the same. The more insistent a person is, the more cautious you should be. Stay away from areas where drug dealing and prostitution occur.

The U.S. and Mexico share a border more than 3,000km (nearly 2,000 miles) long and Americans comprise the vast majority of tourists to Mexico. Because of these countries' close geographic and historical relationship, we recommend that all travelers, from the U.S. or elsewhere, refer to the **U.S. Department of State** travel advisories for Mexico (www.travel.state.gov). The U.S. State

safety IN MEXICO: ONE AUTHOR GIVES HIS TWO CENTS

Stories of murder and mayhem have dominated recent headlines about Mexico. Reports of assassinations, kidnappings, and shootouts sell newspapers but are of little help to tourists evaluating travel risks throughout the country. These incidents are newsworthy in that they document the gravity of the problem Mexico faces in gaining control of its borders and ensuring public safety. The best way to understand the risks of traveling to specific regions in Mexico is to read the travel advisories issued by the U.S. State Department (http://travel.state.gov).

The current situation has changed the way I travel in two ways, beyond the usual precautions (not flashing a lot of money, not wearing an expensive watch, keeping aware of my surroundings, and not driving on the highway at night—for reasons that have more to do with practicalities than issues of crime). The changes I've made can be boiled down to two objectives: Avoid being in the wrong place at the wrong time, and avoid the possibility of mistaken identity. The **first** is largely met by not lingering in Mexico's northern border states (including Durango and the interior of Sinaloa). This is where the immense majority of the violence is occurring. The **second** is meant to minimize any risk of being held up or nabbed by kidnappers, and it is achieved by looking as much like a tourist as possible. Kidnappers in Mexico don't target tourists. They target resident foreigners who have family in the country or business people who have associates. They do this because they need someone to demand the ransom from. The risk here is from small-time gangs who act opportunistically. (Serious kidnappers aren't a threat because they won't do anything without planning and surveillance.) In the last few years, small-time gangs have increased. The best way I know of to avoid this risk is not to carry a briefcase or satchel, which is a business symbol. What's more, by hauling around a backpack, you will automatically escape scrutiny because businesspersons in Mexico never use them. The backpack *(mochila)* in Mexico is a strong cultural identifier. It's associated with students and counterculture types, so much so that the word *mochilero* has come to describe hippies.

—David Baird

Department encourages its citizens to stay in well-known tourist destinations and tourist areas with better security, cooperate fully with Mexican military and other law enforcement checkpoints, and provide an itinerary to a friend or family member not traveling with them.

For emergency numbers, see p. 157.

Crime in Resort Towns

Rapes have been reported in a number of resort areas, usually at night or in the early morning. Women should not walk alone late at night. Although this violence is not explicitly targeted at foreign residents or tourists, visitors to resort areas should be vigilant in their personal safety. Armed street crime is a serious problem in all major Mexican cities. Some bars and nightclubs, especially in resort cities, can be havens for drug dealers and petty criminals.

The U.S. State Department offers specific safety and security information for travelers on spring break in Mexico. Visit http://travel.state.gov/travel/cis_pa_tw/spring_break_mexico/spring_break_mexico_5014.html.

Crime Nationwide—Kidnapping

Kidnapping, including the kidnapping of non-Mexicans, continues to occur sporadically across the country. So-called express kidnappings, such as attempts to get quick cash in exchange for the release of an individual, have occurred in almost all of Mexico's large cities and can target the wealthy as well as the middle class. See "Safety in Mexico: One Author Gives His Two Cents," above.

Highway Safety

The travel warning issued by the U.S. State Department in April 2011 advises that violence along Mexican roads and highways is a particular concern in the northern border region. As of press time, U.S. government employees and their families are not permitted to drive from the U.S.-Mexico border to or from the interior of Mexico. Travel by vehicle is permitted between Hermosillo and Nogales. While violent incidents have occurred at all hours of the day and night on toll highways and on secondary roads, they have occurred most frequently at night on isolated roads. Drivers are strongly advised to travel only during daylight hours and to use toll roads. Fully cooperate with all official checkpoints, which have increased greatly in number, when traveling on Mexican highways.

Bus travel should take place during daylight hours on first-class conveyances. Although bus hijackings and robberies have occurred on toll roads, buses on toll roads have a markedly lower rate of incidents than second-class and third-class buses that travel the less secure "free" highways.

Bribes & Scams

As is the case in many countries around the world, there are the occasional bribes and scams in Mexico, targeted at people believed to be naive, such as obvious tourists. For years, Mexico was known as a place where bribes—called *mordidas* (bites)—were expected; however, the country is rapidly changing. Be aware that offering a bribe today, especially to a police officer, is generally considered an insult, and can land you in deeper trouble.

Many tourists have the impression that everything works better in Mexico if you "tip"; however, in reality, this only perpetuates the *mordida* tradition. If you are pleased with a service, feel free to tip. But you shouldn't tip simply to attempt to get away with something illegal or inappropriate—whether it is evading a ticket that's deserved or a car inspection as you're crossing the border.

Whatever you do, **avoid impoliteness;** you won't do yourself any favors if you insult a Mexican official. Extreme politeness, even in the face of adversity, is the rule in Mexico. Throughout the country, gringos have a reputation for being loud and demanding. By adopting the local custom of excessive courtesy, you'll have greater success in negotiations of any kind. Stand your ground, but do it politely.

While traveling in Mexico, you may encounter several types of **scams** that occur throughout the world. One involves some kind of **distraction** or feigned commotion. While your attention is diverted, a pickpocket may make a grab for your wallet (for example). In another common scam, an **unaccompanied child** pretends to be lost and frightened and takes your hand for safety. Meanwhile the child or an accomplice plunders your pockets. A third involves **confusing currency.** A shoeshine boy, street musician, guide, or other individual might offer you a service for a price that seems reasonable—in pesos. When it comes time to pay, he or she tells you the price is in dollars, not pesos. Be very clear on the price and currency when services are involved. Finally, take caution when using **ATMs in deserted locations;** there have been many reports of card numbers being "skimmed" and information copied, money stolen, or cards fraudulently charged.

SPECIALIZED TRAVEL RESOURCES

LGBT TRAVELERS Mexico is a conservative country, with deeply rooted Catholic traditions. Public displays of same-sex affection are rare and still considered surprising for men, especially outside of urban or resort areas. Women in Mexico frequently walk hand in hand, but anything more would cross the boundary of acceptability. However, gay and lesbian travelers are generally treated with respect and should not experience harassment, assuming they give the appropriate regard to local customs.

Things are changing here. On December 21, 2009, Mexico City became the first Latin American jurisdiction to legalize same-sex marriage, and the 14th in the world, after the Netherlands, Belgium, Spain, Canada, South Africa, Norway, Sweden, and six U.S. jurisdictions.

While much of Mexico is socially conservative, Puerto Vallarta is not. Popular with many gay travelers, the city offer gay-friendly accommodations, bars, and activities. For more information, visit the website of **MexGay Vacations** (www.mexgay.com). Information about gay-friendly accommodations is available at www.gay places2stay.com.

TRAVELERS WITH DISABILITIES Mexico is a challenging destination for travelers in wheelchairs or on crutches. At airports, you may encounter steep stairs before finding a well-hidden elevator or escalator—if one exists at all. Airlines will often arrange wheelchair assistance to the baggage area. Porters are generally available to help with luggage at airports and large bus stations, once you've cleared baggage claim.

Mexican airports are upgrading their services, but it is still occasionally necessary to board a plane from a remote position, meaning you either descend stairs to a bus that ferries you to the plane, which you board by climbing stairs, or you walk across the tarmac to your plane and ascend the stairs. Deplaning presents the same problem in reverse.

Escalators (and there aren't many in the country) are often out of order. Stairs without handrails abound. Few restrooms are equipped for travelers with disabilities; when one is available, access to it may be through a narrow passage that won't accommodate a wheelchair or a person on crutches. Many deluxe hotels (the most expensive) now have rooms with bathrooms designed for people with disabilities. Those traveling on a budget should stick with one-story hotels or hotels with elevators. Even so, there will probably still be obstacles somewhere. Generally speaking, no matter where you are, someone will lend a hand, but you may have to ask for it.

FAMILY TRAVEL   Children are considered the national treasure of Mexico, and Mexicans will warmly welcome and cater to your children. Many parents have been reluctant to bring young children into Mexico in the past, primarily due to health concerns, but I can't think of a better place to introduce children to the exciting adventure of exploring a different culture. One of the best destinations for kids is Puerto Vallarta. Hotels can often arrange for a babysitter.

Before leaving, ask your doctor which medications to take along. Disposable diapers cost about the same in Mexico but are of poorer quality. You can get Huggies Supreme and Pampers identical to the ones sold in the United States, but at a higher price. Many stores sell Gerber's baby foods. Dry cereals, powdered formulas, baby bottles, and purified water are easily available in midsize and large cities or resorts.

Cribs may present a problem; only the largest and most luxurious hotels provide them. However, rollaway beds are often available. Child seats or high chairs at restaurants are common.

Consider bringing your own car seat; they are not readily available for rent in Mexico.

To locate accommodations, restaurants, and attractions that are particularly kid friendly, look for the "Kids" icon throughout this guide.

WOMEN TRAVELERS   Women do not frequently travel alone in Mexico, or drive alone on highways. Walking alone on the street can provoke catcalls, and walking alone at night is not advisable except in well-protected tourist areas. I've known women who have had uncomfortable experiences in crowded places such as subways. In general, however, Mexicans are extremely gracious, and will help a woman carry heavy items, open doors, and provide information, among other courtesies.

SENIOR TRAVEL   Mexico is a popular country for retirees. For decades, North Americans have been living indefinitely in Mexico by returning to the border and recrossing with a new tourist permit every 6 months. Mexican immigration officials have caught on, and now limit the maximum time in the country to 6 months within any year. This is to encourage even partial residents to acquire proper documentation.

AIM-Adventures in Mexico, Apartado Postal 31–70, 45050 Guadalajara, Jalisco, is a well-written, informative newsletter for prospective retirees. Subscriptions are $29 in the United States.

Sanborn Tours, 2015 S. 10th St., PO Box 936, McAllen, TX 78505 (© **800/395-8482;** www.sanborns.com), offers a "Retire in Mexico" orientation tour.

STUDENT TRAVEL Because Mexicans consider higher education a luxury rather than a birthright, there is no formal network of student discounts and programs. Most Mexican students travel with their families rather than with other students, so student discount cards are not commonly recognized.

However, more hostels have entered the student travel scene. The website **www.hostels.com/mexico** offers a list of hostels in Puerto Vallarta, Manzanillo, Guadalajara, and many other cities throughout Mexico.

The U.S. State Department also offers information designated specifically for students traveling abroad. Visit www.students abroad.state.gov.

RESPONSIBLE TOURISM

The diverse geography of the Mexican Riviera and its wealth of eco- and adventure-tour options have made it a natural favorite of travelers interested in ecotourism. This stretch of Mexico's Pacific Coast presents one of the country's most ecologically stunning landscapes. The Costa Alegre, extending between Puerto Vallarta and Manzanillo, has been designated an "Ecological Tourism Corridor" by the state of Jalisco. This largely undeveloped coastline includes the spectacular beaches, jungles, and surrounding mountains of Barra de Navidad Bay, Tenacatita Bay, Careyes Coast, Chamela Bay, and the Majahuas Coast, and is home to an ecological reserve protecting the region's land and marine life. The **Hotel Desconocido** (p. 100), located along this coast, is one of Mexico's most prominent ecotourism resorts.

For hands-on activities with local sea life while in Puerto Vallarta, consider **Dolphin Adventure** (p. 70). Hiking, boating, snorkeling, and scuba diving are all popular activities in Puerto Vallarta and the nearby resorts.

AMTAVE (Asociación Mexicana de Turismo de Aventura y Ecoturismo, A.C.) is an active association in Mexico of eco- and adventure-tour operators dedicated to the operation and promotion of ecotourism and adventure travel in Mexico. They publish an annual catalog of participating firms and their offerings, all of which must meet certain criteria for security, and for quality and training of the guides, as well as for sustainability of natural and cultural environments. For more information, contact AMTAVE (𝄢 **55/5544-7567;** www.amtave.org).

Animal-Rights Issues

The Pacific Coast presents many opportunities to swim with dolphins. The capture of wild dolphins was outlawed in Mexico in 2002. The only dolphins added to the country's dolphin swim programs since then were born in captivity. This law may have eased concerns about the death and implications of capturing wild dolphins, but the controversy is not over. Marine biologists who run the dolphin swim programs say the mammals are thriving and that the programs provide a forum for research, conservation, education, and rescue operations. Animal rights advocates maintain that keeping these intelligent mammals in captivity is nothing more than exploitation. Their argument is that these private dolphin programs don't qualify as "public display" under the Marine Mammal Protection Act because the entry fees bar most of the public from participating.

Visit the websites of the **Whale and Dolphin Conservation Society** (www.wdcs.org) and the **American Cetacean Society** (www.acsonline.org) for further discussion on the topic.

Bullfighting is considered an important part of Latin culture, but before you attend a *correo,* you should know that, in all likelihood, the bulls (at least four) will undergo torture, shed lots of blood, and die before a team of horses drags their carcasses unceremoniously out of the ring. There has been strong opposition to bullfighting on ethical grounds, and you may want to do some research on the controversy surrounding this tradition before making the decision to attend a bullfight. That said, these events provide a window into Mexico's Spanish colonial past, and traditional machismo is on full display. Bullfights take place in towns as different as Tijuana and Puerto Vallarta, and they afford a colorful spectacle like no other, with brass bands playing, matadors sporting traditional costume, spectators shaking their heads at less-than-perfect swipes of the cape, and women throwing roses, jackets, and hats at the matadors' feet.

For information on animal rights issues throughout the world, visit **Tread Lightly** (www.treadlightly.org).

GENERAL RESOURCES FOR
green TRAVEL

In addition to the resources for mid-Pacific Mexico listed above, the following websites provide valuable, wide-ranging information on sustainable travel. For a list of even more sustainable resources, as well as tips and explanations on how to travel greener, visit www.frommers.com/planning.

o **Responsible Travel** (www.responsibletravel.com) is a great source of sustainable travel ideas; the site is run by a spokesperson for ethical tourism in the travel industry. **Sustainable Travel International** (www.sustainabletravel international.org) promotes ethical tourism practices, and manages an extensive directory of sustainable properties and tour operators around the world.

o In the U.K., **Tourism Concern** (www.tourismconcern.org.uk) works to reduce social and environmental problems connected to tourism. The **Association of Independent Tour Operators** (**AITO;** www.aito.co.uk) is a group of specialist operators leading the field in making holidays sustainable.

o In Canada, **www.greenlivingonline.com** offers extensive content on how to travel sustainably, including a travel and transport section.

o **Carbonfund** (www.carbonfund.org), **TerraPass** (www.terra pass.com), and the **CoolClimate Network** (http://cool climate.berkeley.edu) provide info on "carbon offsetting,"

SPECIAL-INTEREST TRIPS
Academic Trips & Language Classes

IMAC (© **866/306-5040;** www.spanish-school.com.mx) offers Spanish-language programs in Guadalajara and Puerto Vallarta. For information about studying Spanish in conjunction with a local university in Puerto Vallarta, visit **Spanish Abroad** (© **888/722-7623;** www.spanishabroad.com/puertovallarta.htm).

To explore your inner Frida or Diego while in Mexico, look into **Mexico Art Tours,** 1233 E. Baker Dr., Tempe, AZ 85282 (© **888/783-1331** or 480/730-1764; www.mexicanarttours.com). Typically led by Jean Grimm, a specialist in the arts and cultures of Mexico, these unique tours feature compelling speakers who are themselves respected scholars and artists. Itineraries include visits to Chiapas, Guadalajara, Guanajuato, Mexico City, Puebla, Puerto or offsetting the greenhouse gas emitted during flights.

○ **Greenhotels** (www.greenhotels.com) recommends green-rated member hotels around the world that fulfill the company's stringent environmental requirements. **Environmentally Friendly Hotels** (www.environmentally friendlyhotels.com) offers more green accommodations ratings. The **Green Key Eco-Rating Program** (www.greenkey global.com) audits the environmental performance of Canadian and U.S. hotels, motels, and resorts.

○ **Sustain Lane** (www.sustainlane.com) lists sustainable eating and drinking choices around the U.S.; also visit **www.eat wellguide.org** for tips on eating sustainably in the U.S. and Canada.

○ For information on animal rights issues throughout the world, visit **Tread Lightly** (www.treadlightly.org). For information about the ethics of swimming with dolphins, visit the **Whale and Dolphin Conservation Society** (www.wdcs.org).

○ **Volunteer International** (www.volunteerinternational.org) has a list of questions to help you determine the intentions and the nature of a volunteer program. For general info on volunteer travel, visit www.goabroad.com/volunteer-abroad or www.idealist.org.

Vallarta, San Miguel de Allende, and Veracruz—and other cities. Special tours involve archaeology, architecture, interior design, and culture—such as a Day of the Dead tour.

The **Archaeological Conservancy,** 5301 Central Ave. NE, Ste. 402, Albuquerque, NM 87108 (✆ **505/266-1540;** www.americanarchaeology.com), presents various trips each year, led by an expert, usually an archaeologist. The trips change from year to year and space is limited; make reservations early.

Adventure & Wellness Trips

AMTAVE (Asociación Mexicana de Turismo de Aventura y Ecoturismo, A.C.) is an association of ecotourism and adventure tour operators. For more information, contact AMTAVE (✆ **55/5544-7567;** www.amtave.org).

Food & Wine Trips

If you're looking to eat your way through Mexico, sign up with **Culinary Adventures,** 6023 Reid Dr. NW, Gig Harbor, WA 98335 (www.marilyntausend.com). It runs a short but select list of cooking tours in Mexico. Culinary Adventures features well-known cooks, with travel to regions known for excellent cuisine. Destinations vary each year. The owner, Marilyn Tausend, is the author of *Cocinas de la Familia* (Family Kitchens), *Savoring Mexico,* and *Mexican,* and co-author of *Mexico the Beautiful Cookbook.*

Volunteer & Working Trips

For numerous links to volunteer and internship programs throughout Mexico involving teaching, caring for children, providing health care, feeding the homeless, and participating in other community and public service, visit www.goabroad.com/volunteer-abroad.

TIPS ON ACCOMMODATIONS
Mexico's Hotel Rating System

The hotel rating system in Mexico is called "Stars and Diamonds." Hotels are awarded stars and diamonds based on facilities, hygiene, and service. All rated hotels adhere to strict standards, though many of the best hotels in Mexico are not certified under this system. These are ranked instead according to the internationally recognized AAA diamond rating and Mobil star rating systems.

Hotel Chains

In addition to the major international chains, you'll run across a number of less-familiar brands as you plan your trip to Mexico. They include:

o **Brisas Hotels & Resorts** (www.brisas.com.mx). These were the hotels that originally attracted jet-set travelers to Mexico. Spectacular in a retro way, these properties offer the laid-back luxury that makes a Mexican vacation so unique. Manzanillo has a Las Brisas property, **Brisas Las Hadas Golf Resort & Marina** (p. 116).

o **Fiesta Americana** and **Fiesta Inn** (www.posadas.com). Part of the Mexican-owned Grupo Posadas company, these hotels set the country's midrange standard for facilities and services. They generally offer comfortable, spacious rooms, and traditional

Mexico lends itself beautifully to the concept of small, private hotels in idyllic settings. They vary in style from grandiose estates to palm-thatched bungalows. **Mexico Boutique Hotels** (© 877/278-8018; www.mexicoboutiquehotels.com) specializes in smaller places to stay with a high level of personal attention and service. Most options have fewer than 50 rooms, and the accommodations consist of entire villas, *casitas,* bungalows, or a combination.

Mexican hospitality. Fiesta Americana hotels offer excellent beach-resort packages. Fiesta Inn hotels are usually more business-oriented. Mid-Pacific Mexico's offerings include Fiesta Americana Grand Guadalajara Country Club, the Fiesta Americana Guadalajara, the Fiesta Inn Guadalajara, and the **Fiesta Americana Puerto Vallarta** (p. 48).

○ **Hoteles Camino Real** (www.caminoreal.com). Hoteles Camino Real remains Mexico's premier hotel chain, with beach resorts, city hotels, and colonial inns scattered throughout the country. Its beach hotels are traditionally located on the best beaches in the area. This chain also focuses on the business market. The hotels are famous for their vivid and contrasting colors. In mid-Pacific Mexico, Camino Real has three hotels: the Camino Real Guadalajara, Camino Real Guadalajara Expo, and the Camino Real Manzanillo.

○ **NH Hoteles** (www.nh-hotels.com). The NH hotels are noted for their family-friendly facilities and quality standards. The beach properties' signature feature is a pool, framed by columns, overlooking the sea. NH Hoteles has only one property in mid-Pacific Mexico, the NH Krystal Puerto Vallarta.

○ **Quinta Real Grand Class Hotels and Resorts** (www. quintareal.com). These hotels are noted for architectural and cultural details that reflect their individual regions. At these luxury properties, attention to detail and excellent service are the rule. Quinta Real is the top-line Mexican hotel brand. The only Quinta Real hotel on the mid-Pacific coast is the **Quinta Real Guadalajara** (p. 130).

House Rentals & Swaps

House and villa rentals and swaps are becoming more common in Mexico, but no single recognized agency or business provides this service exclusively for Mexico. In the following chapters, we provide information on independent services that we have found to be reputable.

You'll find the most extensive inventory of homes at **Vacation Rentals by Owner** (**VRBO;** www.vrbo.com). They have thousands of homes and condominiums worldwide, including a large selection in Mexico. Another good option is **VacationSpot** (© **888/903-7768;** www.vacationspot.com), owned by Expedia and a part of its sister company, Hotels.com. It has fewer choices, but the company's criteria for adding inventory is much more selective and often includes on-site inspections. They also offer toll-free phone support.

SETTLING INTO PUERTO VALLARTA

by Shane Christensen

Puerto Vallarta remains my favorite part of this colorful country, for its unrivaled combination of Mexican warmth, international diversity, and artistic charm. The original city center of Vallarta maintains a small-town feel despite its sophisticated hotels, more than 250 restaurants, and active nightlife. Cool breezes flow down from the mountains along the Río Cuale, which runs through the city center. Fanciful public sculptures enhance the extensive contemporary arts scene, with the finest galleries in all of Mexico clustered together along a few small and charming blocks. As the most gay-friendly city in Mexico, Vallarta is as open-minded as it is laid-back, and folks from Mexico and the world over have relocated here, in part, for its cosmopolitan and open orientation.

Some folks come to Puerto Vallarta for its healing effects. Yoga retreats and fine spas have sprung up all over in recent years. There's something spiritual about a stroll along the *malecón* with its ocean breezes, multihued sunsets, and moonlit views of the bay. Peaceful scenic drives extend north and south of the city along oceanside cliffs and through winding jungle terrain. Those here to rest, read, and relax can choose from 26 miles of beaches, many in pristine coves accessible only by boat and framed by the majestic Sierra Madre mountains.

Dining here is delightful. The fresh fish, locally raised meats, and seasonal ingredients inspire Vallarta's many outstanding chefs, boosting the restaurant scene into one of the country's best. Creative Mexican and international dishes explode with flavor, and service is consistently gracious and warm. Wander through downtown Vallarta for fine sidewalk dining as diverse as the city itself. In Viejo Vallarta, you can enjoy a delicious Mexican meal at a casual eatery steps away from an acclaimed international seafood restaurant. You'll find French, Italian, German, and Asian venues tucked between galleries just on the other side of the Río Cuale.

ESSENTIALS
Getting There

BY PLANE   For a list of international carriers serving Mexico, see "Airline Websites" in chapter 7. International carriers serving Puerto Vallarta include **Alaska Airlines** (© **800/252-7522** in the U.S., or 01-800/252-7522 in Mexico), **American Airlines** (© **800/433-7300** in the U.S., or 01-800/904-6000 in Mexico), **US Airways** (© **800/428-4322** in the U.S., or 01-800/428-4322 in Mexico), **Continental** (© **800/523-3273** in the U.S., or 01-800/900-5000 in Mexico), **Delta** (© **800/241-4141** in the U.S., or 01-800/123-4710 in Mexico), **Frontier** (© **800/432-1359** in the U.S.), and **United** (© **800/538-2929** in the U.S., or 01-800/003-0777 in Mexico).

   Aeroméxico (© **800/237-6639** in the U.S., or 01-800/021-4000 in Mexico) flies from Los Angeles, San Diego, Aguascalientes, Guadalajara, La Paz, León, Mexico City, Morelia, and Tijuana.

   Major car-rental agencies at the airport, including **Alamo, Avis, Budget, Dollar/Thrifty,** and **National,** are open after flight arrivals. After you register, they will send a shuttle to take you to the nearby car-rental lots. Daily rates start at about $40.

BY CAR   The coastal Hwy. 200 is the only choice from Mazatlán (6 hr. north) or Manzanillo (3½–4 hr. south). Hwy. 15 from Guadalajara to Tepic takes 6 hours; to save as much as 2 hours, take Hwy. 15A from Chapalilla to Compostela, bypassing Tepic, and then continue south on Hwy. 200 to Puerto Vallarta. Expect a number of official checkpoints on these highways.

BY BUS   The bus station, **Central Camionera de Puerto Vallarta,** is just north of the airport, approximately 11km (6¾ miles) from downtown. It offers overnight guarded parking and baggage storage. Most major first-class bus lines operate from here, including Estrella Blanca, ETN, TAP, Pacifico, Futura, Turistar, Elite, and Primera Plus, with transportation to points throughout Mexico, including Mazatlán (390 pesos), Manzanillo (230 pesos),

Puerto Vallarta: Hotel Zone & Beaches

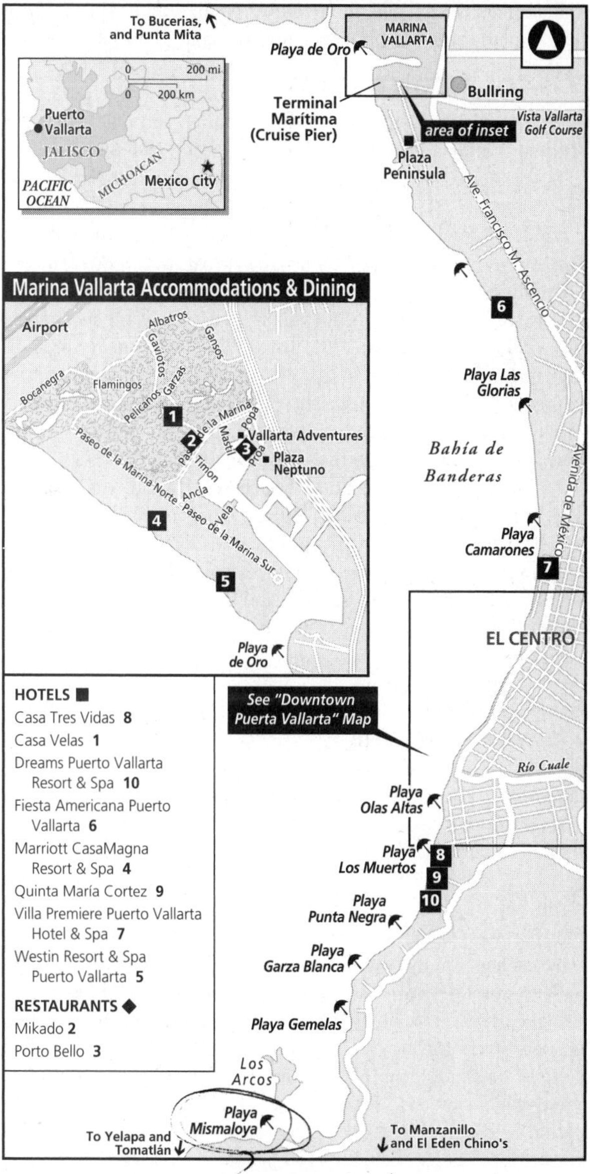

To Bucerias, and Punta Mita
Puerto Vallarta
JALISCO
MICHOACAN
Mexico City
PACIFIC OCEAN
0 200 mi
0 200 km
MARINA VALLARTA
Playa de Oro
Terminal Marítima (Cruise Pier)
Bullring
area of inset
Vista Vallarta Golf Course
Plaza Peninsula
Ave. Francisco M. Ascencio
Marina Vallarta Accommodations & Dining
Airport
Albatros
Gaviotos
Gansos
Bocanegra
Flamingos
Pelicanos
Garzas
Paseo de la Marina
Popa
Mastil
Vallarta Adventures
Proa
Plaza Neptuno
Timon
Ancla
Vela
Paseo de la Marina Norte
Paseo de la Marina Sur
Playa de Oro
Playa Las Glorias
Bahía de Banderas
Avenida de México
Playa Camarones
EL CENTRO
See "Downtown Puerta Vallarta" Map
Río Cuale
Playa Olas Altas
Playa Los Muertos
Playa Punta Negra
Playa Garza Blanca
Playa Gemelas
Los Arcos
Playa Mismaloya
To Yelapa and Tomatlán
To Manzanillo and El Eden Chino's

HOTELS ■

Casa Tres Vidas **8**
Casa Velas **1**
Dreams Puerto Vallarta Resort & Spa **10**
Fiesta Americana Puerto Vallarta **6**
Marriott CasaMagna Resort & Spa **4**
Quinta María Cortez **9**
Villa Premiere Puerto Vallarta Hotel & Spa **7**
Westin Resort & Spa Puerto Vallarta **5**

RESTAURANTS ◆

Mikado **2**
Porto Bello **3**

Guadalajara (350 pesos), Barra de Navidad (185 pesos), and Mexico City (900 pesos). Taxis into town cost approximately $10 and are readily available; public buses operate from 7am to 11pm and regularly stop in front of the arrivals hall.

Visitor Information

Prior to arrival, a useful source of information and publicity is the **Puerto Vallarta Tourism Board** (© **888/384-6822** in the U.S., or 322/224-1175 in Mexico; www.visitpuertovallarta.com). The office is located in the Hotel Canto del Sol in the Zona Comercial Las Glorias. It's open Monday through Friday from 9am to 7pm. If you have questions after you arrive, visit the downtown **Dirección de Turismo** (municipal tourism office) in the corner of the white City Hall building at Juárez and Independencia (© **322/226-8080,** ext. 230), just off the main square. In addition to offering a listing of current events and promotional brochures, the employees can assist with specific questions—there's usually an English speaker on staff. It's open Monday to Saturday from 8am to 8pm, Sunday from 10am to 6pm.

In Marina Vallarta, the **State Tourism Office,** Plaza Marina L 144, 2nd Floor (© **322/221-2676,** -2677, -2678), also offers brochures and can assist with specific questions about Puerto Vallarta and other points in the state of Jalisco, including Guadalajara, Costa Alegre, the town of Tequila, and the program that promotes stays in authentic rural haciendas. It's open Monday through Friday from 9am to 5pm.

Orientation

ARRIVING BY PLANE The airport is close to the north end of town near the Marina Vallarta, about 10km (6¼ miles) from downtown. **Transportes Terrestres Puerto Vallarta** minivans and **Aeromovil** taxis make the trip. They use a zone pricing system, with fares clearly posted at the ticket booths. Fares start at $16 for a ride to Marina Vallarta and go up to $28 for the south shore hotels. Federally licensed airport taxis exclusively provide transportation from the airport, and their fares are more than three times as high as city (yellow) taxi fares. A trip to downtown Puerto Vallarta costs between 200 and 250 pesos, whereas a return trip using a city taxi costs only 120 pesos. Only airport cabs may pick up passengers leaving the airport. You can also buy a ticket for a *colectivo* (a shuttle van that goes every 30 min.) at the official taxi stand which, at only 120 pesos to downtown, is the cheapest option.

Downtown Puerto Vallarta

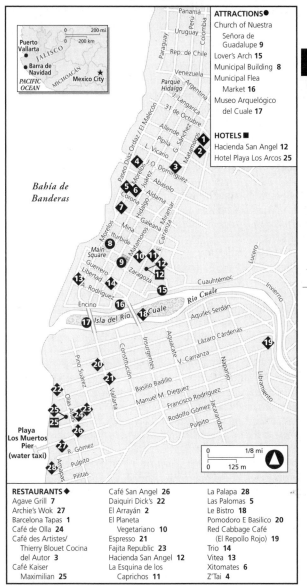

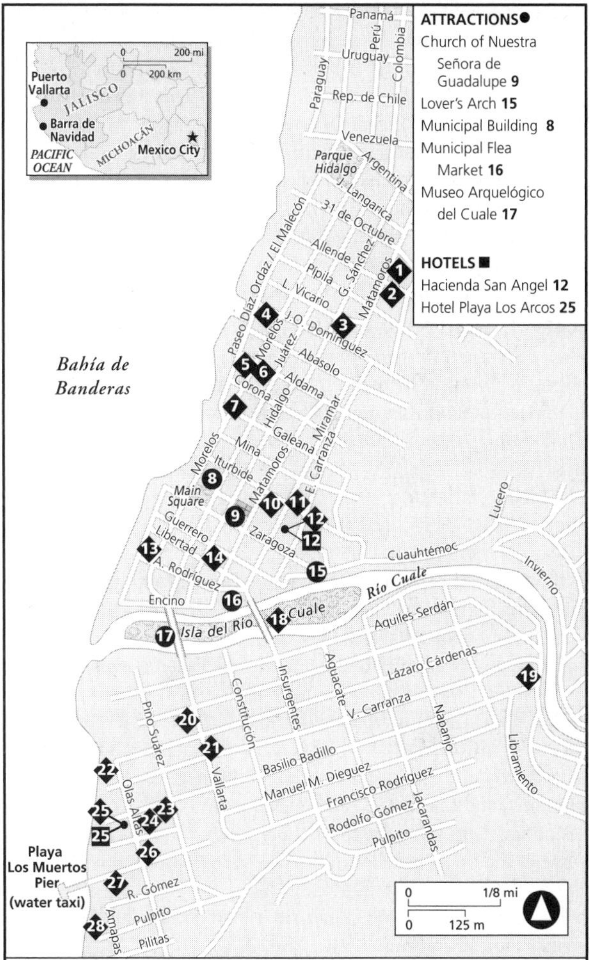
ATTRACTIONS●
Church of Nuestra Señora de Guadalupe 9
Lover's Arch 15
Municipal Building 8
Municipal Flea Market 16
Museo Arquelógico del Cuale 17
HOTELS■
Hacienda San Angel 12
Hotel Playa Los Arcos 25
Puerto Vallarta
JALISCO
Barra de Navidad
MICHOACÁN
Mexico City
PACIFIC OCEAN
0 200 mi
0 200 km
Bahía de Banderas
Playa Los Muertos Pier (water taxi)
Main Square
Parque Hidalgo
Río Cuale
Isla del Río Cuale
Panamá
Perú
Colombia
Uruguay
Paraguay
Rep. de Chile
Venezuela
Argentina
J. Langarica
31 de Octubre
Paseo Díaz Ordaz / El Malecón
Allende
G. Sánchez
Matamoros
Pipila
L. Vicario
J.O. Domínguez
Morelos
Juárez
Abasolo
Corona
Aldama
Hidalgo
Galeana
Miramar
Mina
E. Carranza
Iturbide
Guerrero
Libertad
Zaragoza
A. Rodríguez
Encino
Cuauhtémoc
Lucero
Invierno
Aquiles Serdán
Lázaro Cárdenas
Aguacate
Insurgentes
Constitución
Pino Suárez
V. Carranza
Napanjo
Libramiento
Basilio Badillo
Vallarta
Manuel M. Dieguez
Francisco Rodríguez
Olas Altas
Rodolfo Gómez
Jacarandas
Pulpito
R. Gómez
Amapas
Pilitas
0 1/8 mi
0 125 m

RESTAURANTS ◆

Agave Grill **7**
Archie's Wok **27**
Barcelona Tapas **1**
Café de Olla **24**
Café des Artistes/ Thierry Blouet Cocina del Autor **3**
Café Kaiser Maximilian **25**
Café San Angel **26**
Daiquiri Dick's **22**
El Arrayán **2**
El Planeta Vegetariano **10**
Espresso **21**
Fajita Republic **23**
Hacienda San Angel **12**
La Esquina de los Caprichos **11**
La Palapa **28**
Las Palomas **5**
Le Bistro **18**
Pomodoro E Basilico **20**
Red Cabbage Café (El Repollo Rojo) **19**
Trio **14**
Vitea **13**
Xitomates **6**
Z'Tai **4**

CITY LAYOUT   The seaside promenade, the *malecón,* is a common reference point for giving directions. It's next to **Paseo Díaz Ordaz** and runs north-south through the central downtown area. From the waterfront, the town stretches back into the hills a half-dozen blocks. The areas bordering the **Río Cuale** are the oldest parts of town—the original Puerto Vallarta. The area immediately south of the river, called **Olas Altas** after its main street (and sometimes Los Muertos after the beach of the same name), is home to a growing selection of sidewalk cafes, fine restaurants, espresso bars, and hip nightclubs. In the center of town, nearly everything is within walking distance both north and south of the river. **Bridges** on Insurgentes (northbound traffic) and Ignacio Vallarta (southbound traffic) link the two sections of downtown.

AREA LAYOUT   Beyond downtown, Puerto Vallarta has grown along the beach to the north and south. Linking downtown to the airport is **Avenida Francisco Medina Ascencio,** home of many high-rise hotels (in an area called the **Zona Hotelera,** or Hotel Zone), plus several shopping centers with a variety of dining options.

Marina Vallarta, a resort city within a city, lies at the northern edge of the Hotel Zone, just a few minutes from the airport. It boasts excellent hotels, condominiums, and homes; a huge marina with 450 yacht slips; a golf course; restaurants and bars; and several shopping plazas. Because it was originally a swamp, the beaches are somewhat less desirable, with darker sand and seasonal inflows of cobblestones. The Marina Vallarta peninsula faces the bay and looks south to the town of Puerto Vallarta.

Nuevo Vallarta is a planned resort north of the airport, across the Ameca River in the state of Nayarit (about 13km/8 miles north of downtown). It houses a number of all-inclusive hotels, condominiums, and timeshares, and a yacht marina, with a selection of restaurants and shopping. Most hotels here cater to families, with some of the finest beaches in the bay, but guests usually travel into Puerto Vallarta (about $25 a cab ride) for anything other than poolside or beach action. Regularly scheduled public bus service costs about $2 and runs until 10pm.

Bucerías, a small beachside village of cobblestone streets, villas, excellent seafood restaurants, and just a few art galleries and small hotels, sits farther north along Banderas Bay, 30km (19 miles) beyond the airport. Past Bucerías, following the curved coastline of Banderas Bay, you'll find **La Cruz de Huanaxcle,** a new mega marina project, but still an authentic, colorful seaside town. Continue to the end of the road and you'll reach **Punta Mita.** Once a rustic fishing village, it has been artfully developed as an exclusive luxury destination. Although the fishing village still exists, it has been all but eclipsed by the large gated community of Punta Mita that houses private villas, a few world-class resorts, and two championship golf courses. The site of an ancient celestial observatory, it is an exquisite setting, with white-sand beaches and clear waters. The northern shore of Banderas Bay is emerging as the area's most exclusive address for luxury villas and accommodations, and most of greater Puerto Vallarta's growth is in this direction.

The southern coastal highway stretches south from downtown Vallarta in the direction of Manzanillo and the Costa Alegre. Immediately south of town lies the exclusive residential and rental district of **Conchas Chinas.** Ten kilometers (6¼ miles) south, on **Playa Mismaloya** (where *Night of the Iguana* was filmed), lies the Barceló La Jolla de Mismaloya resort. There's no road on the southern shoreline of Banderas Bay, but three small coastal villages are popular attractions for visitors to Puerto Vallarta: **Las Animas, Quimixto,** and **Yelapa,** all accessible only by boat. The tiny, pristine cove of **Caletas,** site of John Huston's former home, is a popular day- or nighttime excursion (see "Boat Tours" in chapter 3). Dreams Resort also lies south of town at Playa Las Estacas.

Getting Around

BY TAXI   Taxis are plentiful and relatively inexpensive. Most trips from downtown to the northern Hotel Zone and Marina Vallarta cost 65 to 80 pesos; to or from Marina Vallarta to Mismaloya Beach (to the south) costs 195 pesos. Rates are charged by zone and are generally posted in hotel lobbies. Taxis can also be hired by the hour or day for longer trips. Rates run about 200 pesos per hour, with full-day discounts available—consider this an alternative to renting a car.

BY CAR   Rental cars are readily available at the airport, through travel agencies, and through the most popular U.S. car-rental services, but unless you're planning a distant side trip, don't bother. Car rentals are relatively expensive, especially because of insurance rates, and parking around town can be very challenging, unless you opt for one of the two new parking garages constructed on either end of the *malecón* zone (at Park Hidalgo to the north, and adjacent to the northern border of the Cuale River to the south). If you see a sign for a cheap car or jeep rental, be aware that these are lures to get folks to attend timeshare presentations. Unless you are interested in a timeshare, stopping to inquire will be a (possibly annoying) waste of your time.

BY BUS   City buses, easy to navigate and inexpensive, will serve just about all your transportation needs. They run from the airport through the Hotel Zone along Morelos Street (1 block inland from the *malecón*), across the Río Cuale, and inland on Vallarta, looping back through the downtown hotel and restaurant districts on Insurgentes and several other downtown streets. To get to the northern hotel strip from old Puerto Vallarta, take the ZONA HOTELES, IXTAPA, or LAS JUNTAS bus. These buses may also post the names of hotels they pass, such as Krystal, Sheraton, and others. Buses marked MARINA VALLARTA travel inside this area, stopping at the major hotels there.

Other buses operate every 10 to 15 minutes south to either Mismaloya Beach or Boca de Tomatlán (a sign in the front window indicates the destination) from Constitución and Basilio Badillo, a few blocks south of the river. Buses run generally from 6am to 11pm, and it's rare to wait more than a few minutes for one. The fare is about 7 pesos. You do not have to have exact change; the driver will make change.

BY BOAT   The *muelle* (cruise-ship pier), also called Terminal Marítima, is where **excursion boats** to Yelapa, Las Animas, Quimixto, and the Marietas Islands depart. It's north of town near the airport, an inexpensive taxi or bus ride from town. Just take any bus marked IXTAPA, LAS JUNTAS, PITILLAL, or AURORA and tell the driver to let you off at the Terminal Marítima. *Note:* Oddly enough, you must pay a nominal federal tax to gain access to the pier—and your departing excursion boat.

Water taxis to Yelapa, Las Animas, and Quimixto leave multiple times per day starting at 10am and continuing until 6pm from the pier at Los Muertos Beach (south of downtown), on Rodolfo Rodríguez next to the Hotel Marsol. A round-trip ticket to Yelapa (the farthest point, which takes about 45 min. each way) costs 250 pesos. The latest return time is usually 4:45pm, but confirm the pickup time with your water taxi captain. Other water taxis to Yelapa depart from Boca de Tomatlán, about 30 minutes south of town by public bus. These can be a better option if you want more flexible departure and return times from the southern beaches. Generally, they leave on the hour for the southern shore destinations, or more frequently if there is traffic. Prices run about $15 round-trip, with rates clearly posted on a sign on the beach. A private water taxi costs about $35 per hour with a 4-hour minimum, allowing you to come and go on your own time. They'll take up to eight people for that price, so often people band together at the beach to hire one.

There's also water taxi service from Los Muertos Beach to Paradise Village in Nuevo Vallarta for $12 each way.

[FastFACTS] PUERTO VALLARTA

Area Code The telephone area code is **322.**

Climate It's sunny and warm year-round, with tropical temperatures; however, evenings and early mornings in the winter can turn quite cool. Summers are very hot, with an increase in humidity during the rainy season, between May and October. Rains come almost every afternoon in June and July, and are usually brief but strong— just enough to cool off the air for evening activities. In September, heat and humidity are least comfortable and rains heaviest.

Currency Exchange   Banks are found throughout downtown and in the other prime shopping areas. Most banks are open Monday through Friday from 9am to 4pm, with shorter hours on Saturday. ATMs are common throughout Vallarta, including the central plaza downtown. They are becoming the most favorable way to exchange currency, with bank rates plus 24-hour convenience. *Casas de cambio* (money-exchange houses), located throughout town, offer longer hours than the banks, with only slightly lower exchange rates. Most hotels also change money at varying rates.

Drugstores   CMQ Farmacia, Basilio Badillo 365 (☎ **322/222-1330**), is open 24 hours and makes free deliveries to hotels between 11am and 10pm with a minimum purchase of $20. **Farmacias Guadalajara,** Emiliano Zapata 232 (☎ **322/224-1811**), is also open 24 hours.

Embassies & Consulates The **U.S. Consular Agency** office (☎ **322/222-0069;** http://guadalajara.usconsulate.gov) is located in Nuevo Vallarta at Paseo de los Cocoteros 85, in the Paradise Plaza, Local L-7, on the second floor. It's open Monday through Friday from 8:30am to 12:30pm. The **Canadian Consulate** (☎ **322/293-0099,** -0098; 24-hr. emergency line 01-800/706-2900 in Mexico) is located in Plaza Las Glorias, Blvd. Francisco Medina Ascencio 1951, Edificio Obelisco, Loc. 108 (you'll see the Canadian flag hanging from the balcony). It's open Monday through Friday from 9am to 1pm.

Emergencies   Police emergency, ☎ **060** or 066; local police, ☎ **322/290-0513,** -0512; intensive care ambulance, **Cruz Roja (Red Cross),** ☎ **322/222-1533** and **San Javier Marina Hospital Ambulance Service** (☎ **322/226-1010,** ext. 340).

Hospitals   The following offer U.S.-standards service and are available 24 hours: **Ameri-Med Urgent Care,** Avenida Francisco Medina Ascencio at Plaza Neptuno, Loc. D-1, Marina Vallarta (© **322/226-2080;** www.amerimed.com.mx); **San Javier Marina Hospital,** Av. Francisco Medina Ascencio 2760, Zona Hotelera (© **322/226-1010**); and **Cornerstone Hospital,** Av. los Tules 136 (behind Plaza Caracol; © **322/226-3700**).

Internet Access   Most Vallarta hotels have Wi-Fi, and the resorts typically offer business centers. You can also get access at **PV Cafe** (© **322/223-3308**), located in the old town at Olas Altas 246. It's open daily from 8am to midnight and charges 35 pesos per hour for computer use. Next door, **Café Vayan** (© **322/222-0092**), at Olas Altas 350, serves tasty breakfasts and snacks with free Wi-Fi. It's open 8am to 11pm.

Newspapers & Magazines   *Vallarta Today,* a weekly English-language newspaper (© **322/225-3323;** www.vallartatoday.com), is a good source for dining, cultural events, retirement information, real estate, and healthy living in Vallarta. The bilingual quarterly city magazine *Vallarta Lifestyles* (© **322/221-0106;** www.virtualvallarta.com) is also very popular. Both are for sale at area newsstands and hotel gift shops. The weekly English-language *Vallarta Tribune* (www.vallartatribune.com) is distributed free throughout town and offers an objective local viewpoint. *PV Mirror* (www.pvmirror.com) is another English-language city paper and online site that offers local news and visitor information.

Post Office   The *correo* is at Colombia Street, behind Hidalgo Park, and is open Monday through Friday from 9am to 6pm, Saturday from 9am to 1pm.

Safety   Puerto Vallarta enjoys a very low crime rate. Public transportation is safe to use, and Tourist Police (dressed in navy blue and white uniforms) are available to answer questions, give directions, and offer assistance. Most encounters with the police are linked to using or purchasing drugs—so don't. *Note:* The tourist police sometimes conduct random personal searches for drugs. If this happens, you are within your rights to request the name of the officer. Report any unusual incidents to the local consular office.

WHERE TO STAY

Beyond a varied selection of hotels and resorts, Puerto Vallarta offers many alternative accommodations. Oceanfront or marina-view condominiums and elegant private villas can offer families and small groups a better value and more ample space than a hotel. For short-term rentals, check out **Costa Vallarta Boutique Villas** (© **800/728-9098** in the U.S. and Canada, or

01-800/508-7923 in Mexico; www.costavallartaboutiquevillas. com). Office hours are Monday through Friday 9am to 6pm, Saturday 9am to 2pm. Prices start at $100 a night for non-beachside condos and reach into the thousands of dollars for penthouse condos or private villas. This site links to **Mexico Boutique Hotels** (www.mexicoboutiquehotels.com), which is an association of luxury boutique inns across the country, including **Hacienda San Angel** (p. 49). Upon request, the association organizes personalized trips in the region. **Bayside Properties** (② **322/222-8148;** www.baysidepropertiespv.com) located at Francisco Rodríguez 160, on the corner of Olas Altas, rents condos, villas, and hotels for individuals and large groups, including gay-friendly accommodations. Another reputable full-service travel agency is **Puerto Vallarta Villas** (② **415/704-0455** in the U.S., or 322/221-5495; www.puertovallartavillas.com). For the ultimate, indulge in a Punta Mita Villa rental within this exclusive resort. Contact **Mita Residential** (② **877/561-2893** toll-free in the U.S., or 329/291-5300; www.mitaresidential.com).

This section lists hotels from the airport south along Banderas Bay.

Marina Vallarta

Marina Vallarta is the most modern and deluxe area of hotel development in Puerto Vallarta. Located immediately south of the airport and just north of the cruise ship terminal, it's a planned development whose centerpiece is a 450-slip modern marina.

In addition to the hotels reviewed below, an excellent choice is **Casa Velas,** on the golf course at Pelícanos 311 (www.hotel casavelas.com; ② **866/529-8813** in the U.S., or 322/226-6688). High-season rates start at $210 per person, all-inclusive.

Marriott CasaMagna Resort & Spa ★★ ☺   Set on a lovely stretch of beach in Marina Vallarta, the family-friendly CasaMagna underwent a $10.7-million renovation in 2008. Guest rooms, all of which are accessed through open-air hallways, were upgraded with contemporary Mexican styling, marble floors, and flower accents, and bougainvillea hangs from each balcony overlooking the pool and bay. Pool activities and beach watersports are offered throughout the day, and there's a luxurious yet reasonably priced spa. Among the many diversions for children is a turtle-preservation program that runs from June to November and provides guests the chance to release baby turtles into the sea. The resort houses four restaurants, including the teppanyaki-style **Mikado** (p. 53), as well as the colonial-designed Mexican La Estancia. Executive Chef

Fred Ruiz offers interactive cooking classes (about $60 per person), beginning with a tour of the hotel's own chile, herb, and cactus garden.

Paseo de la Marina Norte 435, Marina Vallarta, 48354 Puerto Vallarta, Jal. www. puertovallartamarriott.com. ℂ **800/223-6388** in the U.S., or 322/226-0000. Fax 322/226-0060. 433 units. High season $229 and up double, $459–$479 suite; low season $159 and up double, $359–$389 suite. AE, DC, MC, V. Free parking. **Amenities:** 4 restaurants; deli; 3 bars; concierge; golf privileges at Marina Vallarta Golf Club; kids' club; state-of-the-art fitness center and spa w/classes (fee), sauna, steam room, and whirlpool; oceanside pool; room service; 2 lighted grass tennis courts. *In room:* A/C, flatscreen TV, iHome, hair dryer, minibar, Wi-Fi.

Westin Resort & Spa Puerto Vallarta ★★ ☺ Stunning architecture and vibrant colors are the hallmark of this award-winning property. Despite the spacious grounds, the warm service creates the feeling of an intimate resort. Hammocks are strung between the palms closest to the beach, where there are also private beach cabañas. All rooms have oceanview balconies, "Heavenly" beds, oversize wood furnishings, tile floors, and original art. Eight junior suites and some double rooms have Jacuzzis, and the five grand suites consist of two levels, with spacious living areas. Two floors of rooms make up the Royal Beach Club with VIP services, including a private lounge with continental breakfast and evening drinks included. There's an excellent spa and fitness center, as well as an exclusive beach area with pergolas available for daily rent.

Paseo de la Marina Sur 205, Marina Vallarta, 48354 Puerto Vallarta, Jal. www. starwoodhotels.com/westin. ℂ **800/228-3000** in the U.S., or 322/226-1100. Fax 322/226-1144. 280 units. $155 and up double. AE, DC, MC, V. Free parking. **Amenities:** 2 restaurants; 3 bars; beach club; concierge; kids' club; gallery arcade; golf privileges at Marina Vallarta Golf Club; 2 free-form pools; room service; full-service spa and health club w/sauna and steam room; 3 lighted grass tennis courts. *In room:* A/C, TV, hair dryer, minibar, Wi-Fi.

The Hotel Zone

The main street running between the airport and town is Avenida Francisco Medina Ascencio. The hotels here offer excellent wide beachfronts with generally tranquil waters for swimming. From here it's a quick 50-peso taxi or bus ride to downtown.

Fiesta Americana Puerto Vallarta ★★ ☺ The Fiesta Americana's towering, three-story, thatched *palapa* lobby is a landmark in the Hotel Zone, and the resort is known for its excellent beach, quality rooms, and friendly service. An abundance of plants, splashing fountains, constant breezes, and comfortable seating areas in the lobby create a casual South Seas ambience. The nine-story terra-cotta building embraces a large beachfront plaza and pool bustling with activities. Marble-trimmed rooms in neutral tones with pastel accents contain carved headboards and comfortable rattan-and-wicker furniture. All have private balconies with ocean and pool views. Beachside massages continue from morning to sunset, and there's a full-service spa.

Av. Francisco Medina Ascencio Km 2.5, 48300 Puerto Vallarta, Jal. www.fiesta americana.com. ✆ **322/226-2100.** Fax 322/224-2108. 291 units. $150 and up double; $300 and up suite. AE, DC, MC, V. Limited free parking. **Amenities:** 3 restaurants; 3 bars; kids' club; fitness center; large pool w/activities; room service; full-service spa. *In room:* A/C, TV, hair dryer, minibar, Wi-Fi.

Villa Premiere Puerto Vallarta Hotel & Spa ★★   Located a few blocks north of the start of the *malecón*, the Premiere is within walking distance of downtown restaurants, shops, galleries, and clubs. With a first-rate spa and a policy that restricts guests to ages 16 and older, it's a place that caters to relaxation. Rooms are decorated in warm colors with tile floors and light wood furnishings. Deluxe rooms have ocean views, a small seating area with comfortable chairs, and a sizable private balcony. Spa suites offer Jacuzzis in the bedrooms. The stunning bi-level spa is the real attraction of this hotel—scented with aromatherapy and glowing with candlelight, it uses top-notch, 100% natural products, most based on Mexico's natural treasures such as coconut, aloe, and papaya. The Premiere also offers an all-inclusive option.

San Salvador 117, behind the Buenaventura Hotel, Col. 5 de Diciembre, 48350 Puerto Vallarta, Jal. www.premiereonline.com.mx. ✆ **877/886-9176** in the U.S., or 322/226-7001, -7040. Fax 322/226-7043. 83 units. Room only: High season $185–$430 double; low season $135–$370 double. All-inclusive rates are approximately double. AE, MC, V. Limited street parking. Children 15 and younger not accepted. **Amenities:** 3 restaurants; fitness center; outdoor pool; room service; full spa w/sauna and steam room; yoga classes and meditation workshops. *In room:* A/C, TV, hair dryer, minibar, Wi-Fi.

Downtown to Los Muertos Beach

This part of town has undergone a renaissance; economical hotels and good-value guesthouses dominate. Several blocks off the beach, you can find numerous budget inns offering clean, simply furnished rooms; most offer discounts for long-term stays. Many hotels in Viejo Vallarta (the old town, south of the Río Cuale) are gay- and straight-friendly.

Hacienda San Angel ★★★ 🎁   This renowned boutique hotel has a more formal feel than most Vallarta accommodations.

Although not on the beach, you'll hardly miss the surf since it offers beautiful vistas of the city and Bay of Banderas. Once the home of Richard Burton, the Hacienda lies just behind Puerto Vallarta's famed church and, in fact, looks somewhat like a church itself (guests can request to stay in Burton's former room, "Celestial"). The inn consists of four rustic colonial villas; the first two are joined to the third villa by a path that winds through a lovely terraced tropical garden with statuary and a fountain. An old chapel across the street offers seven guest rooms decorated in rich colonial furnishings and tapestries; many have antiques and claw-foot tubs. One of the heated pools and a deck lie next to the elegant open-air restaurant, and a second sun deck overlooks the church and sea beyond. Continental breakfast is served outside your suite at the hour you request or in the memorable open-air restaurant (p. 54).

Miramar 336, Col. Centro, 48300 Puerto Vallarta, Jal. www.haciendasanangel. com. ☏ **877/815-6594** or 322/222-2692. 19 units. High season $535 and up double; low season $435 and up double. All rates include daily continental breakfast. Rates for the entire Hacienda or separate villas consisting of 3 suites each are also available. AE, MC, V. Very limited street parking available. **Amenities:** 3 outdoor pools; en-suite spa services available; assistance w/activities and tours; concierge; free Internet. *In room:* A/C, TV/DVD, CD player, hair dryer.

Hotel Playa Los Arcos ★★ This perennially popular hotel has a stellar location in the heart of Los Muertos Beach, central to the Olas Altas sidewalk-cafe action. The lovely four-story structure is U-shaped and faces the ocean. Guest rooms are small but comfortable, and draped in white, with carved wooden furniture. They have balconies that overlook the courtyard pool that virtually extends into the lobby. The hotel grounds include a *palapa* beachside bar with occasional live entertainment, a gourmet coffee shop, and Kaiser Maximilian's gourmet restaurant (p. 58). The hotel is 7 blocks south of the river in the old section of downtown.

Olas Altas 380, 48380 Puerto Vallarta, Jal. www.playalosarcos.com. ☏ **800/648-2403** in the U.S., or 322/226-7100. Fax 322/226-7104. 171 units. $120–$150 double; $150–$200 suite. All-inclusive packages available. MC, V. Limited street parking. **Amenities:** Restaurant; lobby bar; outdoor pool; Wi-Fi (in lobby). *In room:* A/C, TV.

South to Mismaloya

Casa Tres Vidas ★★ 🏷 Set on a stunning private cove, Tres Vidas gives you the experience of your own private villa, complete with service staff. It offers outstanding value for the location— close to town, with panoramic views from every room. Each villa has at least two levels and over 460 sq. m (4,951 sq. ft.) of mostly open living areas, plus a private swimming pool, heated whirlpool, and air-conditioned bedrooms. The Vida Alta penthouse villa has three bedrooms, plus a rooftop deck with pool and bar. Vida Sol villa's three bedrooms sleep 10 (two rooms have two king-size beds each). Directly on the ocean, Vida Mar is a four-bedroom villa, accommodating eight. The staff prepares gourmet meals in your villa twice a day—you choose the menu and pay only for the food. Service is consistently excellent.

Sagitario 132, Playa Conchas Chinas, 48300 Puerto Vallarta, Jal. www.casatresvidas.com. ☏ **888/640-8100** toll-free in the U.S., or 322/221-5317. Fax 322/221-53-27. 3 villas. High season $900–$950 villa; low season $550–$600 villa. Rates include services such as housekeeping and meal preparation. Special summer 1- or 2-bedroom rates available; minimum 5 nights during high season. AE, MC, V. Limited street parking. **Amenities:** 2 prepared daily meals; concierge; private outdoor pool. *In room:* A/C, TV, Wi-Fi.

Dreams Puerto Vallarta Resort & Spa ☺

The all-inclusive Dreams Resort sits on a beautiful beach with soft white sand in a private cove. Set apart from other properties, with a lush mountain backdrop, it's only a 10-minute ride to town. The hotel consists of two buildings: the 250-room main hotel, which curves gently with the shape of the Playa Las Estacas, and the newer 11-story Club Tower, also facing the beach and ocean. Standard rooms in the aging main building are large; some have sliding doors opening onto the beach, and others have balconies. Preferred Club suites have access to a private lounge, expanded marble bathrooms with upgraded amenities, and balconies with whirlpool tubs. All rooms feature ocean views, vibrant colors, marble floors, and local artwork. The grounds include two swimming pools, a health club, and a spa; activities are offered day and night. The Explorer's Club for Kids (ages 3–12) offers your basic arts and crafts activities and sandcastle contests, as well as your not-so-basic outdoor movies on the beach and weekly campout. Food served in the resort is so-so.

Carretera Barra de Navidad Km 3.5, Playa Las Estacas, 48300 Puerto Vallarta, Jal. www.dreamsresorts.com. ☏ **866/237-3267** in the U.S. and Canada, or 322/226-5000. Fax 322/221-6000. 337 units. All-inclusive rates are per person and include all meals, premium drinks, activities, airport transfers, tips, and taxes. $380 and up double; $540 and up junior suite; $700 and up oceanview suite. AE, DC, MC, V. Free secured parking. **Amenities:** 6 restaurants; 4 bars; pool bar; kids' club; fully equipped health club; 3 outdoor pools w/daytime activities; room service; shows at night in high season; spa; 2 lighted grass tennis courts; nonmotorized watersports; yoga. *In room:* A/C, TV, MP3 players, hair dryer, Internet, minibar.

Quinta María Cortez ★★ 🏠

An eclectic, imaginative B&B on the beach, this is Puerto Vallarta's most original place to stay—and one of Mexico's most memorable inns. Most of the seven large suites, uniquely decorated with antiques, whimsical curios, and original art, have a kitchenette and balcony. Sunny terraces, a small pool, and a central gathering area with fireplace and *palapa*-topped dining area (where an excellent full breakfast is served) occupy different levels of the seven-story house. A rooftop terrace offers another sunbathing alternative—and is among the best sunset-watching spots in town. The Quinta sits on a beautiful cove on Conchas Chinas beach. A terrace fronting the beach accommodates chairs for taking in the sunset.

Sagitario 132, Playa Conchas Chinas, 48300 Puerto Vallarta, Jal. www.quinta-maria.com. © **888/640-8100** in the U.S., or 322/221-5317. Fax 322/221-5327. 7 units. High season $170–$320 double; low season $155–$195 double. Rates include breakfast. AE, MC, V. Very limited street parking. Children 17 and younger not accepted. **Amenities:** Concierge; small outdoor pool; Wi-Fi (in common areas). *In room:* A/C, fridge, hair dryer.

Yelapa

Verana ★★★ 📷   Verana is a secluded retreat tucked in the hills overlooking sleepy Yelapa, a natural paradise with spectacular views of the tropical landscape and ocean before it. The adults-only clientele are spread out among eight accommodations ranging from the tranquil two-bedroom "stone house" to the more expensive "tea house" that resembles an enchanted open-air treehouse with a private pool. The houses feature king-size beds with mosquito nets, beautiful bathrooms, and private terraces, and while there are no TVs or telephones, Wi-Fi is available. Guests have access to an unforgettable "Jungle Spa," where most of the treatments and programs take place in a tranquil outdoor setting; kayaks; and snorkeling equipment. The European-trained chef prepares exquisite cuisine. Verana is reached via a 30-minute water taxi from Boca de Tomatlán (south of Puerto Vallarta, p. 44) followed by a 10-minute hike up a fairly steep trail from the boat launch (mules can be arranged for people with mobility difficulties). The town of Yelapa lies about a half-hour walk from the inn.

Calle Zaragoza 404, 48304 Yelapa, Jal. www.verana.com. © **866/687-9358** or 310/455-2425 in the U.S., or 322/222-0878. 8 villas. Winter/high season $360–$480 villa per night with 5-night minimum; $750 3-bedroom Casa Grande per night; extra person $70 per night. AE, MC, V. Optional daily breakfast, lunch, and dinner $95 per person; alcoholic beverages extra. Shorter stays based on availability. Closed during summer months. Management helps arrange transportation from Puerto Vallarta to Boca. **Amenities:** Restaurant/bar; morning yoga classes; library; outdoor pool; spa w/massage services; snorkeling equipment; kayaks; Wi-Fi. *In room:* No phone.

WHERE TO EAT

Puerto Vallarta has an exceptional dining scene. Over 250 restaurants serve cuisines from around the world, in addition to fresh seafood and regional dishes. Chefs from France, Switzerland, Germany, Italy, and Argentina have come for visits and stayed to open restaurants. In celebration of this diversity, Vallarta's culinary community hosts a gourmet dining festival each November. Prices below include the 16% IVA tax.

Of the inexpensive local spots, one favorite is **El Planeta Vegetariano,** Iturbide 270, just down from the main church (**☏ 322/222-3073**), serving an inexpensive and delicious vegetarian buffet, which changes for breakfast and lunch/dinner. It's open daily. Breakfast (50 pesos) is served from 8am till noon; the lunch and dinner buffets (75 pesos) are served from noon to 10pm; no credit cards are accepted.

Marina Vallarta

Most of the best restaurants in the Marina are in hotels, but a number of quality options line the boardwalk bordering the marina yacht harbor, as well.

Expensive

Mikado ★ ☺ JAPANESE   Surrounded by koi ponds next to the CasaMagna Marriott, this fun teppanyaki-style restaurant is a favorite among families and celebratory groups. Up to eight people gather around each of the communal tables with a built-in steel grill, as the Mexican-turned-Japanese chef puts on a culinary show of juggling spatulas, flying shrimp, tossed eggs, and steaming onion volcanoes that will delight children and adults alike. Order a la carte or a complete progressive dinner, which includes miso soup and salad along with your choice of chicken, beef, shrimp, or fish prepared flaming in front of your eyes. Each complete dinner is served with steamed or fried rice and fresh grilled vegetables, topped off with green tea and sorbet. Mikado also offers sushi, sashimi, nigiri, and noodle dishes, and there are a few non-teppanyaki tables for those who prefer more private dining.

Paseo de la Marina Norte 435, Marina Vallarta (Marriott CasaMagna). **☏ 322/226-0000**. Reservations recommended. Main courses 179–431 pesos; complete dinner 420–431 pesos. AE, MC, V. Daily 6–11pm.

Porto Bello ★★ ITALIAN   One of the first restaurants in the marina, Porto Bello serves flavorful Italian dishes to the backdrop of docked sailboats and motor yachts. For starters, the fried cala-mari is delicately seasoned, and the grilled vegetable antipasto could easily serve as a full meal. Signature dishes include fusilli prepared with artichokes, black olives, lemon juice, basil, olive oil, and Parmesan cheese; and sautéed fish filet with white wine, spin-ach, and arugula. I love the lightly broiled butterfly shrimp served with spaghetti or, for a splurge, the pecan-crusted rack of French lamb. The elegant indoor dining room is air-conditioned, and there's also open-air seating with white linen tables. Porto Bello recently opened a second restaurant in Nuevo Vallarta (✆ 322/297-6719), next to the Mayan Palace.

Marina Sol, Loc. 7 (Marina Vallarta *malecón*). ✆ **322/221-0003.** www.portobello vallarta.com. Reservations recommended for dinner. Main courses 195–410 pesos. AE, MC, V. Daily noon–11pm.

Downtown
EXPENSIVE
Café des Artistes/Thierry Blouet Cocina del Autor ★★★
FRENCH/INTERNATIONAL   The award-winning chef and owner, Thierry Blouet, is both a member of the French Academie Culinaire and a Maitre Cuisinier de France. The Café des Artistes includes the upscale Constantini martini and piano bar and the expensive Thierry Blouet Cocina del Autor dining area. The cafe's menu consists of French gourmet bistro fare, drawing on Chef Blouet's French training and incorporating regional specialty ingre-dients. Noteworthy entrees include sea bass served with a Swiss chard mousse, and roasted duck glazed with honey, soy, and ginger. At the elegant Cocina del Autor, fashionable diners choose from the fixed-priced tasting menu (prices depend on the number of plates you select, from 4 to 12). Choose any combination of start-ers, entrees, and desserts. Portions are generally small. For a par-ticularly romantic setting, reserve a table on the lush, candlelit terrace. After dining, you're invited to the cognac and cigar room, an exquisite blend of old adobe walls, flickering candles, and ele-gant leather chairs. Service is professional, if a bit stiff.

Guadalupe Sánchez 740, corner with Vicario. ✆ **322/222-3228,** -3229, -3230. www.cafedesartistes.com. Reservations recommended. Main courses 210–405 pesos; Cocina del Autor tasting menu 650–1,450 pesos without wine, 1,050–2,100 pesos with wine. AE, DC, MC, V. Daily 6–11:30pm. Lounge until 1am.

MODERATE
Hacienda San Angel ★★★ MEXICAN   The exquisite beauty
of the Hacienda, as well as the city lights and shimmering bay, are proudly displayed for diners at this special location. The menu

Tapas, Anyone?

Certainly much of modern Mexico's culture draws on the important influence of Spain, so it only makes sense that Spanish culinary traditions would be evident as well. Of the many options, these are my favorites: the long-standing **Barcelona Tapas,** Matamoros and 31 de Octubre streets (✆ **322/222-0510**), a tapas bar located up a set of stairs on a hillside, with sweeping views of the bay. In addition to tapas and a selection of Spanish entrees, including paella, it offers sangria and a fine selection of wines from noon to 11:30pm. **La Esquina de los Caprichos,** Miramar 402, corner of Iturbide (✆ **322/222-0911**), is a tiny place near Hacienda San Angel known as having the most reasonably priced (35–85 pesos) tapas in town, and perhaps the tastiest. Hours are Monday through Saturday from 8:30am to 10pm; cash only. It closes in August.

changes periodically and features Mexican-infused international cuisine. Starters include crispy fried calamari with a selection of sauces; grilled seasonal vegetables in a tomato, olive oil, and basil balsamic vinaigrette; and a shrimp and coconut cream soup accented with brandy. The house specialty is the grilled *Cabreria,* a tender bone-in steak, served with garlic mashed potatoes, a portobello mushroom ragout, and a three-chile sauce. Other standouts include chicken *mole* and the herb-crusted rack of lamb in a green-pepper sauce. Top this memorable dinner off with apple raviolis smothered in butterscotch and almonds. Start the evening by arriving between 7:30 and 9:30pm for a sunset cocktail hour often featuring live mariachi music—you may also enjoy strolling the grounds. Service is wonderful.

Miramar 336, Centro. ✆ **322/222-2692.** www.haciendasanangel.com. Reservations required. Main courses $15–$40, with 20% gratuity added to all checks. AE, MC, V. Daily 6–10pm.

Las Palomas ★ MEXICAN   One of Puerto Vallarta's first restaurants, this is the power-breakfast place of choice—and a popular hangout for everyone else throughout the day. Authentic in atmosphere and menu, it's one of Puerto Vallarta's few genuine Mexican restaurants. Breakfast is the best value. The staff pours mugs of steaming coffee spiced with cinnamon as soon as you're seated. Try classic *huevos rancheros* or *chilaquiles* (tortilla strips, fried and topped with red or green spicy sauce, cream, and cheese, with fried eggs or shredded chicken). Lunch and dinner offer traditional Mexican specialties, such as chiles rellenos, enchiladas, fajitas, and carne asada. The best places for checking out the *malecón* and watching the sunset while sipping an icy margarita are the spacious bar and the upstairs terrace. You may need some drinks to participate in (or even just listen to) the nightly karaoke.

Paseo Díaz Ordaz 610. ⟐ **322/222-3675.** www.laspalomaspvr.com. Breakfast 50–125 pesos; lunch and dinner 135–325 pesos. AE, MC, V. Daily 8am–1am.

Trio ★★★ 🏠 INTERNATIONAL   Trio is the darling of Vallarta restaurants, with diners beating a path to the modest but stylish cafe where chef-owners Bernhard Güth and Ulf Henricksson's undeniable passion for food imbues each dish. They call it "Mediterranean food cooked with love," and indeed Trio is noted for its perfected melding of Mexican and Mediterranean flavors and exquisite presentation. Consider starting with the cilantro-ginger-marinated calamari with avocado and a jalapeño salsa. For a main course, I recommend the ricotta spinach ravioli with sun-dried tomatoes, or the oven-roasted rabbit with Italian vegetables. These dishes may not be on the menu when you arrive, though—it's a constantly changing work of art. In high season, the rooftop dining area allows for a more comfortable wait for a table or for after-dinner coffee, and a trio plays live music during dinner. Most locals will tell you this is their favorite restaurant in town. The same owners run **Vitea** (p. 57).

Guerrero 264. ⟐ **322/222-2196.** www.triopv.com. Reservations recommended. Main courses 175–320 pesos. AE, MC, V. Daily 6–11:30pm.

INEXPENSIVE

Agave Grill ★ MEXICAN   Agave Grill has gradually taken over the space at the Casa de Tequila in central downtown. The location is lovely, in a beautiful garden setting within a classic hacienda-style building. Start with fresh salsa made at your table (spiced to your preference), and follow with the *pulpo* (octopus) sautéed to tenderness in a delectable chile and garlic sauce. My favorite main courses include seafood enchiladas, and beef tenderloin prepared with *mole*. For a sweet finish, you'll love the chocolate "tamal" served with homemade vanilla ice cream. All tortillas and savory salsas are handmade. An elegant bar serves Vallarta's most original selection of fine tequilas, many from small distilleries.

Morelos 589. ⟐ **322/222-2000.** Reservations not accepted. Main courses 148–298 pesos; chef's tasting menu 300 pesos. MC, V. Mon–Sat noon–11:30pm; Sun 5–11:30pm.

El Arrayán ★★★ 🍴 MEXICAN   The spirited Arrayán, up a steep sidewalk, offers rewarding, authentic Mexican cuisine. The casual open-air dining area surrounds a cozy courtyard, while its exposed brick walls and funky-chic decor showcase a modern view of Mexican classics. Start with an order of delicious ceviche, sumptuous plantain empanadas filled with black beans, or a traditional salad of diced *nopal* cactus paddles with fresh cheese. Favorite main courses include chicken *mole,* chiles rellenos packed with shrimp, and Mexican duck *carnitas* served in an *arrayán*-orange sauce. (*Arrayán*, the namesake of the place, is a small sweet-and-sour fruit native to the region.) Any dish can be made vegetarian. The homemade ice creams and sorbets make for a tasty and refreshing finish to your meal. The full bar offers an extensive selection of original cocktails (check out the "mojo-basil grapefruit mojito"), tequilas, Mexican wines, and nonalcoholic *aguas frescas*—a blended drink of fresh fruit and water. Expect excellent service.

Allende 344, just past Matamoros, on the corner with Miramar. ✆ **322/222-7195.** www.elarrayan.com.mx. Reservations recommended. Main courses 160–230 pesos. AE, MC, V. Wed–Mon 5:30–11pm. Closed Tues.

Vitea ★★ 🍴 INTERNATIONAL   This artistic bistro is run by the acclaimed chef/owners of **Trio** (see above), whom many consider to serve Vallarta's best food. It's no surprise then that the fresh, healthy dishes here make Vitea another favorite among locals. Due to strategically placed mirrors on the back wall, every seat has a view of the ocean, while the interior is cheerful and inviting. Starters include succulent shrimp tempura with pumpkinseeds, spicy garlic, and chile or a fresh Greek salad that just explodes with flavor. Main courses change regularly and may include barbecue red snapper with wilted spinach, eggplant ravioli with portobello mushrooms, or Angus beef tips sautéed with wine. Dinner selections offer a choice of smaller or larger portions. Lunch offers lighter fare, and breakfast is now served as well.

Malecón no. 2, at Libertad. ✆ **322/222-8703.** www.viteapv.com. Reservations recommended during peak dining hours. Main courses 155–285 pesos. MC, V. Daily 8am–midnight.

South of the Río Cuale to Olas Altas

South of the river is the densest restaurant area, where you'll find Basilio Badillo. A second main dining drag has emerged along Calle Olas Altas, with a variety of cuisines and price categories. Cafes and espresso bars, generally open from 7am to midnight, line its wide sidewalks, and there are a number of casual seafood eateries open along the beachfront during high season. A wonderful farmers market takes place on Olas Altas Saturdays from 10am to 2pm.

EXPENSIVE

Archie's Wok ★★★ 🎁 ASIAN/SEAFOOD Since 1986, Archie's has been legendary in Puerto Vallarta for serving original cuisine influenced by the intriguing flavors of Southeast Asia, and today the restaurant remains as impressive as ever. Archie was Hollywood director John Huston's private chef during the years he spent in the area. Today his family upholds his legacy at this tranquil Asian-inspired retreat, where fountains trickle and table candle lights flicker by night. The Thai Mai Tai and other tropical drinks, made from only fresh fruit and juices, are a good way to kick off a meal, as are the consistently crispy and delicious Filipino spring rolls. The popular Singapore fish filet features lightly battered filet strips in sweet-and-sour sauce; the delicious barbecue pork riblets are baked for 5 hours and then served with a rich oyster sauce. Friday and Saturday from 7:30 to 10:30pm, there's live classical harp and flute in Archie's Oriental garden.

Francisca Rodríguez 130 (a half-block from the Los Muertos pier). © **322/222-0411.** Main courses 125–225 pesos. MC, V. Mon–Sat 2–11pm. Closed Sept.

Café Kaiser Maximilian ★★ INTERNATIONAL Designed to resemble a 19th-century Viennese cafe, Kaiser Maximilian presents a distinctly European, not Mexican, atmosphere. It's the prime place to go if you want to combine exceptional food with great people-watching. Austrian-born owner Andreas Rupprechter is almost always on hand to ensure that the service is impeccable and the food delicious. Indoor, air-conditioned dining takes place at cozy tables; sidewalk tables are larger and great for groups of friends. The cuisine merges old-world European preparations with regional fresh ingredients (think Wiener schnitzel with a Mexican touch). Recommended mains include filet of trout with a horseradish crust; rack of lamb wrapped in bacon; and seared scallops with butternut squash purée. The gourmet coffees and desserts made in the adjacent cafe and pastry shop are famous throughout the town: I'd try the warm pecan chocolate bourbon tart if I were you.

Olas Altas 380-B (at Basilio Badillo, in front of the Hotel Playa Los Arcos), Zona Romántica. © **322/223-0760.** www.kaisermaximilian.com. Reservations recommended in high season. Main courses 195–328 pesos. AE, MC, V. Mon–Sat 6–11pm.

Daiquiri Dick's ★★★ PACIFIC RIM/MEDITERRA-
NEAN While Puerto Vallarta is replete with ideal "people-
watching" perches, come to Daiquiri Dick's if you want to enjoy
some fantastic "food-watching." Each dish is festively prepared,
served steaming hot from the kitchen and bursting with color and
artistic garnishes. You'll be tempted to try each dish that passes
your table. For light fare, try the Asian chicken salad, which blends
tender chicken, crunchy vegetables, and a savory ginger sesame
dressing. For something more substantial, the barbecue pork
spareribs as well as the crispy cornmeal-crusted perch with toasted
garlic-ancho chile vinaigrette remain house favorites. Don't forget
to order a daiquiri with your meal. The restaurant lies at the northern edge of Viejo Vallarta, set against a lovely section of beach with
palm trees wrapped in white lights that provide a warm glow at
dinner. Live music accompanies the Sunday brunch, which offers
excellent value.

Olas Altas 314. ✆ **322/222-0566.** www.ddpv.com. Main courses 185–265 pesos;
Sunday brunch 145 pesos. MC, V. Daily 9am–10:30pm. Closed Sept.

Espresso ITALIAN This popular eatery is one of Vallarta's late-
night dining options. The two-level restaurant sits on one of the
town's busiest streets—across from El Torito's sports bar—meaning that traffic noise is a factor but not a deterrent. The food is
reliable, the service attentive, and the prices reasonable. Owned by
a partnership of lively Italians, it serves authentic Italian food, from
thin-crust, brick-oven pizza to savory homemade pastas and oven-
baked breads. Excellent calzones and *paninis* are also options. I
prefer the rooftop garden area for dining, but many patrons gravitate to the air-conditioned downstairs, which features major sports
and entertainment events on satellite TV. Espresso also has full bar
service and draft beer.

Ignacio L. Vallarta 279. ✆ **322/222-3272.** Entrees 98–189 pesos. MC, V. Daily
noon–1am.

Fajita Republic MEXICAN/SEAFOOD/STEAKS Fajita
Republic has hit on a winning recipe: delicious food, ample portions, welcoming atmosphere, and low prices. The specialty is, of
course, sizzling fajitas, grilled to perfection in every variety: steak,
fish, chicken, vegetarian, shrimp, combo, and occasionally lobster.
This "tropical grill" also serves sumptuous barbecued ribs, Mexican
molcajetes with incredibly tender strips of marinated beef filet,
and grilled shrimp. Starters include fresh guacamole served in a
giant spoon and the ever-popular Maya cheese sticks (breaded and

deep-fried). Try an oversize mug or pitcher of Fajita Rita Mango Margaritas.

Basilio Badillo 188, 1 block north of Olas Altas. ☎ **322/222-3131.** Main courses 82–188 pesos. MC, V. Daily 5–11pm.

La Palapa ★★ 👔 SEAFOOD/MEXICAN   This beachside *palapa* restaurant defines enchantment, a decades-old favorite with beautiful amber lamps, candles, and lanterns illuminating the night. With each visit, I've been impressed by the quality of the food and service. For lunch and dinner, seafood is the specialty; dishes include miso Chilean sea bass, pepper-crusted yellowfin tuna, grilled shrimp in coconut and tequila, and—for those looking for a break from seafood—pork tenderloin stuffed with chorizo, pecans, and goat cheese. The Palapa's location on Los Muertos Beach makes dinner especially enticing for moon watching over the bay. The bar opens to the dining area and features acoustic guitars and vocals nightly from 8 to 11pm. The restaurant doubles as a beach club during the day.

Pulpito 103. ☎ **322/222-5225.** www.lapalapapv.com. Reservations recommended for dinner in high season. Breakfast 60–130 pesos; main courses 190–400 pesos. AE, MC, V. Daily 8am–11:30pm.

MODERATE

Le Bistro ★★ INTERNATIONAL   I love this place, a French-inspired bistro with a large garden deck set right over the river. Le Bistro's specialty is crepes, with delicious options such as shrimp with broccoli or chicken with squash blossoms. The lunch-and-dinner menu offers fine international cuisine, including filet mignon, duck in a blackberry sauce, and rock Cornish hen stuffed with herbed rice, dried tropical fruit, and nuts, finished in mango-cilantro sauce. Tasty Mexican dishes like crab enchiladas and grilled steak with guacamole are also on order. An extensive wine list and selection of specialty coffees complement the menu, and romantic jazz music plays Thursday through Saturday nights. Le Bistro is also a lovely spot to linger over breakfast.

Isla Río Cuale 16-A (just east of northbound bridge). ☎ **322/222-0283.** www.lebistro.com.mx. Reservations recommended for dinner in high season. Breakfast 48–155 pesos; main courses 115–275 pesos. AE, MC, V. Mon–Sat 9am–midnight.

INEXPENSIVE

Café de Olla ★★ 🎁 MEXICAN   One of my favorite Vallarta restaurants, the Café de Olla serves up the most consistently delicious Mexican food in town. The atmosphere is simple and festive, and the typically packed dining room is served by a staff that's quick and efficient. Large portions of enchiladas, quesadillas, chiles rellenos, fajitas, and tacos come sizzling hot out of the open kitchen and grill. Although not on the menu, you can also order a terrific seafood platter for two. I recommend an order of fresh, thick guacamole to kick off your meal. The margaritas light up the night. Don't come here for romance or refinement, but do come here for great authentic fare, friendly service, and a fun experience. Only cash is accepted.

Basilio Badillo 168. (*) **322/223-1626.** Main courses 70-230 pesos. No credit cards. Wed-Mon 9am-11pm. Closed Tues.

Café San Angel ★ CAFE   This eclectic sidewalk cafe is a favorite gathering place from sunrise into the wee hours. For breakfast, choose a three-egg Western omelet, such Mexican classics as huevos rancheros or *chilaquiles*, or a tropical fruit plate. Deli sandwiches, flavorful salads, sweet and savory crepes, and simple Mexican plates like burritos and quesadillas round out the menu. The cafe also serves exceptional fruit smoothies, iced blended coffees, and other coffee drinks. Although service is occasionally slow, keep in mind that this place affords the best people-watching in the area. Bar service and Internet access are available.

Olas Altas 449 (at Francisco Rodríguez). (*) **322/223-1273.** Breakfast 35-85 pesos; main courses 58-105 pesos. No credit cards. Daily 8am-2am.

Pomodoro E Basilico ★★ ITALIAN   This unobtrusive Italian restaurant is one of Vallarta's best, a delightful table in Vallarta's old town. Choose from Mediterranean salads, fish carpaccios, homemade pastas, and thin-crust pizzas. The hand-tossed pies come as "red" or "white" depending on whether there's a tomato base, with the white pizzas considered more gourmet. My favorite is Patate Provola Pancetta, made with potatoes, Provola smoked cheese, mozzarella, bacon, and rosemary. Daily specialties, including the fish of the day, are listed on a blackboard. The owners hail from Rome, with the mostly Italian staff serving just a dozen alfresco tables. An excellent selection of Italian wines accompanies the simple, delectable menu.

Vallarta 228 (at Lázaro Cárdenas), Zona Romántica. (*) **322/223-6188.** Pizzas and pastas 110-140 pesos; main dishes 120-210 pesos. No credit cards. Tues-Sat 4:30-11:30pm; Sun 6-11:30pm.

Red Cabbage Café (El Repollo Rojo) ★★★ 📖 MEXICAN   The tiny, hard-to-find cafe is worth the effort—a visit here will reward you with exceptional traditional Mexican cuisine and a whimsical crash course in contemporary culture. The small room is covered wall-to-wall with photographs, paintings, movie posters, and news clippings about the cultural icons of Mexico. Frida Kahlo figures prominently in the decor, and a special menu duplicates dishes she and husband Diego Rivera prepared for guests. Specialties from all over Mexico include *chiles en nogada* (poblanos stuffed with ground beef, pine nuts, and raisins, topped with a sweet walnut cream sauce sprinkled with pomegranates and served cold); intricate chicken *mole* from Puebla; and a hearty Mexican plate with steak, a chile relleno, quesadilla, guacamole, rice, and beans. In addition, the vegetarian menu is probably the most diverse and tasty in town.

Calle Rivera del Río 204A (across from Río Cuale). *✆* **322/223-0411.** www. redcabbagepv.com. Main courses 110–240 pesos. No credit cards. Mon–Sat 5–10:30pm.

EXPLORING PUERTO VALLARTA & BEYOND

by Shane Christensen

Puerto Vallarta's welcoming atmosphere is complemented by its wealth of natural beauty and man-made pleasures. Beyond the cobblestone streets, graceful cathedral, bustling malecón (boardwalk), and festive *zócalo* (town square), the city boasts a thriving arts community, sizzling nightlife, and wide variety of ecotourism attractions.

Galleries, boutique shops, and outdoor markets blanket the town's cobblestone streets. You can walk everywhere, pausing along the way at a beachside cafe or on a boardwalk bench. Life here revolves around the ocean, with activities including deep-sea fishing, snorkeling, long-board surfing, and swimming with dolphins. Sign up for a jungle canopy tour, visit a protected island preserve, or test your sight at bird-watching. Ease yourself into an ocean kayak, watch whales migrating, or put on your scuba gear and dive with giant mantas in Banderas Bay. The range of activities in this earthly heaven is astounding.

Nighttime entertainment transforms the *malecón* into a modern Mexican party, where hipsters pack fashionable clubs, dancers swing to salsa, midnight revelers chase back tequila, and celebrations spill into the streets. A number of more chilled-out bars cater to the wine and margarita crowd. Even snowbirds jam to oldies not far from the hottest clubs. The old town is filled with fun-loving gay and gay-friendly bars. As with every aspect of this lively and lovely city, there is something for everyone.

Puerto Vallarta's unabated growth has continued northward into neighboring Nayarit. With 185 miles of coastline, the **Riviera Nayarit,** as marketing wizards have aptly named it, offers spectacular geography, recreation, and biodiversity. Bird-watchers marvel at the hundreds of species that flock to the region, a collision of jungle and tundra habitats. Small sacred surf spots dot the coastline, including the beginners break in (what used to be) sleepy **Sayulita. Bucerías,** a fishing-village-turned-snowbird-capital, offers charming strolls and an expanding selection of quality restaurants. Next door, exclusive **Punta Mita** sets the gold standard for luxury accommodations and activities. Majestic vistas, world-class golf courses, a burgeoning sailing community, and thrilling adventure sports round out this gentle and rich slice of Mexico.

BEACHES, ACTIVITIES & EXCURSIONS

Travel agencies can provide information on what to see and do in Puerto Vallarta and can arrange tours, fishing trips, and other activities. Most hotels have a tour desk on-site. Of the many travel agencies in town, I highly recommend **Tukari Servicios Turísticos,** Av. España 316 (© **322/224-7177;** www.tukari.net), which specializes in ecological and cultural tours. Another source is **Xplora Adventours** (© **322/226-6349**), in the Huichol Collection shop on the *malecón*. It has listings of all locally available tours, with photos, explanations, and costs; however, be aware that a timeshare resort owns the company, so part of the information you receive will be an invitation to a presentation, which you may decline. One of the tour companies with the largest—and best-quality—selection of boat cruises and land tours is **Vallarta Adventures ★★★** (© **888/526-2238** in the U.S., or 322/297-1212; www.vallarta-adventures.com). I can highly recommend any of their offerings.

The Beaches

For years, beaches were Puerto Vallarta's main attraction. Although visitors today are exploring more of the surrounding geography, the sands are still a powerful draw. Over 42km (26 miles) of beaches extend around the broad Bay of Banderas, ranging from action-packed party spots to secluded coves accessible only by boat.

IN TOWN The easiest to reach is **Playa Los Muertos** (also known as Playa Olas Altas or Playa del Sol), just off Calle Olas

Altas, south of the Río Cuale. The water can be rough, but the wide beach is home to a diverse array of *palapa* restaurants that offer food, beverage, and beach-chair service. The most popular are the adjacent El Dorado and La Palapa, at the end of Pulpito Street. On the southern end of this beach is a section known as "Blue Chairs"—the most popular gay beach. Vendors stroll Los Muertos, and beach volleyball, parasailing, and jet-skiing are all popular pastimes. The **Hotel Zone** is also known for its broad, smooth beaches, accessed through the resorts.

SOUTH OF TOWN   **Playa Mismaloya** is in a beautiful sheltered cove about 10km (6¼ miles) south of town along Hwy. 200. The water is clear and ideal for snorkeling off the beach. Entrance to the public beach is just to the left of the **Barceló La Jolla de Mismaloya** (© **322/226-0600**). This is where the *Night of the Iguana,* the movie that made Puerto Vallarta famous with the international jet set, was filmed.

The beach at **Boca de Tomatlán,** just down the road, houses numerous *palapa* restaurants where you can relax for the day—you buy drinks, snacks, or lunch, and you can use their chairs and *palapa* shade. The boat to **Verana** (p. 52) also goes from here.

The two beaches are accessible by public buses, which depart from Basilio Badillo and Insurgentes every 15 minutes from 5:30am to 10pm and cost about 7 pesos.

Las Animas, Quimixto, and **Yelapa** beaches are the most secluded, accessible only by boat (see "Getting Around" in chapter 2 for information about water-taxi service). They are larger than Mismaloya, offer intriguing hikes to jungle waterfalls, and are similarly set up, with restaurants fronting a wide beach. Overnight stays are available at Yelapa (see "Side Trips from Puerto Vallarta," later in this chapter).

NORTH OF TOWN   The beaches at **Marina Vallarta** are the least desirable in the area, with darker sand and seasonal inflows of stones. The entire northern coastline from Bucerías to Punta Mita is a succession of sandy coves alternating with rocky inlets. For years the beaches to the north, with their long, clean breaks, have been the favored locale for surfers. The broad, sandy stretches at **Playa Anclote, Playa Piedras Blancas,** and **Playa Destiladeras,** which all have *palapa* restaurants, have made them favorites with local residents looking for a quick getaway.

You can also hire a *panga* (small motorized boat) at Playa Anclote to take you to the **Marietas Islands ★★★** just offshore. These uninhabited islands are a great place for bird-watching, diving, snorkeling, or just exploring. Blue-footed booby birds (found only here and in the Galápagos) dawdle along the islands' rocky coast, and giant mantas, sea turtles, and colorful tropical fish swim among the coral cliffs. The islands are honeycombed with caves and hidden beaches—including the stunning Playa de Amor (Beach of Love) that appears only at low tide. Humpback whales congregate around these islands during the winter months, and *pangas* can be rented for a do-it-yourself whale-watching excursion. Trips cost about $40 per hour. You can also visit these islands aboard one of the numerous day cruises that depart from the cruise ship terminal in Puerto Vallarta.

Organized Tours

BOAT TOURS   Puerto Vallarta offers a number of boat trips, including sunset cruises and snorkeling, swimming, and diving excursions. They generally travel one of two routes: to the **Marietas Islands,** a 30- to 45-minute boat ride off the northern shore of Banderas Bay, or to **Yelapa, Las Animas,** or **Quimixto** along the southern shore. The trips to the southern beaches make a stop at **Los Arcos,** an island rock formation south of Puerto Vallarta, for snorkeling. Prices range from $45 for a sunset cruise or a trip to one of the beaches with open bar, to $85 for an all-day outing with open bar and meals. Travel agencies sell tickets and distribute information on all cruises.

One of the best outings is a day trip to **Las Caletas ★★**, the cove where John Huston made his home for years. **Vallarta Adventures** (© **888/526-2238** in the U.S., or 322/297-1212; www.vallarta-adventures.com) has done an excellent job of restoring Huston's former home, adding exceptional day-spa facilities, and landscaping the beach, which is wonderful for snorkeling. The trip ($85 per person, $70 for children 4–11) sets out every Monday through Saturday from Nuevo Vallarta at 8:30am or from Vallarta's Maritime Terminal at 9am, and includes a light continental breakfast, buffet lunch, open bar, snorkeling and kayaking equipment, and guided tours.

Whale-watching tours become more popular each year. Viewing humpback whales is almost a certainty from mid- to late November to March. The majestic whales have migrated to this bay for centuries (in the 17th c. it was called "Humpback Bay") to bear their calves. The noted local authority is **Open Air Expeditions,** Guerrero 339 (© **322/135-9260;** www.vallartawhales.com). It offers ecologically oriented, oceanologist-guided 4-hour tours on the soft boat *Prince of Whales,* the only boat in Vallarta specifically designed for whale-watching. Cost is $95 for adults, $82 for children 5 to 10, and travel is in a group of up to 12 (there's a discount for booking online). The tour departs at 9:30am.

LAND TOURS   **Tukari Servicios Turísticos** (see "Beaches, Activities & Excursions," above) can arrange an unforgettable morning at **Terra Noble Art & Healing Center** ★★ (© 322/223-0308; www.terranoble.com), a mountaintop day spa and center for the arts where participants can get a massage, *temazcal* (ancient indigenous sweat lodge—available only for groups), or treatment; work in clay and paint; and have lunch in a heavenly setting overlooking the bay. Hotel travel desks and travel agencies, including Tukari, also book popular **Tropical Tour** or **Jungle Tours** ($95), a basic orientation to the area. These excursions are expanded city tours that include the workers' village of Pitillal, the affluent neighborhood of Conchas Chinas, the cathedral, the market, the Taylor-Burton houses, and lunch at a jungle restaurant.

The **Sierra Madre Expedition** is an excellent tour offered by **Vallarta Adventures** (see "Boat Tours," above). The excursion offered Monday through Thursday travels in Mercedes all-terrain vehicles north of Puerto Vallarta through jungle trails, stops at a small town, ventures into a forest for a brief nature walk, and winds up on a pristine secluded beach for lunch and swimming. The $78 outing is worthwhile because it takes tourists on exclusive trails into scenery that would otherwise be off-limits.

Active Pursuits

DIVING & SNORKELING   Underwater enthusiasts, from beginner to expert, can arrange scuba diving or snorkeling through **Vallarta Adventures** (© 888/526-2238 in the U.S., or 322/297-1212, ext. 3; www.vallarta-adventures.com), a five-star PADI dive center. You may snorkel or dive at Los Arcos, a company-owned site at Caletas Cove (where you'll dive in the company of sea lions), Quimixto Coves, the Marietas Islands, or the offshore La Corbeteña, Morro, and Chimo reefs. The company runs a full range of certification courses. **Chico's Dive Shop** (© 322/222-1895; www.chicos-diveshop.com), with its main shop at Díaz Ordaz 772–5, near Punto V bar, offers similar diving and snorkeling trips and is also a PADI five-star dive center. Chico's is open daily from 8am to 10pm, with branches at the Barceló, Fiesta Americana, and Playa Los Arcos. You can also snorkel off the beaches at Mismaloya and Boca de Tomatlán; elsewhere, there's not much to see besides a sandy bottom. Expect to pay about $70 for a two-tank boat dive to Los Arcos, and about $30 for a snorkeling trip there.

ECOTOURS & ACTIVITIES   **Open Air Expeditions** (www. vallartawhales.com) offers nature-oriented trips, including birding and ocean kayaking in Punta Mita. **Ecotours de México**

(© **322/222-6606;** www.ecotoursvallarta.com), in Marina Vallarta, runs eco-oriented tours, including whale-watching, snorkeling, sea kayaking, hiking, and seasonal (Aug–Dec) trips to a turtle preservation camp where you can witness hatching baby Olive Ridley turtles.

A popular Vallarta adventure activity is **canopy tours.** You glide from treetop to treetop, getting an up-close-and-personal look at a tropical rainforest canopy and the trails far below. Tours depart from the **Vallarta Adventures** (see "Diving & Snorkeling," above) offices in both Marina Vallarta and Nuevo Vallarta at 8am, returning at 2pm. The price ($79 for adults, $55 for children 8–11) includes the tour, bottled water, and light snacks.

A second option is available in the southern jungles of Vallarta, over the Orquidias River, through **Canopy Tours de Los Veranos** (© **877/563-4113** toll-free in the U.S., or 322/223-6060; www.canopytours-vallarta.com). Shuttle locations include the Canopy office (in front of the Pemex Conchas Chinas), in front of Le Kliff Restaurant in Mismaloya, at Hacienda Palma Real in Nuevo Vallarta, or at Collage Disco in Marina Vallarta. Departures are on the hour, from 9am to 2pm. In addition to the 14 cables—the longest being a full 350m (1,148 ft.)—it offers climbing walls and water slides. Price is $79 for adults, or $58 for children ages 6 and older.

FISHING   Arrange fishing trips through travel agencies or through the **Cooperativa de Pescadores (Fishing Cooperative),** on the *malecón* north of the Río Cuale, next door to the Rosita Hotel (© **322/222-1202**). Fishing charters cost from $300 to over $1,000, depending on the size of the boat and trip duration (4–8 hr.). Smaller boats (7m/24 ft.) can accommodate up to four people, while larger boats (12m/40 ft.) can accommodate up to 10. It's open daily from 8am to 9pm, but make arrangements by phone a day ahead. You can also arrange fishing trips at the Marina Vallarta docks, or by calling **Fishing with Carolina** (© **322/224-7250;** www.fishingwithcarolina.com), which uses a 9m (30-ft.) Uniflite sportfisher, fully equipped with an English-speaking crew. There are 4-, 6-, and 8-hour fishing trips starting at about $350 for four people. The waters are filled with marlin, sailfish, dorado (mahimahi), and tuna.

GOLF   Puerto Vallarta is an increasingly popular golf destination. The Joe Finger–designed private course at the **Marina Vallarta Golf Club** (© **322/221-0073;** www.marinavallartagolf.com) is an 18-hole, par-71 course that winds through the Marina Vallarta peninsula and affords ocean views. It's for members only, but most luxury hotels in Puerto Vallarta have memberships for their guests.

Beaches, Activities & Excursions

EXPLORING PUERTO VALLARTA & BEYOND

Greens fees are $130 year-round, and $100 after 2pm. Fees include golf cart, range balls, and tax. A caddy costs about $15 plus tip.

North of town in the state of Nayarit, about 15km (9¼ miles) beyond Puerto Vallarta, is the 18-hole, par-72 **Los Flamingos Club de Golf** (© **329/296-5006;** www.flamingosgolf.com.mx). It features beautiful jungle vegetation and is open from 7am to 7pm daily, with a full pro shop and *palapa* restaurant and bar. The daylight greens fee is $140, which drops to $90 after 2pm. It includes the use of a golf cart; hiring a caddy costs $20 plus tip, and club rental is $35 to $45. Free transportation is offered to and from local hotels.

There are two breathtaking Jack Nicklaus Signature courses at the **Punta Mita Golf Club ★★★** (© **329/291-6000;** www.fourseasons.com/puntamita/golf). The original Pacífico course features eight oceanfront holes and an ocean view from every hole. The second and more-challenging course, Bahía, intertwines with the original course and also affords stunning seaside holes; its finishing hole is adjacent to the St. Regis Resort. The courses are open only to members or guests staying in the Punta Mita resorts, or to other golf club members with a letter of introduction from their pro. Greens fees are $210 for 18 holes and $135 for 9 holes, including cart but excluding taxes, with (Calloway) club rentals for $60.

Another Jack Nicklaus course is located at the **Vista Vallarta Golf Club** (© **322/290-0030;** www.vistavallartagolf.com), along with one designed by Tom Weiskopf. These courses were the site of the 2002 PGA World Cup Golf Championships. A round costs $196 per person, including cart, or $136 after 2pm. Club rentals are available for $55. A caddy costs about $15 plus tip.

The Robert von Hagge–designed **El Tigre** course at Paradise Village (© **866/843-5951** in the U.S., or 322/297-0773; www.eltigregolf.com), in Nuevo Vallarta, is a 7,239-yard course on a relatively flat piece of land, but the design incorporates challenging bunkers, undulating fairways, and water features on several holes. Greens fees are $150 a round, or $98 if you play after 2pm. Club rentals are $45.

HORSEBACK-RIDING TOURS Travel agents and local ranches can arrange guided horseback rides. **Rancho Palma Real,** Carretera Vallarta, Tepic 4766 (© **322/222-0501**), has an office 5 minutes north of the airport; the ranch is in Las Palmas, 40 minutes northeast of Vallarta. It is by far the nicest horseback-riding tour in the area. The price ($75; cash only) includes continental breakfast, drinks, and lunch.

Another excellent option is **Rancho el Charro,** Av. Francisco Villa 895 (② **322/224-0114,** or cell 044-322/294-1689; www.ranchoelcharro.com), which has beautiful, well-cared-for horses and a variety of rides for all levels, departing from their ranch at the base of the Sierra Madre Mountains. Rides range in length from 3 to 8 hours, and in price from $62 to $120. Rancho el Charro also has multiple-day rides—check their website for details. **Rancho Ojo de Agua,** Cerrada de Cardenal 227, Fracc. Las Aralias (② **322/224-0607;** www.ranchojodeagua.com), also offers high-quality tours, from its ranch located 10 minutes by taxi north of downtown toward the Sierra Madre foothills. The rides last 3 hours (10am and 3pm departures) and take you up into the mountains overlooking the ocean and town. The cost is $62. Both of the ranches listed above have other tours available, as well as their own comfortable base camp for serious riders who want to stay out overnight.

SWIMMING WITH DOLPHINS Dolphin Adventure ★★★ (② **888/526-2238** in the U.S., or 322/297-1212; www.vallarta-adventures.com) operates an interactive dolphin-research facility—considered the finest in Latin America—that allows limited numbers of people to swim with dolphins Monday through Saturday at scheduled times. Cost for the **Dolphin Signature Swim** is $129. Reservations are required, and they generally sell out at least a week in advance. **Dolphin Encounter** ($79) allows you to touch and learn about the dolphins in smaller pools, so you're ensured up-close-and-personal time with them. The **Dolphin Kids** program, for children ages 4 to 8, is a gentle introduction to dolphins, featuring the Dolphin Adventure baby dolphins and their mothers interacting with the children participants ($75).

TENNIS Many hotels in Puerto Vallarta offer excellent tennis facilities; they often have clay courts. The full-service **Canto del Sol Tennis Club** (② 322/226-0123; www.cantodelsol.com) is at the Canto del Sol hotel in the Hotel Zone. It offers indoor and outdoor courts, a full pro shop, lessons, clinics, and partner matches. Courts cost about $15 per hour.

A Stroll Through Town

Puerto Vallarta's streets retain a cobblestone charm that weaves its way through time; they're full of tiny shops, rows of windows edged with curling wrought iron, and vistas of red-tile roofs and the sea. One of the greatest pleasures to be had in Puerto Vallarta is simply wandering its streets, but there are a few key sights that any visitor should see. For a map of the attractions mentioned below, see the "Downtown Puerto Vallarta" map on p. 41.

Start with a walk up and down the *malecón*. Among the sights you should see is the **municipal building** on the main square (next to the tourism office), which has a large Manuel Lepe mural inside in its stairwell. Nearby, right up Independencia, sits the picturesque **Church of Nuestra Señora de Guadalupe,** Hidalgo 370 (© **322/222-1326**), topped with a curious crown held in place by angels—a replica of the one worn by Empress Carlota during her brief time in Mexico as Emperor Maximilian's wife. On its steps, women sell religious mementos; across the narrow street, stalls sell native herbs for curing common ailments. Services in English are held each Saturday at 5pm and Sunday at 10am. Regular hours are Monday through Saturday from 7:30am to 8:30pm, Sunday from 6:30am to 7:30pm. Note that the entrance is restricted to those properly attired—no shorts, sleeveless shirts, or cellphones allowed. Three blocks south of the church, head east on Libertad, lined with small shops and pretty upper windows, to the **municipal flea market** by the river. After exploring the market, cross the bridge to the island in the river; sometimes a painter is at work on its banks. Walk down the center of the island toward the sea, and you'll come to the tiny **Museo Arquelógico del Cuale** (no phone; Tues–Sat 10am–2pm and 3–6pm; free admission), which has a small but impressive permanent exhibit of pre-Columbian figurines.

Retrace your steps to the market and Libertad, and follow Calle Miramar to the brightly colored steps up to Zaragoza. Up Zaragoza to the right 1 block is the famous pink arched bridge that once connected Richard Burton's and Elizabeth Taylor's houses, commonly referred to as **"Lover's Arch."** In this area, known as **"Gringo Gulch,"** many Americans have houses.

SHOPPING

For years, shopping in Puerto Vallarta was concentrated in small, eclectic shops rather than impersonal malls. Although plenty of independent stores still exist, it's now home to large, modern shopping centers between the marina and hotel zone areas as well. Vallarta is known for having the most diverse and impressive selection of **contemporary Mexican fine art** outside Mexico City. It also has an abundance of **silver jewelry,** beachwear, and Mexican souvenirs.

The Shopping Scene

The key shopping areas are central downtown, the Marina Vallarta *malecón,* the popular *mercados,* and the beach—where the merchandise comes to you. Some of the more attractive shops are 1 to

A huichol ART PRIMER

Puerto Vallarta offers the best selection of Huichol art in Mexico. Descendants of the Aztecs, the Huichol are one of the last remaining indigenous cultures in the world that has remained true to its traditions, customs, language, and habitat. Huichol art falls into two main categories: yarn paintings and beaded pieces. All other items you might find in Huichol art galleries are either ceremonial objects or items used in everyday life.

Yarn paintings are made on a wood base covered with wax and meticulously overlaid with colored yarn. Designs represent the magical vision of the underworld, and each symbol gives meaning to the piece. Paintings made with wool yarn are more authentic than those made with acrylic; however, acrylic yarn paintings are usually brighter and more detailed because the threads are thinner. It is normal to find empty spaces where the wax base shows. Usually the artist starts with a central motif and works around it, but it's common to have several independent motifs that, when combined, take on a different meaning.

Beaded pieces are made on carved wooden shapes depicting different animals, wooden eggs, or small bowls made from gourds. The pieces are covered with wax, and tiny *chaquira* beads are applied one by one to form designs. Usually the beaded designs

2 blocks in **back of the *malecón.*** Start at the intersection of Corona and Morelos streets—interesting shops spread out in all directions from here. **Marina Vallarta** has two shopping plazas, Plaza Marina and Neptuno Plaza, on the main highway from the airport into town, which offer a limited selection of shops, with Plaza Neptuno primarily featuring home decor shops.

Plaza Peninsula (located on Av. Francisco Medina Ascencio 2485, just south of the cruise ship terminal and north of the Ameca River bridge; no phone number or website), in front of a large waterfront condominium development of the same name, is home to more than 30 businesses, including Vallarta's first **Starbucks,** as well as art galleries, boutiques, and a varied selection of restaurants. The **Galerías Vallarta,** on Av. Francisco Medina Ascencio 2920, adjacent to Wal-Mart and directly across from the cruise ship terminal (© **322/209-1520;** www.galeriasvallarta.com.mx), is a large shopping and entertainment mall anchored by the high-end Mexican department store Liverpool. It houses a variety of boutiques, including Levi's, Nine West, and United Colors of Benetton. Among the selections for dining are Chili's, Subway, and represent animals; plants; the elements of fire, water, or air; and certain symbols that give a special meaning to the whole. Deer, snakes, wolves, and scorpions are traditional elements; other figures, such as iguanas, frogs, and any animals not indigenous to Huichol territory, are incorporated by popular demand. Beadwork with many small designs that do not exactly fit into one another is more time-consuming and has a more complex symbolic meaning.

You can learn more about the Huichol at **Huichol Collection,** Morelos 490, across from the sea-horse statue on the *malecón* (© 322/223-2141; daily 9am–10:30pm). This shop offers an extensive selection of Huichol art in all price ranges, and has a replica of a Huichol adobe hut, informational displays explaining more about their fascinating way of life and beliefs, and usually a Huichol artist at work. However, this is a timeshare sales location, so don't be surprised if you're hit with a pitch for a "free" breakfast and property tour. **Peyote People,** Juarez 222 (© 322/222-2302, -6268; www.peyotepeople.com; Mon–Fri 10am–9pm, Sat–Sun 10am–6pm), is a more authentic shop specializing in Huichol yarn paintings and bead art from San Andres Cohamiata, one of the main villages of this indigenous group, high up in the Sierra Madres.

Sirloin Stockade. For entertainment, there's a 10-screen movie theater. The mall is open daily from 8am to 2am; most stores are open from 11am to 9pm.

Puerto Vallarta's **municipal flea market** is just north of the Río Cuale, where Libertad and A. Rodríguez meet. The *mercado* sells clothes, jewelry, serapes, shawls, leather accessories and suitcases, papier-mâché parrots, stuffed frogs and armadillos, and, of course, T-shirts. The market is open daily from 9am to 6pm. Upstairs, a **food market** serves inexpensive Mexican meals. An **outdoor market** is along Río Cuale Island, between the two bridges. Stalls sell crafts, jewelry, gifts, folk art, and clothing.

Clothing

Vallarta's locally owned department store, **LANS,** has branches downtown at Juárez 867 (© 322/226-9100; www.lans.com.mx) and in both Plaza Peninsula and Plaza Caracol. LANS offers a wide selection of name-brand clothing, accessories, footwear, cosmetics, and home furnishings.

Contemporary Art

Known for sustaining one of the stronger art communities in Latin America, Puerto Vallarta has an impressive selection of fine galleries featuring quality original works. Several dozen galleries get together to offer art walks every Wednesday from 6 to 10pm between November and April. Most of the participating galleries serve complimentary cocktails during the art walks. It's a very popular weekly event among the local expat residents.

Ana Romo   This contemporary gallery opened in 2009 featuring works of Guadalajara artist Ana Romo. You'll find an impressive selection of abstract paintings, blown-glass vases, and glass sculptures—all at very reasonable prices when compared with galleries featuring art of similar quality. Open Monday through Saturday noon to 2pm and 4 to 9pm. Guadalupe Sanchez 803A, next to Pipila. ✆ **322/223-5666.** www.anaromoart.com.

Corsica   Among the best of Vallarta's galleries, Corsica features an exquisite collection of sculptures, installations, and paintings from world-renowned contemporary artists from Mexico. There are two locations—at Guadalupe Sanchez 735 and Leona Vicario 230. Open Monday through Saturday 11am to 2pm and 5 to 10pm. ✆ **322/223-1821.** www.galeriacorsica.com.

Galería des Artistes   This stunning gallery features contemporary painters and sculptors from throughout Mexico, Europe, and Latin America, including the renowned original "magiscopes" of Feliciano Bejar. Paintings by Vallarta favorite Evelyn Boren, as well as a small selection of works by Mexican masters, including Orozco, can be found here. There's an impressive new collection of sculptures from Guadalajara as well. It's open Monday to Saturday 11am to 10pm. Just across the street, affiliate **Galería Omar Alonso** exhibits photography by internationally renowned artists. It's also open Monday through Saturday 11am to 10pm. Leona Vicario 248. ✆ **322/222-5587.**

Galería Pacífico   Since opening in 1987, Galería Pacífico has been considered one of the finest galleries in Mexico. On display is a wide selection of sculptures and paintings in various mediums by midrange masters and up-and-comers alike. The gallery is a short walk inland from the fantasy sculptures on the *malecón*. Among the artists whose careers Galería Pacífico has influenced are rising talents Alfredo Langarica and Brewster Brockman, renowned sculptor Ramiz Barquet, and David Leonardo. Gallery owner Gary Thompson offers public sculpture walks on Tuesdays at 9:30am in high season. Open Monday through Saturday from 10am to 8pm, Sunday by appointment. Between June and October, check for reduced hours or vacation closings. Aldama 174, 2nd floor, above La Casa del Habano cigar store. ✆ **322/222-1982.** www.galeriapacifico.com.

Galería Uno   One of Vallarta's first galleries, the Galería Uno features an excellent selection of contemporary paintings by Latin American artists, plus a variety of posters and prints. In a classic adobe building with open courtyard, it's also a casual, salon-style gathering place for friends of owner Jan Lavender. Open Monday through Saturday from 10am to 8pm. Morelos 561 (at Corona). ✆ **322/222-0908.**

Gallería Dante   This gallery-in-a-villa showcases contemporary art including sculptures and paintings against a backdrop of gardens and fountains. Works by more than 100 Mexican and international artists are represented, including the acclaimed Oscar Solis, Guillermo Gomez, Israel Zzepda, Alejandro Colunga, and Tellosa. The gallery, which is the largest in Puerto Vallarta, is open during the winter Monday through Friday from 10am to 5pm, and by appointment. Basilio Badillo 269. ✆ **322/222-2477.** www.galleriadante.com.

Crafts & Gifts

Alfarería Tlaquepaque   Opened in 1953, this is Vallarta's original source for Mexican ceramics and decorative crafts, all at excellent prices. Open Monday through Saturday 9am to 9pm and Sunday from 9am to 3pm in high season, with reduced hours in low season. Av. México 1100. ✆ **322/223-2121.**

Safari Accents   Flickering candles glowing in colored-glass holders welcome you to this highly original shop overflowing with creative gifts, one-of-a-kind furnishings, and reproductions of paintings by Frida Kahlo and Botero. Open daily from 10am to 11pm. Olas Altas 224, Loc. 4. ✆ **322/223-2660.**

Decorative & Folk Art

Banderas Bay Trading Company ★   This shop features fine antiques and one-of-a-kind decorative objects for the home, including contemporary furniture, antique wooden doors, mirrors, Talavera, religious-themed items, original art, hand-loomed textiles, glassware, and pewter. Open Monday to Saturday 10am to 6pm. There's also a *bodega* (warehouse) annex of the shop, with the same hours, located at Constitución 319 (at Basilio Badillo; ✆ **322/223-9871**). Lázaro Cárdenas 263 (near Ignacio L. Vallarta). ✆ **322/223-4352.** www.banderasbaytradingcompany.com.

Tequila Sun Rising

You can tug on Superman's cape, you can spit into the wind, but don't ever mess with tequila in Mexico. Tequila lovers savor the subtle flavors of the agave spirit and prefer to take it like wine, sip by sip, over the course of an entire meal. They will likely gasp in horror if you throw back a shot of Jose Cuervo like a coed on spring break, and pity you when you wake with a monster hangover.

The makers of tequila—all but one still based in Jalisco—have formed an association to establish standards for labeling and denomination. The best tequilas are 100% agave, made with a set minimum of sugar to prime the fermentation process. These tequilas come in three categories, based on how they were stored: *Blanco* is white tequila aged very little, usually in steel vats; *reposado* (reposed) is aged in wooden casks for between 2 months and a year; *añejo* (aged) has been stored in oak barrels—often reused whiskey barrels from the U.S.—for at least a year. A good way to ease into the world of tequila appreciation is to order a *bandera* (flag), which consists of a shot of tequila and shots of lime and tomato juice. Each glass represents a color in the Mexican flag.

Lucy's CuCu Cabaña 🎁 Owners Lucy and Gil Gevins have assembled an entertaining and eclectic collection of Mexican folk art. Each summer they travel through Mexico and personally select the handmade works created by over 200 indigenous artists and artisans. Open Monday through Friday from 10am to 8pm, and Saturday from 10am to 3pm. Basilio Badillo 295 (at Constitución). © **322/222-1220.**

Olinala This shop contains two floors of fine indigenous Mexican crafts and folk art, including a collection of museum-quality masks and original contemporary art by gallery owner Brewster Brockman. Open Monday through Friday from 10am to 6pm, Saturday 10am to 2pm. Lázaro Cárdenas 274. © **322/222-4995.**

Puerco Azul Set in a space that actually has a former pig-roasting oven, Puerco Azul features a whimsical and eclectic selection of art and home accessories, much of it created by owner and artist Lee Chapman (aka Lencho). Open Monday to Saturday from 10am to 6pm. Constitución 325. © **322/222-8647.**

Querubines 🎁 Owner Marcella García travels across the country to select the items, which include exceptional artistic silver jewelry, embroidered and hand-woven clothing, bolts of loomed fabrics, tin mirrors and lamps, glassware, pewter frames and trays, high-quality wool rugs, straw bags, and Panama hats. Open Monday through Saturday from 9am to 9pm. Juárez 501A (at Galeana). ✆ **322/223-1727.**

Tequila & Cigars

La Casa del Habano This fine tobacco shop has certified quality cigars from Cuba, along with humidors, cutters, elegant lighters, and other smoking accessories. It's also a local cigar club, with a walk-in humidor for regular clients. In the back, you'll find comfy leather couches, TV sports, and full bar service. Open Monday through Saturday from noon to 9pm. Aldama 170. ✆ **322/223-2758.**

La Casa del Tequila ★ Here you'll find an extensive selection of premium tequilas, plus information and tastings. Also available are books, tequila glassware, and other tequila-drinking accessories. The shop has been downsized to accommodate the **Agave Grill** (p. 56) in the back. Open Monday through Saturday from noon to 11pm, and Sunday from 4 to 11pm. Morelos 589. ✆ **322/222-2000.**

PUERTO VALLARTA AFTER DARK

Puerto Vallarta's spirited nightlife reflects the town's dual nature—part resort, part colonial town. In the past, Vallarta was known for its live music scene, but in recent years the nocturnal action has shifted to DJ clubs with an array of eclectic, contemporary music. Happy hour offering two-for-one drinks usually takes place between 3 and 7pm. A concentration of spirited bars, lounges, and nightclubs line the *malecón,* with more traditional cantinas, sports bars, and gay clubs and bars found south of the Río Cuale in Viejo Vallarta (old town).

Performing Arts & Cultural Events

Opened in March 2010 in downtown Puerto Vallarta, the 912-seat **Teatro Vallarta,** Uruguay 184 (✆ **322/222-4475;** www.teatro vallarta.com) has since hosted such diverse performers as the Russian State Ballet, the Mexican comedian Teo Gonzalez, and the Drums of Okinawa, a Okinawan folkloric dance production. It's also the home of the music and dance spectacular **Fandango,** which celebrates the region's cultural history from the pre-Hispanic era through the present day. See the theater's website, as well

as the events page of **http://visitpuertovallarta.com**, for performances and dates.

The visual arts are big in Puerto Vallarta; the opening of an
exhibition carries considerable social and artistic significance.
Puerto Vallarta's gallery community comes together in the central
downtown area to present biweekly **art walks** from late October
to April, where new exhibits are presented, featured artists attend,
and complimentary cocktails are served. Check listings in the daily
English-language newspaper *Vallarta Today,* or the events section of
www.virtualvallarta.com.

3 Fiesta Nights

Major hotels in Puerto Vallarta feature frequent fiestas for tourists—extravaganzas with open bars, Mexican buffet dinners, and
live entertainment. Some are fairly authentic and make a good
introduction for first-time travelers to Mexico.

Rhythms of the Night (Cruise to Caletas) ★★ ◉   This is
an unforgettable evening under the stars at John Huston's former
home at the pristine cove called Las Caletas. The smooth, fast
Vallarta Adventures catamaran travels here, entertaining guests
along the way. Tiki torches and drummers dressed in native costumes greet you at the dock. There's no electricity—you dine by
the light of candles, the stars, and the moon. The evening includes
dinner, open bar, and entertainment. The buffet dinner is delicious—steak, seafood, and generous vegetarian options. The entertainment showcases indigenous dances in contemporary style. The
cruise departs at 6pm from the Vallarta Adventure Center in
Nuevo Vallarta or at 6:30pm from the Puerto Vallarta Maritime
Terminal and returns by 11pm. ℰ **888/526-2238** in the U.S., or 322/297-
1212. www.vallarta-adventures.com. Cost $89 (includes cruise, dinner, open bar,
and entertainment).

The Club & Music Scene
RESTAURANTS & BARS

Constantini Martini and Piano Bar ★   The most sophisticated martini bar in Vallarta is set in the elegant eatery **Café des
Artistes** (p. 54). Settle into one of the plush sofas and choose from
a fabulous list of champagnes or wines by the glass, signature martinis, and specialty drinks. An ample appetizer and dessert menu
makes it appropriate for late-night dining and drinks. Open daily
from 6pm to 1am. Guadalupe Sánchez 740. ℰ **322/222-3229.**

La Bodeguita del Medio   This authentic Cuban restaurant
and bar is known for its casual energy, terrific live Cuban music,

and mojitos. It's a branch of the original Bodeguita in Havana (reputedly Hemingway's favorite restaurant there), which opened in 1942. If you can't get to that one, the Vallarta version has successfully imported the essence—and has a small souvenir shop that sells Cuban cigars, rum, and other items. The food is not memorable, so I recommend coming just for drinks and dancing. A Cuban band plays salsa, cumbia, and other tropical rhythms nightly (except Mon) from 10pm to 2am. Kitchen open daily from 11:30am to 1am; bar open until 3am. Paseo Díaz Ordaz 858 (malecón), at Allende. ✆ **322/223-1585.**

Punto V ★ Having replaced Carlos O'Brien's in 2009, Punto V quickly became one of Vallarta's top nightspots. The grand open-air bar and restaurant overlooks the *malecón* and sea, transforming as the night wears on into a sizzling dance club popular with a 30- and 40-something crowd. Crystal chandeliers, faux Greek statues, video screens, and tables and sofas fill the main room; the upstairs sky bar also has daybeds. Live bands often play, too. Open daily from 11am to 3am. Open bar Sunday and Wednesday nights for 450 pesos. Paseo Díaz Ordaz (malecón) 786, at Pípila. ✆ **322/322-1444.**

Z'Tai Z'Tai is a stunning array of spaces that span an entire city block. Enter from the *malecón,* and you'll discover ZBar, an upstairs lounge with chill-out music, backlit orange lighting, bay views, and comfortable banquettes to relax on. Venture farther into this club, and you'll find an expansive open-air garden area that serves cocktails, as well as Asian-inspired dining and snacking options, accompanied by electronic music at a level still appropriate for conversation. There's an enormous selection of wines, but the favorite drink here is their signature cucumber martini. Open daily for food service from 6pm to midnight, with bar service until 2am or later. Valet parking available. Morelos 737, Col. Centro. ✆ **322/222-0306.** www.ztai.com.

ROCK, JAZZ & BLUES

El Faro Lighthouse Bar ★ A circular cocktail lounge at the top of the Marina lighthouse, El Faro is one of Vallarta's most romantic nightspots. Live guitar plays in high season, and the music's not so loud as to interrupt conversations. Drop by at twilight for the magnificent panoramic views, but don't expect anything other than a drink and, if you get lucky, some popcorn. Open daily from 5pm to 1:30am. Royal Pacific Yacht Club, Marina Vallarta. ✆ **322/221-0541,** -0542.

Hard Rock Cafe Vallarta's iconic Hard Rock Cafe features live rock music nightly starting at 10:30pm. Standard American fare and bar service are available throughout the day. Packed with rock memorabilia, the Hard Rock also sells merchandise in the adjacent shop. The bar is more popular with tourists than with locals. It's open daily from 11am to 2am. Paseo Díaz Ordaz (malecón) 652 ✆ **322/222-2230.** www.hardrock.com.

NIGHTCLUBS & DANCING

A few of Vallarta's clubs charge admission (typically in high season and on weekends), but more generally you pay just for drinks: about 60 pesos for a margarita, 45 pesos for a beer, and a bit more for mixed drinks. Keep an eye out for discount passes frequently available in hotels, restaurants, and other tourist spots. Along with clubs listed below, **Carlos 'n Charlie's, Hard Rock Cafe,** and **Señor Frog's** are also here. Most clubs are open from 10pm to 3am or later.

Collage Club   A multilevel monster of nighttime entertainment, Collage includes a pool salon, bowling alley, and the Disco Bar, with frequent live entertainment. It's just past the entrance to Marina Vallarta, air-conditioned, and very popular with a young, mainly local crowd. Calle Proa s/n, Marina Vallarta. ✆ **322/221-0505.** Cover up to 350 pesos, including open bar.

Hilo   You'll recognize Hilo by the giant sculptures that practically reach out the front entrance, including somewhat ironic faux-bronze statues of *campesinos* (Mexican farmers). This high-energy club playing extremely loud music ranging from house and electronic to rock remains a favorite with the 20-something set. The later the hour, the more crowded the club becomes. Open daily from 4pm to 6am. Malecón, btw. Aldama and Abasolo sts. ✆ **322/223-5361.** Cover $10 weekends and holidays. No cover weekdays.

Hyde   Formerly Christine's, this dazzling club draws a crowd with laser-light shows, pumped-in dry ice, flashing lights, and large-screen video panels. Once a disco—in the true sense of the word—it is now a modern dance club, with techno, house, and hip-hop the primary tunes played. The sound system is amazing, and the mix of music can get almost anyone dancing. Dress code: no tennis shoes or flip-flops, no shorts for men. Open weekends from 10:30pm to 6am. In the Krystal Vallarta hotel, north of downtown off Av. Francisco Medina Ascencio. ✆ **322/224-0202.** Cover $20 men, free for women.

J & B Salsa Club   This is a popular place to dance to Latin music—from salsa to samba, the dancing is hot and the atmosphere electric. On Fridays, Saturdays, and holidays, the air-conditioned club hosts live bands. Open daily from 8pm to 5am. Av.

Francisco Medina Ascencio Km 2.5 (Hotel Zone). ☏ **322/224-4616.** Cover 100 pesos.

La Vaquita   A giant dancing cow dominates the bar of this hot addition to the Vallarta club scene. In fact, paintings of flying cows and cattle in any number of amusing poses decorate this raging bar, with couches and daybeds upholstered like spotted cows. A sexy crowd moves to the grooves of the DJ into the wee hours. It's located next to Zoo (see below). Calle Morelos 535 (at Paseo Diaz Ordaz). No phone. Cover 100 pesos.

Mandala   The sister club to Hilo is geared toward a slightly more sophisticated crowd. There are giant Buddha sculptures situated throughout the Pan Asian–inspired club, and the three-level bar and dance club has ongoing music video screens and oversize windows overlooking the *malecón*. But there's little meditating here amid the din of house and Latin pop. This place attracts a sleek and suntanned crowd. Open daily from 6pm to 6am. Paseo Díaz Ordaz (malecón) 600 at Abasolo. ☏ **322/223-0966.** Cover 200 pesos.

Roo ★★★   Vallarta's hottest club at press time, Roo attracts a sexy crowd dressed in designer clothes. Giant chandeliers hang over the multilevel nightclub, with a killer sound system, dancing cages, and indoor and outdoor bars. It gets started at 8pm and continues until breakfast time. Expect a line during peak periods, and lots of stolen glances. Morelos 771. ☏ **322/223-3052,** -3053. Cover 200 pesos.

Zoo   This is your chance to be an animal and get wild in the night. A giant elephant head emerges out of a jungle-themed mural near the entrance, and the Zoo even has cages to dance in if you're feeling unleashed. This packed club boasts a killer sound system and a hot variety of dance music, including techno, reggae, and rap. Every hour's happy hour, with two-for-one drinks from 5 to 11pm. Zoo opens daily at 5pm and closes around 4am. Paseo Díaz Ordaz (malecón) 630. ☏ **322/222-4945.** www.zoobardance.com. Cover 100 pesos.

A Sports Bar

Andale's   Andale's is the most happening sports bar in town. The kitschy joint, decorated with an egg carton ceiling, stuffed animals, and comical life-size dolls, attracts a mixed-age English-speaking crowd. Sports play on various screens to the backdrop of classic rock. It's open from 7am to 3am. Olas Altas 425 in the Zona Romántica. ☏ **322/222-1054.** www.andales.com.

Gay & Lesbian Clubs

Vallarta has a vibrant gay community with a wide variety of clubs and nightlife options, including special bay cruises and evening excursions to nearby ranches. Most of the gay nightlife happens in so-called *Zona Romántica* (also called *Viejo Vallarta* or old town) on the south side of the Río Cuale, where the busiest street lined with restaurants, cafes, and bars is Olas Altas. The free **Gay Guide Vallarta** (www.gayguidevallarta.com) specializes in gay-friendly listings, including weekly specials and happy hours. Another excellent resource for gay travelers to Puerto Vallarta is **www.gogay puertovallarta.com**.

Casanova　This small club, decorated with leather sofas, red lights, and disco balls, usually gets going after midnight. There's a small stage featuring strip shows nightly from 11pm to 3am. The club itself is open daily from 10pm until the last customers leave. Lázaro Cárdenas 302 (corner of Constituciones). No phone. Cover 100 pesos.

La Noche　La Noche is a casual, intimate "neighborhood bar" catering to a gay clientele, with great prices on drinks and a menu of martinis and tequila cocktails. Beers are always two-for-one. Open daily from 6pm to 2am. Lázaro Cárdenas 263 (2 doors from Ignacio Vallarta). ☏ **322/222-3364.**

Mañana ★　Located in the Zona Romántica, the town's oldest and most popular gay club offers two dance floors, a pool with a waterfall, and candlelit tables. Weekends bring drag shows and stripteases. Open daily from 10pm to 6am. Venustiano Carranza 290. ☏ **322/222-7772.** www.manana.mx. Cover 200 pesos weekends, 100 pesos weekdays.

SIDE TRIPS FROM PUERTO VALLARTA
Yelapa: Robinson Crusoe Meets Jack Kerouac ★

It's a cove straight out of a tropical fantasy, and only a 45-minute trip by boat from Puerto Vallarta. Yelapa has no cars and one paved (pedestrian-only) road, and it only acquired electricity in the past 10 years. It's accessible only by boat. Its tranquillity, natural beauty, and seclusion make it a popular home for hipsters, artists, writers, and a few expats (looking to escape the stress of the world, or perhaps the law). Yelapa remains casual and friendly—you're unlikely to ever meet a stranger.

To get there, travel by excursion boat or inexpensive water taxi (see "Getting Around" in chapter 2). You can spend an enjoyable day, but I recommend a longer stay—it provides a completely different perspective.

Once you're in Yelapa, you can lie in the sun, swim, snorkel, eat fresh grilled seafood at a beachside restaurant, or sample the local moonshine, *raicilla*. The beach vendors specialize in the most amazing pies you've ever tasted (coconut, lemon, or chocolate). You can tour this tiny town or hike up a river to see one of two waterfalls; the closest to town is about a 5-minute walk straight up from the pier. *Note:* If you use a local guide, agree on a price before you start out. Horseback riding, guided birding, fishing trips, and paragliding are also available.

For overnight accommodations, local residents frequently rent rooms, and there's also the rustic **Hotel Lagunita ★** (www.hotel lagunita.com; ✆ **322/209-5056,** -5055). Its 29 cabañas have private bathrooms, and the hotel has electricity, a saltwater pool, massage service, an amiable restaurant and bar, the Barracuda Beach lounge and brick-oven pizza cafe, and a gourmet coffee shop. Though the prices are high for what you get, it is the most accommodating place for most visitors. Double rates run up to $120 during high season and up to $90 in the off season. Special rooms are available for honeymooners, for $135 in high season. MasterCard and Visa are accepted. Lagunita is a popular spot for yoga retreats.

If you wish to splurge, look into staying at **Verana ★★★** (www. verana.com; ✆ **800/530-7176** in the U.S., or 322/222-2360). See p. 52 for details.

If you stay over on a Wednesday or Saturday during the winter, don't miss the biweekly dinner-dance at the **Yelapa Yacht Club ★** (no phone). Typically tongue-in-cheek for Yelapa, the "yacht club" consists of a cement dance floor and a disco ball, but the DJ spins a great range of tunes, attracting all ages and types. Dinner (80–160 pesos) is a bonus—the food may be the best anywhere in the bay. The menu changes depending on what's fresh. Ask for directions; it's in the main village, on the beach.

Nuevo Vallarta & North of Vallarta: All-Inclusives

Many people assume Nuevo Vallarta is a suburb of Puerto Vallarta, but it's a stand-alone destination over the state border in Nayarit. It was designed as a mega resort development, complete with marina, golf course, and luxury hotels. Although it got off to a slow start, it has finally come together, with a collection of mostly all-inclusive hotels catering particularly to families on one of the widest, most attractive beaches in the bay. The biggest resort, Paradise Village, has a full marina and an 18-hole golf course inland from the beachside strip of hotels, plus a growing selection of condos and homes for sale. The Mayan Palace also has an 18-hole course here. The most expensive all-inclusive resort here is **Grand Velas All Suites & Spa Resort** (www.vallarta.grandvelas.com; ✆ **322/226-8000**) at Av. Cocoteros, 98 Sur. The Paradise Plaza shopping center, next to Paradise Village, amplifies the area's shopping, dining, and services. It's open daily from 10am to 10pm. To get to the beach, you travel down a lengthy entrance road from the highway, passing by a few remaining fields (which used to be great for birding) but mostly real estate under construction.

A 26km (16-mile) trip into downtown Puerto Vallarta takes about 30 minutes by taxi, costs about 250 pesos, and is available 24 hours a day. The ride is slightly longer by public bus, which costs 15 pesos and operates from 7am to 11pm.

Marival Resort & Suites   This casual all-inclusive hotel sits at the northernmost end of Nuevo Vallarta. Designed in Mediterranean style, it offers a complete vacation experience, including extensive land sports, watersports, and daytime activities for kids, teenagers, and adults. There are a large variety of room types, ranging from studios to one-, two-, and three-bedroom suites. Rooms and suites have balconies or terraces with garden, pool, or ocean views. The broad white-sand beach is one of the real assets here. The nearby Marival Residences & World Spa is one of Nuevo Vallarta's most luxurious all-inclusive clubs, offering modern condo-like accommodations, an innovative spa, and outstanding dining facilities. This is a better option for those looking for quiet, upscale amenities, and pampering.

Paseo de los Cocoteros and Bulevar Nuevo Vallarta s/n, 63732 Nuevo Vallarta, Nay. www.marival.com. ✆ **877/222-0302** in the U.S., 322/297-0100, or 322/226-8200. Fax 322/297-0262. 499 units. $210 and up double; $279 and up suite. Rates are all-inclusive. Ask for seasonal specials. AE, MC, V. Free parking. From the Puerto Vallarta airport, enter Nuevo Vallarta from the 2nd entrance; Marival is the 1st resort to your right on Paseo de los Cocoteros. **Amenities:** 6 restaurants; 7 bars; kids' club; 4 outdoor pools and an adults-only whirlpool; spa; 4 lighted tennis courts; extensive watersports, land sports, and daytime activities. *In room:* A/C, TV, hair dryer, Wi-Fi.

Paradise Village ★   The collection of pyramid-shaped buildings, designed in Maya-influenced style, houses well-designed all-suite accommodations in studio and one-, two-, and three-bedroom configurations. All have sitting areas and kitchenettes, making the resort ideal for families or groups of friends. Truly a village, this self-contained resort set on an exquisite stretch of beach offers a full array of services. The Maya theme extends to both oceanfront pools, with mythical creatures forming water slides and waterfalls. The spa is reason enough to book a vacation here, with treatments, hydrotherapy, massage (including massage on the beach), and fitness and yoga classes. A compelling attraction is the nearby El Tigre golf course (see "Active Pursuits," earlier in this chapter); their on-site marina continues to draw a growing number of boats and yachts. Paradise Village has begun to feel a bit dated around the edges.

Paseo de los Cocoteros 001, 63731 Nuevo Vallarta, Nay. www.paradisevillage.com. ℭ **866/334-6080** in the U.S., or 322/226-6770. Fax 322/226-6713. 700 units. $150-$300 junior or 1-bedroom suite; $220-$400 2-bedroom suite; $335-$600 3-bedroom suite. All-inclusive rates available for $89 additional per person. AE, DC, MC, V. Free covered parking. **Amenities:** 3 restaurants; 2 beachside snack bars; kids' club; petting zoo; access to championship golf club w/18-hole course; complete fitness center; basketball court; beach volleyball; 2 beachside pools; lap pool; European spa; 2 tennis courts; watersports center; marina; Wi-Fi in lobby. *In room:* A/C, TV, hair dryer, minibar.

Bucerías: A Coastal Village ★

Only 18km (11 miles) north of the Puerto Vallarta airport and adjacent to Nuevo Vallarta, Bucerías (Boo-seh-*ree*-ahs, meaning "place of the divers") is a trendy coastal town on the Nayarit side of Banderas Bay. Lovely villas, art galleries, and gourmet restaurants line the main street in Bucerías Sur, the gentrified south side of town bustling with expatriates and suburban commuters. Across a walking bridge lies the north side of Bucerías, colloquially referred to as "el pueblo," a traditional fishing village where more of the local population lives.

To reach the town center by car, take the exit road from the highway out of Vallarta and drive down the shaded, divided street that leads to the beach. Turn left when you see a line of minivans and taxis (which serve Bucerías and Vallarta). Go straight ahead 1 block to the main plaza. The beach, with a lineup of restaurants, is a half-block farther. You'll see cobblestone streets leading from the highway to the beach, and hints of villas and town homes behind high walls.

If you take the bus to Bucerías, exit when you see the minivans and taxis to and from Bucerías on the street that leads to the beach. To use public transportation from Puerto Vallarta, take a minivan or bus marked BUCERIAS (they run 6am–9pm). The last minivan stop is Bucerías's town square. There's also 24-hour taxi service.

EXPLORING BUCERÍAS

Come here for a day trip from Puerto Vallarta just to enjoy the long, wide, uncrowded beach, along with the fresh seafood served at the beachside restaurants or at one of the cafes listed below. On Sundays, many of the streets surrounding the plaza are closed to traffic for a *mercado* (street market)—where you can buy anything from tortillas to neon-colored cowboy hats. There's also an art walk every second Thursday of the month from 7 to 9pm (www.thebucerias artwalk.com).

Bucerías doesn't offer much in the way of hotels—many people who come here rent condominiums or other vacation properties. One reliable option is the **Hotel Palmeras** (www.hotelpalmeras. com; © **329/298-1288**), on Lázaro Cárdenas 35, with simple, comfortable rooms generally under $100, just a block off the beach.

The **Coral Reef Surf Shop,** Heroe de Nacozari 114 (© **329/298-0261**), sells a great selection of surfboards and gear, and offers surfboard and Boogie board rentals, and a surf package that includes transport to Punta Mita or La Lancha and a lesson there for $85. Surfboards rent for $20 per day and $100 per week, double that for stand-up paddle boards. The shop is on the main highway heading south out of town.

WHERE TO EAT

In addition to the restaurants mentioned below, many seafood restaurants front the beach. The local specialty is *pescado zarandeado*, a whole fish (usually red snapper) smothered in tasty sauce and slow-grilled, and the ceviche and lobster are excellent here, too. Most fine-dining options here are open only for dinner.

Eva's Brickhouse ★★ INTERNATIONAL   Kent oversees the preparation of the delicious fresh fish and aged steaks while his wife, Eva, takes care of the desserts (the Key lime pie, chocolate volcano cake, and carrot cake are all irresistible). Jazz fills the air of the palm-filled outdoor patio, with hanging coconut lamps, Maya-inspired tablecloths, and ribbon-woven flowers with each place-setting. The tender steaks are aged in-house for 14 days and then cooked to order over the mesquite-wood fire; a peppercorn brandy sauce covers the New York strip. Mahimahi (caught locally and served as a thick filet) and sea bass are on the menu, and the flavorful Mediterranean preparation includes shrimp, garlic, tomatoes, onions, peppers, capers, and olives. On Saturdays, Kent slow-roasts pork for 7 hours and serves it with garlic mashed potatoes and homemade apple sauce.

Galeana 15 (at Lázaro Cárdenas). © **329/298-2238.** www.evasbrickhouse.com. Main courses 249–349 pesos. No credit cards. Daily 4–11pm. *Mondays?*

Le Fort ★★★ 📷 FRENCH   An evening here begins with champagne smiles as privileged diners watch chef-owner Gilles Le Fort prepare their gourmet meal. The U-shaped bar adjacent to the kitchen accommodates the guests, who sip *kir royales* and nibble on homemade terrine while the master works. Chef Le Fort is the winner of numerous culinary awards, and his warm conviviality is the real secret ingredient of this unusual experience. Once dinner is served in the adjacent open-air dining room, Le Fort and his wife, Margarita, join the table, which seats up to 16. He owns the most extensive wine cellar in the bay—some 2,000 bottles of French and Mexican varieties. Three delicious courses are served (the menu is chosen by the first group to reserve for that night), followed by a presentation of fine liquors (available for purchase). I cannot imagine a more creative, social dining experience along this beautiful stretch of coast.

Calle Lázaro Cárdenas 71, 1 block from the Hotel Royal Decameron. © **329/298-1532.** www.lefort.com.mx. Reservations required. Cooking class, 3-course dinner, wines, and recipes $60 per person. MC, V. Daily 8–10:30pm. Closed for a month in summer.

Mark's ★★ 🍴 MEDITERRANEAN   It's worth a special trip to Bucerías just to eat at this open-air patio restaurant. The most popular dinner spot in town, Mark's serves sophisticated cuisine alongside simpler thin-crust pizzas and flatbreads, baked in a brick oven and seasoned with fresh herbs grown in the garden. The bustling kitchen focuses on fresh local and organic products—favorite starters include the roasted beet and apple salad with goat cheese and the tender chicken masala and vegetable spring roll. Among the most tempting entrees are the macadamia-crusted red snapper filet, fresh poached lobster, and grass-fed filet mignon with blue-cheese ravioli. A four-course wine-tasting menu is available for 400 pesos. Multitalented chef Jan Marie (Mark's charming wife and business partner) runs an adjacent boutique (www.jan marieboutique.com), featuring elegant home accessories, art, and gifts. The small restaurant bar televises all major sporting events.

Calle Lázaro Cárdenas 56 (a half-block from the beach). ☎ **329/298-0303.** www.marksbucerias.com. Reservations recommended. Pizza and pasta 175–245 pesos; main courses 210–365 pesos. MC, V. Daily 5–11pm. From the highway, turn left just after bridge, where there's a small sign for Mark's; double back left at next street (immediately after you turn left) and turn right at next corner; Mark's is on the right.

Mezzogiorno ★★ ITALIAN The owners of this popular oceanfront trattoria built a reputation with their Mezzaluna restaurant in Vallarta and then moved the business to their former home in Bucerías. It's one of the most attractive dining options north of Vallarta, in a sleekly restored home overlooking the bay. Despite the stunning setting, it takes second place to the flavorful dishes. Large, flavorful salads overflow with fresh ingredients—my favorite combines grilled chicken with mixed greens, sun-dried tomatoes, goat cheese, and a currant-balsamic vinaigrette. For main dishes, pasta takes center stage, with bestsellers that include carbonara, fettuccini salmone, and lasagna, as well gnocchi. The black fettuccine topped with shrimp, scallops, and fish is also delicious. A few candlelit tables sit on the beach in high season and offer the best views of all. The restaurant operates a beach club here by day.

Av. del Pacífico 33. ☎ **329/298-0350.** www.mezzogiorno.com.mx. Reservations recommended. Main courses 95–215 pesos. MC, V. Daily 5–11pm (lunch sometimes offered in high season).

Punta Mita: Exclusive Seclusion ★★★

At the northern tip of the bay lies an arrowhead-shaped, 600-hectare (1,482-acre) peninsula bordered on three sides by the ocean, called Punta de Mita. Considered a sacred place by the Indians, this is the point where Banderas Bay, the Pacific Ocean, and the Sea of Cortez come together. It's magnificent, with quiet beaches and coral reefs just offshore. Stately rocks jut out along the shoreline, and the water is a dreamy translucent blue. Punta Mita has evolved into Mexico's most exclusive development, an enormous gated resort community next to the original little town that to this day has a few authentic restaurants and shops. The luxury community's master plan includes a couple world-class resorts, multi-million dollar villas and residences, and two championship golf courses. You'll find the elegant Four Seasons Resort, St. Regis, and two Jack Nicklaus Signature golf courses here along with plenty of exclusive real estate for sale to the highest bidders.

Casa de Mita ★★ 🎁 This hotel isn't technically in Punta Mita, but it's near enough to convey a sense of the area's relaxed seclusion. It's located on the back road that runs from Punta Mita to Sayulita, on the small, pristine Careyeros Bay. The six rooms and two suites are set in a villa overlooking the exquisite beach. The villa itself is a work of white stucco walls, hand-painted tiles and stone mosaics, thatch and tile roofs, and guayaba-wood balcony detailing. Interiors of the guest rooms are simple and elegant, with touches such as carved armoires, headboards, and doors from Michoacán. Private balconies with ocean views surround the pool, which features canopy daybeds and a small fountain. A big plus here is the delicious dining.

Playa Careyeros, 63734 Punta de Mita, Nay. www.casademita.com. © **866/740-7999** in the U.S., or 329/298-4114. Fax 329/298-4112. 8 units. High season $645-$795 double; low season $505-$635 double. Rates include all meals and drinks. Minimum 3-night stay required. AE, DC, MC, V. Limited street parking. **Amenities:** Restaurant; entertainment room w/TV and DVD; universal gym station; small outdoor pool; spa; tour services, including horseback riding, paddle boarding, and surfing lessons; Wi-Fi. *In room:* A/C, minibar, no phone.

Four Seasons Resort Punta Mita ★★★ The Four Seasons Punta Mita is one of the world's most spectacular resorts, offering refinement, seclusion, and impeccable service. Accommodations lie in three-story casitas surrounding the main building, which houses the stunning open-air lobby, cultural center, restaurants, shopping arcade, and oceanfront infinity pool. Guest rooms offer ocean or garden views from large terraces or balconies. Suites include a private plunge pool, sitting room with a sofa bed, separate bedroom, bar, and a powder room. Rooms are plush and spacious, with a king or two double beds, seating area, and luxurious bathroom. The resort also has an adults-only tranquillity pool, with a sushi and tapas bar surrounded by cabañas available for daily rent, as well as an incredible lazy river pool with inner tubes for kids and adults to float around. The resort rents out magnificent four- and five-bedroom villas with private butlers, and there are two Jack Nicklaus championship golf courses, a full-service spa, and tennis center. Service is unerringly warm and unobtrusive throughout this little paradise, and each of the resort's gourmet restaurants is fantastic.

63734 Bahía de Banderas, Nay. www.fourseasons.com/puntamita. © **800/332-3442** in the U.S., or 329/291-6000. Fax 329/291-6060. 173 units. High season $545-$1,175 double, $1,685-$16,000 suite; low season $375-$925 double, $1,025-$8,750 suite. AE, DC, MC, V. Free valet parking. **Amenities:** 3 restaurants; lobby bar; beachfront bar; children's programs; concierge; cultural center w/lectures, cooking classes, Spanish classes, dance classes, and other daily activities; full-service fitness center; horseback riding; Jacuzzi; oceanfront pool; adults-only pool surrounded by private cabañas; lazy river pool; room service; European-style spa; tennis center w/10 courts of various surfaces; watersports equipment; yacht charter; yoga. *In room:* A/C, flatscreen TV/DVD, i-Home, hair dryer, Internet, minibar.

St. Regis ★★   Opened in late 2008, this ultraexclusive St. Regis is the first in Latin America, set on a stunning expanse of beach in Punta Mita. Guest rooms and suites are almost hidden amid the 33 two-story casitas spread throughout the property, where palm-filled gardens and three infinity pools compete with the endless ocean for guests' attention. Beautifully appointed rooms incorporate handmade tiles, custom Mexican furnishings, and large marble bathrooms with indoor and outdoor showers. Other features include flatscreen TVs, Remède bath amenities, and the St. Regis signature butler service. Throughout the resort, touches of Provence combine with chic Mexican designs that draw on river stone, marble, onyx, wood, and clay. The resort's spa merits special mention for its pampering service. Although there's a kids' program, the resort targets adults looking for privacy and usually feels very quiet. The three gourmet restaurants give you variety, so you never need to leave the property.

Lote H-4 Carretera Federal 200, Km 19.5, Punta de Mita, 63734, Nayarit. www. stregis.com/puntamita. ✆ **800/598-1863** in the U.S., or 329/291-5800. Fax 329/291-5801. 120 units. $480 and up double; $1,140 and up suite. AE, DC, MC, V. Free valet parking. **Amenities:** 3 restaurants; 3 bars; babysitting; kids' club; concierge; full-service spa and fitness center; Jacuzzi; Internet room; 3 pools; room service; 8 tennis courts and access to the Jack Nicklaus Signature courses Pacífico and Bahía; watersports equipment. *In room:* A/C, flatscreen TV, hair dryer, Internet, minibar.

Sayulita: A Surfers' Paradise

Sayulita sits only 40km (25 miles) northwest of Puerto Vallarta, on Hwy. 200 to Tepic, yet it feels like a world apart. It captures the simplicity and tranquillity of beach life that has long since left Vallarta—but hurry, because it's exploding in popularity. For years, Sayulita has been principally a surfers' destination—the main beach in town is known for its consistent break and long, ridable waves. Visitors and locals who find Vallarta to be too cosmopolitan have started to flock here. Although Sayulita has only 5,800 residents, it swells to nearly 40,000 visitors in high season. You'll now find more real estate offices than surf shops, and more fine-jewelry stores than juice bars, but Sayulita is still holding on to its charms.

An easygoing attitude prevails in this beach town, despite the niceties popping up amid the basic accommodations, inexpensive Mexican food stands, and handmade, hippie-style-bauble vendors. You may encounter a Huichol Indian family that has come down from the Sierra to sell their wares. Yet it's quickly becoming gentrified with new cafes, sleek shops, aromatherapy-infused spas, and elegant villas for rent.

Sayulita is most popular for surfing. Any day, you'll witness a swarm of surfers seeking perfect swells offshore from the main beach. Numerous other surf spots dot the coastline—some more secret than others—and a reliable long-boarders' break can be found at La Lancha and Punta Mita, about half an hour away (most surf shops will organize trips there). Other ocean activities, such as whale-watching, fishing, and snorkeling trips, can be arranged through **Riviera Nayarit Magical Tours** (© 329/291-2065), located at the corner of Avenita Revolución and Calle Delfin.

To get to Sayulita, you can rent a car or take a taxi from the airport or downtown Vallarta. The rate is about $70 to get to the town plaza. The taxi stand is on the main square, or you can call for pickup at your hotel. The trip to the airport from Sayulita costs about $60. Guides also lead tours to Puerto Vallarta, Punta Mita, and other surrounding areas, including a Huichol Indian community. There's also a bus that operates between Sayulita and Puerto Vallarta every 15 minutes between 5:30am and 8:15pm for only 25 pesos each way.

SURFING

There are two main surf spots in Sayulita—the most popular is the "point" break fronting the main beach in the village, which is a right long board break. A faster, left break is found just north of the river mouth, in front of the campground. There's also a calmer spot toward the beach's south end where lessons are usually given. Surf instruction and board rentals are available at **Lunazul Surf School** (© 329/291-2009; www.lunazulsurfschool.com), located at Marlin 4, where this street ends at the beachfront. The 90-minute surf lessons cost 450 pesos for individual instruction, or 350 pesos per person for group instruction. This includes a rash guard and an hour free board rental after the lesson. Board rentals (including hard and soft short and long boards) through Lunazul are 50 pesos per hour or 200 pesos for the day; you'll need to leave an ID as a deposit. Stand-up paddle boards and Boogie boards are also available. You'll find several other surf schools on the beach during high season. Most surf shops also organize trips to La Lancha, a popular surf spot near Punta Mita with slow-rolling waves perfect for long boarders. Four-hour excursions there cost about $65 per person, including transportation and board rental.

WHERE TO STAY

Along with the hotels listed below, Sayulita has two hostels, a beachside campground, and a number of private homes to rent.

Hotel La Casona ★ 🍷   Just half a block from Sayulita's main surfing beach, this cheerful hotel houses nine individually designed rooms decorated in bleached white, terra cotta, and turquoise with colorful Mexican accents. Five rooms—Sky (which has a full ocean view), Amor, Coco, Lily, and Peacock—offer their own balconies with hammocks, and all rooms have private bathrooms with showers only. The communal kitchen and "living lounge" tend to bring guests together, and there are a number of daybeds and couches interspersed throughout the corridors perfect for reading. For breakfast, organic coffee, teas, fresh squeezed orange juice and fruit, granola, and freshly baked muffins are offered. Expect a very friendly vibe here. One drawback: The surrounding streets can be quite noisy, especially in high season.

Calle Delfin 7, 63734 Sayulita, Nay. www.lacasonasayulita.com. ☎ **415/683-3244** in the U.S., or 329/291-3629. 9 units. $75–$140 high season; low season discounts available. Rates include continental breakfast. AE, MC, V. **Amenities:** Communal kitchen and lounge; massage service; help w/tours and activities; Wi-Fi. *In room:* A/C (in some), fan.

Playa Escondida ★★★ 🎒   Just above an idyllic beach cove, a handful of uniquely designed bungalows dot the lush tropical grounds of Playa Escondida. A waterfall rains warm water into the oceanfront infinity pool, set next to the *palapa* restaurant and open-air spa. The casual, friendly staff gets to know many of the guests at this gorgeous yet unpretentious resort. It's not the Four Seasons—activities are limited, there are no air conditioners, and Mother Nature sometimes visits the open-air bungalows (which have fans and mosquito nets). But for those who want a peaceful vacation off the beaten track and don't mind sacrificing a bit of commercial convenience for enchanted natural beauty, this place is unforgettable. Choose from among individually designed beachfront casitas, bungalows in the jungle, or imported teak houses from Thailand constructed in a spectacular bird canyon. The open-air spa offers outstanding massages for a great value. Sayulita is a winding 10-minute drive from this splendid resort.

Playa Escondida, 63732 Sayulita, Nay. www.playa-escondida.com. ☎ **805/709-1470** in the U.S., or 329/291-3641. 26 units. High season $220–$475 double; low season $115–$250 double. $100 mandatory fee per guest for food and beverages. AE, MC, V. **Amenities:** Restaurant; bar; oceanfront pool; Jacuzzi; horseback riding; open-air spa; private beach w/watersports equipment; yoga; walking trails; Wi-Fi (in reception and restaurant areas). *In room:* Fan, fridge (full kitchen in houses in bird canyon).

Villa Amor ★★   Resembling an enchanted private villa, Villa Amor is a collection of guest rooms perched on a bluff by the sea.

Owner Rod Ingram and his design team carefully crafted each space and individual suite with careful attention to detail. Beach chic rooms may have canopy beds, rattan furnishings, stone floors, original Mexican artwork, and organic bathroom amenities. One- and two-bedroom "villa" suites include fully equipped kitchenettes, plus open-air seating and—in the case of some—private plunge pools. The exterior walls open to breathtaking ocean views all around. Outdoor candlelit tables and the *palapa* bar framed by tiki torches tempt you not to leave the property, even though down- town Sayulita lies just a short walk away. A small private beach sits just in front. Note that many stairs and steep walkways zigzag the property.

Camino Playa Los Muertos s/n, 63732 Sayulita, Nay. www.villaamor.com. Ⓒ **619/819-5407** in the U.S., or 329/291-3010. Fax 329/291-3018. 34 units. High season $110–$260 1-bedroom villa, $380–$550 2-bedroom villa, $750 3-bed- room villa; low season $55–$130 1-bedroom villa, $190–$275 2-bedroom villa, $375 3-bedroom villa. MC, V. **Amenities:** Restaurant; bar; concierge w/tour ser- vices; kayaks; room service; Wi-Fi. *In room:* A/C (in some), fan.

WHERE TO EAT

Fine dining is hard to come by in Sayulita, but you'll find tasty seafood eateries and fish taco stands around town and by the beach. For the best burrito of your life, stop by **Burritos Revolu- ción** just off the main plaza at Revolución 40 (no phone). There's almost always a line here for the cooked-to-order "surf" (marlin, mahimahi, or shrimp) and "turf" (chicken, beef, or carnitas) burri- tos, and a sign advises you to smile, pay cash, and not ask for any substitutions. This no-nonsense burrito shack is open Tuesday to Sunday from 10am to 6pm. The best fish tacos are made at the aptly named **Sayulita Fish Taco** (Ⓒ **329/291-3272**), also serv- ing over 200 tequilas at Mariscal 13. **Ruben's Deli** (Ⓒ **322/183- 0692**), located at the corner of Revolución and Delfin, prepares yummy deli sandwiches daily from 10am to 5pm.

Don Pedro's INTERNATIONAL   Sayulita's best-known res- taurant features an enticing beachfront location, which is the main reason to come here. Choose between an open-air dining area or shaded tables on the beach for breakfast, lunch, or dinner. Although the food quality varies, the grilled artichoke, scallop sushi, and fresh salads are all reliable starters. For main courses, I recommend the thin-crust pizza, fresh fish, and variety of savory pasta and meat dishes, such as the mesquite grilled leg of lamb with couscous. Homemade flatbread accompanies your meal. At night, torches and clay pot fireplaces warm the beachfront tables. In the bar area, TVs broadcast wide-ranging sports events. A Cuban band plays salsa Monday nights.

Marlin 2, on the beachfront. ℂ **329/291-3090.** Main courses 145–285 pesos. MC, V. Daily 8am–10:30pm.

El Costeño SEAFOOD   They say you haven't been to Sayulita if you haven't eaten at El Costeño, the oldest restaurant here dating from 1964. The sandy, sun-drenched eatery right on the main beach invites you to nibble on tortilla chips and ceviche while watching surfers glide across waves just in front. Grab one of the plastic tables and chairs on the large open-air patio or right on the beach—you can come for lunch or an early dinner and sit for as long as you like. Start with an order of guacamole and an outrageously large, potent margarita. The fish tacos are simple and delicious, as are the shrimp quesadillas. Whole fish comes topped with butter, garlic, or spicy "Diablo" sauce, with shrimp and octopus prepared any number of ways. The laid-back waitstaff seems as timeless as the ocean before you, and is never too rushed.

On the main beach. No phone. Dishes 60–110 pesos. No credit cards. Fri–Wed noon–8pm. Closed Thurs.

Restaurant Bar Leyza ★★ 🗝 MEXICAN   Sayulita's most authentic Mexican restaurant sits off the main square and incorporates traditional Huichol dishes, such as *sopes* and *huaraches,* into its creative but no-nonsense menu. Other delectable dishes include chiles rellenos stuffed with shrimp, fish fajitas, *arrachera* beef, chicken *mole,* and enormous combination platters with enchiladas, burritos, and tostadas. There are vegetarian options, too. The perfectly spiced food is cooked in olive oil and served on beautiful ceramic dishes; everything at this family-run restaurant tends to be healthy, cheap, and delicious. Try one of the fresh fruit waters to accompany your meal, and don't miss the hot salsa with fresh tomatoes, chiles, garlic, and shallots. You can sit inside, on the sidewalk patio, or on the rooftop terrace. If you can't get a table here, quality Mexican food is also served next door at Carmelita.

Next to the main square. ℂ **322/100-9373.** Dishes 60–239 pesos. No credit cards. Daily 8am–midnight.

Rollie's ★ INTERNATIONAL   Resident expats love this eclectic restaurant, where the menu welcomes "travelers, strangers, and lovely locals." Known for its good value breakfasts, Rollie's serves, among other items, Adriana's Rainbow (an omelet with cheese, tomatoes, green peppers, and onions) and my personal favorite, Indian Pipe Pancakes. All breakfasts come with lightly seasoned, pan-fried new potatoes. Rollie's also serves dinner, with live music in high season. Specialties include taco salads, paella, and creative hamburgers (such as those with shrimp or mahimahi). An espresso bar opens in the mornings, and terrific Mexican coffee is available all day.

Av. Revolución 58, 2 blocks west of the main square. ✆ **329/291-3567,** -3075. Breakfast 55–75 pesos; dinner 65–135 pesos. No credit cards. Nov–Apr daily 7:30am–noon and 5:30–9pm. Closed for dinner Mon nights; closed May–Oct.

NIGHTLIFE

Nightlife in Sayulita is as laid-back by night as by day, and much of the action just happens out on the street and around the main square. Locals seem to gravitate to a different locale each night, so when you arrive, ask around to see where the evening's hot spot will be. For salsa in Sayulita, **La Bodeguita del Medio** (✆ 329/291-3866), located at Av. Revolución 30-A, offers live Cuban music from 8pm until midnight and serves potent *mojitos*. It's open daily from noon to 2am. Housed upstairs under a big *palapa* next to the main plaza, **Calypso** (✆ 329/291-3704), at Revolución 44, is a popular bar/restaurant serving consistently high quality Mexican dishes and excellent salads alongside a full collection of tequilas. Traditional Mexican music plays in the background. It's open daily from 5 to 11pm. **Tekari** ✆ 329/291-3828), on Calle Manuel Navarrete at the corner of Gaviottas, is basically a big beach shack playing live music weekends and DJ mixes during the week. It's open from 8pm into the wee hours, although the place really gets going after midnight.

San Sebastián: A Mountain Hideaway ★★★

If you haven't heard about San Sebastián yet, it probably won't be long—its remote location and historic appeal have made it the Mexican media's new darling destination. Originally discovered in the late 1500s and settled in 1603, the town peaked as a center of mining operations, swelling to a population of over 30,000 by the mid-1800s. Today, with roughly 600 year-round residents, San Sebastián retains all the charm of a village locked in time, with an old church, a coffee plantation, and an underground tunnel system—and wholly without a T-shirt shop.

GETTING THERE

By car, it's a 2-hour drive up the Sierra Madre from Puerto Vallarta on a recently improved road, but it can be difficult during the summer rainy season, when the road washes out frequently.

A number of tour operators offer day trips to San Sebastián from Puerto Vallarta (see below). It's worth taking a guided tour, as tour guides are generally highly knowledgeable and a large part of San Sebastián's appeal is its fascinating history.

GUIDED TOURS

Vallarta Adventures (© **888/526-2238** in the U.S., or 322/297-1212; www.vallarta-adventures.com) runs 7-hour long day trips from Puerto Vallarta. The cost is $84 including round-trip transportation by air-conditioned van, lunch at a traditional restaurant, a guided tour of the town, and bottled water. The tour includes a visit to the coffee factory **La Quinta Mary,** the local church, and the **Casa Museo de Doña Conchita,** a small family-run museum full of personal and historical artifacts curated by the very knowledgeable daughter of the late Doña Conchita. On the way back from San Sebastián, the bus stops at a tequila distillery in the village of La Estancia, where visitors are given a tour of the distillery and the opportunity to sample—and purchase, if they wish—the various types of tequila and *raicilla* (a local mezcal similar to tequila, but produced from a different type of agave plant).

WHERE TO STAY

There are two places to stay in San Sebastián. The first is the very basic **El Pabellón de San Sebastián,** which faces the town square. Its nine simply furnished rooms surround a central patio. Don't expect extras here; rates run $40 per double. The town's central phone lines handle reservations—you call (© **322/297-0200**) and leave a message or send a fax, and hopefully the hotel will receive it. Except on holidays, there is generally room at this inn. No credit cards.

A more enjoyable option, the stately **Hacienda Jalisco ★★** (© **322/222-9638;** www.haciendajalisco.com), built in 1850, was once the center of mining operations in town. The beautifully landscaped, rambling old hacienda is near the airstrip, a 15-minute walk from town. The five extra-clean rooms have wood floors, rustic furnishings and antiques, and working fireplaces; some are decorated with pre-Columbian reproductions. The ample bathrooms are beautifully tiled and have skylights. Hammocks grace the upstairs terrace, while a sort-of museum on the lower level attests to the celebrity guests and importance the hacienda has enjoyed over the years. Because of its remote location, all meals are included. Rates are around $80 per person per night with full breakfast and dinner, or $60 per person per night with breakfast only;

alcoholic beverages are extra. Reserve by e-mail (info@hacienda jalisco.com), by phone, or on their website. Group rates and discounts for longer stays are available. No credit cards are accepted. Guided horseback, walking, or mine tours can be arranged through the Hacienda.

COSTA ALEGRE: PUERTO VALLARTA TO BARRA DE NAVIDAD

by Shane Christensen

4

In my view, the Costa Alegre (also spelled Costalegre) is Mexico's most spectacular coastal area, a 232km (144-mile) stretch that connects tropical forests with a series of dramatic cliff-lined coves and exclusive accommodations. Tiny outpost towns line the coast, while dirt roads trail down to a succession of magical coves with pristine beaches, most of them steeped in privileged exclusivity. The sunset vistas and nighttime stargazing here are incredible—without any light pollution, it feels like you can reach up and grab the stars. Considered one of Mexico's greatest undiscovered treasures, this coast is becoming a favored hideaway for publicity-fatigued celebrities and those in search of natural seclusion. However, don't be surprised to hear about major development plans for this region as the economy recovers.

The area is referred to as **Costa Alegre (Happy Coast)**—the marketer's term—and **Costa Careyes (Turtle Coast),** after the many sea turtles that nest here. It is home to an eclectic array of the most captivating and exclusive places to stay in Mexico, with a selective roster of activities that includes championship golf and polo. Along the line, however, you will encounter the funky beach towns that were the original lure for travelers who discovered the area.

Costa Alegre & the Central Pacific Coast

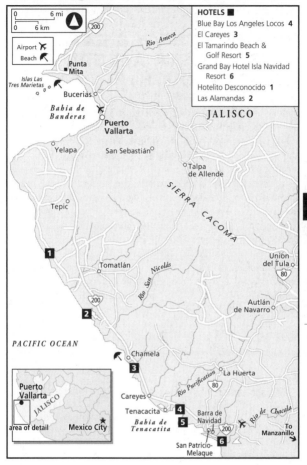

0   6 mi
0   6 km

Airport ✈
Beach ⚓

HOTELS ■
Blue Bay Los Angeles Locos **4**
El Careyes **3**
El Tamarindo Beach &
   Golf Resort **5**
Grand Bay Hotel Isla Navidad
   Resort **6**
Hotelito Desconocido **1**
Las Alamandas **2**

Rio Ameca

Punta
Mita

Islas Las
Tres Marietas

Bucerías

Bahía de
Banderas

Puerto
Vallarta

JALISCO

Yelapa

San Sebastián

Talpa
de Allende

Tepic

SIERRA CACOMA

Tomatlán

Rio San Nicolás

Union
del Tula
80

Autlán
de Navarro

PACIFIC OCEAN

Chamela

La Huerta

Rio Purification
80

Careyes

Tenacacita

Bahía de
Tenacatita

Barra de
Navidad

Rio de Chacala

To
Manzanillo

San Patricio-
Melaque

Puerto
Vallarta

JALISCO

area of detail

Mexico City ★

4

COSTA ALEGRE

Introduction

EXPLORING COSTA ALEGRE Hwy. 200, as it meanders between Puerto Vallarta to the north and Manzanillo to the south, is a beautiful winding road with breathtaking ocean, mountain, and jungle vistas trading places along the way. A handful of Mexican villages dot the route, while most of the beaches are tucked into coves accessible by dirt roads that can extend for a few kilometers. If you drive along this coast, Hwy. 200 is safe and well paved, but it's not lit and parts of it curve through the mountains, making daytime driving preferable. A few buses travel this route, but they stop only at the towns that line the highway; many of them are several kilometers inland from the resorts along the coast. For more information about traveling to this area, visit **www.costalegre.ca.**

WHERE TO STAY & EAT ALONG COSTA ALEGRE (NORTH–SOUTH)

Hotelito Desconocido 📷   After having been closed and completely renovated, the Hotelito re-opened in mid-2011 as a luxury eco-resort under new management. The enchanted bungalows, called *palafitos,* offer handcrafted furnishings, richly colored Mexican art, canopy beds, and luxuriously appointed bathrooms with solar-heated showers. Three family-friendly villas are built on stilts with large terraces overlooking the canals, lagoon, and beach. Located 96km (60 miles) south of Puerto Vallarta, Hotelito sits on 40 hectares (100 acres) of private reserve, which includes trails leading past organic gardens and gorgeous Pacific coastline. Among the activities are a holistic spa with a wellness center, yoga program, and aqua gym; a bio-center with programs on marine turtles, indigenous plants, and birds; beachfront horseback riding; an observatory; and a private beach with watersports. The tropical grounds are as serene as they are spectacular, lit up at night by torches, candles, and lanterns. The resort uses renewable energy, including ecofriendly air conditioners in the bungalows, as well as 100% organic food in the gourmet restaurants. The rates include lodging, meals, nonalcoholic beverages, and airport transportation.

Playón de Mismaloya s/n, Cruz de Loreto, 48360 Tomatlán, Jal. www.hotelito. com. ✆ **800/851-1143** in the U.S. and Canada, or 01-800/013-1313 in Mexico. 30 units. High season $580–$1,025 double; low season $485–$855 double. Meal plan high season $160; low season $140. All activities are subject to an extra charge. AE, MC, V. Free parking. Take Hwy. 200 south for 1 hr., turn off at exit for Cruz de Loreto, and continue on clearly marked route on unpaved road for about 25 min. Children allowed in villas but not bungalows. **Amenities:** 2 restaurant/ bars; horseback riding; Internet; Jacuzzi; outdoor pool; extensive spa w/yoga and other fitness programs. *In room:* Eco air-conditioning, no phone.

Las Alamandas ★★★ 📷   Almost equidistant between Manzanillo (2 hr.) and Puerto Vallarta (2 hr.) lies one of the world's most exquisite resorts. The privileged guests, served by over 80 employees, enjoy the seclusion of the magnificent grounds, which boast 1,500 acres of gardens, lakes, lagoons, and four stunning private beaches. The owner's commitment to the environment includes a turtle preservation program and bird sanctuary with over 100 species sighted (birding boat tours are available). Palms, jasmine, bougainvillea, and the bright yellow Alamanda flower dominate the landscape. The seven distinctly Mexican villas house 16 suites splashed in pinks, yellows, and blues with brick dome roofs, handcrafted furniture, regional artwork, tiled verandas, gorgeous ocean or garden views, and many with private Jacuzzis. Activities include a massage and yoga spa, tennis court and gym, mountain bikes, beach toys, complimentary horseback rides, and rooftop lounge with a telescope. The food here is excellent, with most of the organic products grown right on the property.

Hwy. 200, Km 83 48850 Manzanillo–Puerto Vallarta, Jal. Mailing address: Domicilio Conocido Costa Alegre QUEMARO Jalisco, Apdo. Postal 201, 48980 San Patricio Melaque, Jal. www.alamandas.com. ℰ **888/882-9616** in the U.S. and Canada, or 322/285-5500. Fax 322/285-5027. 16 units. High season $488–$2,070 double; low season $371–$1,499 double. Meal plans $135. AE, MC, V. Free parking. **Amenities:** Restaurant; 2 bars; mountain bikes; concierge; exercise room; horseback riding; 18m (59-ft.) outdoor pool; room service; lighted tennis court; watersports equipment. *In room:* A/C, TV w/DVD/VCR available upon request, minibar.

Careyes

El Careyes ★ El Careyes sits quietly tucked in a pristine cove between dramatic cliffs. The view over the calm waters, particularly at sunset, is simply magnificent and the resort's primary draw. Most guests come for seclusion, although families also feel welcome here. Room facades are awash in scrubbed pastels and form a U around the center lawn and free-form pool. Palms, banana leaves, and bougainvillea dominate the subtropical landscape. Cheerful, if dated, accommodations face the pool or ocean and come in seven categories, including a number with private plunge pools. Luxurious bathroom amenities, including exfoliating scrubs, use natural local products. The hotel lies roughly 150km (93 miles) south of Puerto Vallarta and 85km (53 miles) north of Manzanillo on Hwy. 200, and is about an hour's drive from the Manzanillo airport (a $110 taxi ride).

Hwy. 200 Km 53.5, 48970 Careyes, Jal. CP. Mailing address: Apdo. Postal 24, 48970 Cihuatlán, Jal. www.elcareyesresort.com. ℰ **888/433-3989** in the U.S. and Canada, or 315/351-0000. Fax 315/351-0100. 51 units. High season $385 double, $575–$1,379 suite; low season $281 double, $448–$936 suite. AE, MC, V. Free parking. **Amenities:** Restaurant; bar; deli; mountain bikes; children's programs (during Christmas and Easter vacations only); horseback riding; large beachside pool; hot and cold plunge pools; room service; spa w/massage rooms, Jacuzzis, steam room, sauna, and fitness center; 2 tennis courts; watersports rentals. *In room:* A/C, TV/DVD, CD player, minifridge, hair dryer, minibar, Wi-Fi.

Tenacatita Bay

Located an hour (53km/33 miles) north of the Manzanillo airport, this jewel of a bay is accessible by an 8km (5-mile) dirt road that passes through a small village set among banana plants and coconut palms. Sandy, serene beaches dot coves around the bay (frolicking dolphins are a common sight), and exotic birds fill a coastal lagoon. Swimming and snorkeling are good, and the bay is a popular stop for luxury yachts. Just south of the entrance to Tenacatita is a sign for the all-inclusive **Blue Bay Los Angeles Locos,** as well as the exclusive **El Tamarindo Beach & Golf Resort** (see below). There is no commercial or shopping area, and dining options outside hotels are limited to a restaurant or two that may emerge during the winter months (high season).

El Tamarindo Beach & Golf Resort ★★★ 👜 The most beautiful resort I know in Mexico, El Tamarindo is a romantic haven amid magnificent jungle surroundings, with exquisite facilities, attentive service, and absolute tranquillity. Enchanted thatched-roof villas feature a wraparound splash pool, hammock, and open-air sitting and dining area that overlooks a private lawn. The bedrooms—with dark hardwood floors and intricately designed furnishings—can be closed off for air-conditioned comfort, but the remaining areas are open to the sea breezes and tropical air. A bottle of wine, fresh fruit, and L'Occitane amenities are included. There are also three luxurious four-bedroom beachfront residences that can accommodate up to eight adults. El Tamarindo boasts a championship 18-hole golf course designed by David Fleming, with 7 oceanside holes and dramatic views. The spa services are exceptional, and the open-air restaurant serves delicious fresh fish. At night, subtle lighting through the jungle and around the casitas transforms El Tamarindo into a truly enchanted retreat. On over 809 hectares (2,000 acres) of nature preserve extending along 3.2km (2 miles) of oceanfront—complete with hiking trails and bird-watching tours—you'll feel as if you've found your own personal bit of heaven here. The laid-back beach town of Barra de Navidad lies 30 minutes away.

Carretera Barra de Navidad–Puerto Vallarta Km 7.5, 48970 Cihuatlán, Jal. www.eltamarindoresort.com. 📞 **866/717-4316** in the U.S., or 315/351-5031. Fax 315/351-5070. 29 casitas. High season $720–$1,875 villa; low season $285–$1,160 villa. Beachfront residences $3,000–$7,995. AE, MC, V. Free valet parking. From Puerto Vallarta (3 hr.) or the Manzanillo airport (45 min.), take Hwy. 200, and then turn west at the clearly marked exit for El Tamarindo; follow signs for about 25 min. **Amenities:** Restaurant; bar; mountain bikes; kids' club (in high season); high-tech fitness center; beachside pool w/whirlpool; room service; spa services; *temazcal* (pre-Hispanic sweat lodge); 2 clay tennis courts and 1 grass court; watersports equipment; Wi-Fi (in lobby and restaurant). *In room:* A/C, TV, CD player, hair dryer.

Where to Stay & Eat Along Costa Alegre

COSTA ALEGRE

Barra de Navidad Bay Area

HOTELS ■

Grand Bay Hotel Isla Navidad Resort **9**
Hotel Alondra **6**
Hotel Barra de Navidad **5**
Hotel Cabo Blanco **2**

RESTAURANTS ◆

Ambar d'Mare **8**
Deli & Espresso **7**
Mar y Tierra **4**
Restaurant Ramón **3**
Sea Master **1**

Melaque

Barra de Navidad

Bahía de la Navidad

BARRA DE NAVIDAD & MELAQUE

This pair of rustic beach villages (just 5km/3 miles apart) has been attracting travelers for decades. Only 30 minutes north of Manzanillo's airport and about 100km (62 miles) north of downtown Manzanillo, Barra has cobblestone streets, inexpensive seaside hotels and restaurants, and funky beach charm. All of this lies incongruously next to the superluxurious Grand Bay Hotel, which sits on a bluff across the inlet from Barra.

In the 17th century, Barra de Navidad was a harbor for the Spanish fleet; from here, galleons first set off in 1564 to find China. Located on a crescent-shaped bay with curious rock outcroppings, Barra de Navidad and neighboring Melaque are connected by a continuous beach on the same wide bay. It's safe to say that the only time Barra and Melaque hotels are full is during Easter and Christmas weeks. **Barra de Navidad** has more charm, more tree-shaded streets, better restaurants, more stores, and more conviviality between locals and tourists. Barra is very laid-back; faithful returnees adore its lack of flash. Other than the Grand Bay Hotel, on the cliff across the waterway in what is called Isla Navidad (although it's not on an island), nothing is new or modern. But there's a bright edge to Barra, with more good restaurants and limited—but existent—nightlife.

Melaque, on the other hand, is larger, sun baked, treeless, and lacking in attractions. It does, however, have plenty of cheap hotels available for longer stays, and a few restaurants. Although the beach between the two is continuous, Melaque's beach, with deep sand, is more beautiful than Barra's. Both villages appeal to those looking for a quaint, quiet, inexpensive retreat rather than a modern, sophisticated destination.

Grand Bay Isla Navidad Resort (p. 106) has a manicured 27-hole golf course and the super luxurious Grand Bay Hotel, but the area's pace hasn't quickened as fast as expected. The golf is challenging and delightfully uncrowded, with another exceptional course at nearby **El Tamarindo** (p. 102). It's a serious golfer's dream.

Essentials

GETTING THERE Regional buses from Manzanillo frequently run up the coast along Hwy. 200 on their way to Puerto Vallarta and Guadalajara. Most stop in the central villages of Barra de Navidad and Melaque. First-class **ETN** buses (www.etn.com.

mx) make the 4-hour ride to and from Guadalajara for about 350 pesos each way. From the Manzanillo airport, it's only 30 minutes to Barra, and **taxis** are available. The taxi fare from Manzanillo to Barra is around 450 pesos; from Barra to Manzanillo, 350 pesos. From Manzanillo, the highway twists through some of the Pacific Coast's most beautiful mountains. Puerto Vallarta is 3 hours by **car** and 4 to 5 hours by bus, north on Hwy. 200 from Barra. A taxi from Barra to Puerto Vallarta costs about 1,700 pesos.

VISITOR INFORMATION   The **tourism office** for both villages is at Jalisco 67 (btw. Veracruz and Mazatlán), Barra (© **315/355-5100;** www.costalegre.com); it's open Monday through Friday from 9am to 5pm and will help with hotel reservations as well as with a general orientation to the towns.

ORIENTATION   In Barra, hotels and restaurants line the main beachside street, **Legazpi.** From the bus station, beachside hotels are 2 blocks straight ahead, across the central plaza. Two blocks behind the bus station and to the right is the lagoon side. More hotels and restaurants are on its main street, **Morelos/Veracruz.** Few streets are marked, but 10 minutes of wandering will acquaint you with the village's entire layout. There's a taxi stand at the intersection of Legazpi and Sinaloa streets. Legazpi, Jalisco, Sinaloa, and Veracruz streets border Barra's **central plaza.**

Activities on & off the Beach

Swimming and enjoying the attractive beach and bay views take up most tourists' time. You can hire a small boat for a coastal ride or fishing in two ways. Go toward the *malecón* on Calle Veracruz until you reach the tiny boatmen's cooperative, with fixed prices posted on the wall, or walk two buildings farther to the water taxi ramp. The water taxi is the best option for going to Colimilla (5 min.; 30 pesos) or across the inlet (3 min.; 20 pesos) to the Grand Bay Hotel. Water taxis make the rounds regularly, so if you're at Colimilla, wait, and one will be along shortly. At the cooperative, a 30-minute **lagoon tour** costs 300 pesos, with other boat tours available. **Sportfishing** costs 500 pesos per hour for up to four people in a small *panga* (open fiberglass boat).

Isla Navidad Country Club (© **314/337-9024;** www.isla navidad.com) has a 27-hole, 7,053-yard, par-72 **golf course** that is open to the public (daily 7am–7pm). Greens fees are $140 for 18 holes plus tax, $160 for 27 holes plus tax (discounts are available for hotel guests). Prices include a motorized cart. Caddies are available for $30 and rental clubs for $46. The clubhouse is stocked with Cuban cigars and premium tequila.

Where to Stay

Low season in Barra is any time except Christmas and Easter weeks. Except for those 2 weeks, it doesn't hurt to ask for a discount at the inexpensive hotels.

VERY EXPENSIVE

Grand Bay Hotel Isla Navidad Resort ★★★ ☺ Situated on its own island, this palatial resort spreads out over 480 hectares (1,186 acres) next to a 27-hole golf course. The Spanish-style Grand Bay overlooks the village, bay, and fresh water Navidad lagoon with mountains in the background. The hotel's swimming pools are simply spectacular, and a narrow beach faces the lagoon. Large guest rooms are luxuriously outfitted with marble floors and columns, beautiful bathrooms, hand-carved wood furnishings, and balconies. Outdoor activities abound, and the spa offers an extensive array of facial and body treatments. The hotel is a short water-taxi ride across the inlet from Barra de Navidad. It's worth a visit even if you're not staying here, although the hotel is closed to non-guests at night unless they're coming for dinner.

Circuito de los Marinos s/n, 28830 Isla Navidad, Col. www.wyndham.com. ✆ **877/999-3223** in the U.S., 01-800/849-2373 in Mexico, or 314/331-0500. Fax 314/331-0570. 199 units. $175 and up double; $300 and up suite. AE, DC, DISC, MC, V. Free parking. **Amenities:** 4 restaurants; 2 bars; babysitting; kids' club; concierge; small exercise room; golf club w/pro shop and driving range; 27-hole, par-72 golf course; Jacuzzi; marina w/private yacht club; 3 outdoor pools, including 1 w/waterslides and swim-up bar; room service; full spa; 3 lighted grass tennis courts. *In room:* A/C, TV, hair dryer, minibar, Wi-Fi.

MODERATE

Hotel Alondra Located next to the church on the main strip of restaurants, shops, and bars, and with a little beach just in front, this place sits in the heart of the action. Guest rooms are spread out in two buildings, one oceanfront called "Casa Club" and the other just across the street. Splashed in hues of blue, yellow, and white, the light-filled rooms feature marble floors and small bathrooms; junior suites have kitchenettes. This hotel, which is especially popular with Canadians, has a small infinity pool in front of the beach, as well as an open-air bar on the fifth floor with a lovely view.

Sinaloa 16, 48987 Barra de Navidad, Jal. www.alondrahotel.com. ✆ **315/355-8373.** 73 units. 1,250–1,340 pesos double; 1,490 pesos oceanview double. MC, V. **Amenities:** Restaurant; bar; outdoor pool; Wi-Fi. *In room:* A/C, TV, kitchenette (in some rooms).

INEXPENSIVE

Hotel Barra de Navidad At the northern end of Legazpi, this comfortable beachside hotel remains a favorite among value-seeking visitors. It has friendly management and basic rooms, some with balconies overlooking the beach and bay. Other, less-expensive rooms afford only a street view. Three bungalows offer king-size beds, kitchenettes, and separate sitting areas. A beachside swimming pool lies off the lobby, and there's a popular restaurant here called the Banana Cafe.

Legazpi 250, 48987 Barra de Navidad, Jal. ✆ **315/355-5122.** Fax 315/355-5303. 60 units. 860–1,000 pesos double; 1,550 pesos bungalow. MC, V. Free parking. **Amenities:** Restaurant; bar; outdoor pool. *In room:* A/C and TV in some rooms.

Hotel Cabo Blanco ★ ☺ Located on the point where you cross over to Isla Navidad, the Cabo Blanco is an easy-going option for longer-term stays. Comfortable though basic rooms have tile floors, large tile tubs with showers, and stucco walls. The Cabo Blanco overlooks the canal, and it's a 10-minute walk to the hotel's **Mar y Tierra** beach club (below), which is open Friday through Sunday. The beamed-ceiling lobby is in its own building; rooms are in hacienda-style buildings surrounded by gardens. The atmosphere is festive, especially during weekends and Mexican holidays, when this hotel tends to fill up. The website has its own theme song celebrating the hotel, and offers all-inclusive packages.

Armada y Bahía de la Navidad s/n, 48987 Barra de Navidad, Jal. www.hotel caboblanco.com. ✆ **01-800/710-5690** in Mexico, or 315/355-6495, -6496. Fax 315/355-6494. 101 units. 700 pesos double; 1,450 pesos all-inclusive option. AE, MC, V. Limited street parking. **Amenities:** Restaurant; 2 outdoor pools (1 adults only); tennis court. *In room:* A/C, TV.

Where to Eat

Ambar d'Mare ★★ CREPES/ITALIAN/FRENCH This cozy beachside restaurant is open to the breezes, and the food is as wonderful as the ambience. The crepes are named after towns in France; the delicious *crêpe Paris*, for example, is filled with chicken, potatoes, spinach, and green sauce. A rich selection of salads and carpaccios are available as starters. Main dishes include grilled fish prepared with olive oil and herbs, lobster kabob in white wine, and beef medallions with a green peppercorn sauce. Pastas and pizzas are also served. Owner Veronique Bourdet's inviting restaurant includes a wine cellar and bar, with live music in high season as well as free Internet. She also rents out a couple of studio lofts—inquire directly with her.

López de Legazpi 150 (corner of Jalisco), across from the church. ✆ **315/355-8169.** Crepes 125–210 pesos; main courses 100–350 pesos. No credit cards. Daily 5pm–midnight.

Mar y Tierra INTERNATIONAL Hotel Cabo Blanco's beach club is also a popular restaurant and bar, and a great place to spend a day at the beach. Shaded *palapas* and beach chairs dot the sand. Open during the daytime only, the colorful restaurant is decorated with murals of mermaids. Perfectly seasoned shrimp fajitas come in plentiful portions.

In Hotel Cabo Blanco (p. 107), Legazpi s/n (at Jalisco). 📞 **315/355-5028.** Main courses 120–220 pesos. MC, V. Fri–Sun 10am–6pm.

Restaurant Ramón 🦐 SEAFOOD/MEXICAN   It seems that all the English speakers in town eat regularly at Ramón's, where the chips and fresh salsa arrive unbidden, and service is prompt and friendly. The food tastes great, although many options are fried. Try fresh shrimp with french fries, fish and chips, chicken nuggets, fish tacos, or any daily special that features vegetable soup or chicken-fried steak. Ramón, proud of the fried specialties, is often on hand to greet guests.

Legazpi 260. 📞 **315/355-6435.** Main courses 75–150 pesos. No credit cards. Daily 7am–11pm.

Sea Master ★ SEAFOOD   Sea Master's creative allure stems from its own private gallery, located at the entrance to the restaurant. Original paintings, artistic lighting, and brilliant colors spill out from the gallery to the cafe and waterfront dining room, and all the tables here afford beautiful sea views. Big, succulent shrimps dominate the menu, with selections such as the "Sea Master pineapple" stuffed with shrimp, cheese, brandy, and Kahlúa, and the "Sea Master roll" with fresh fish filled with shrimp, bacon, nuts, and garlic cream. Filet mignon, rib-eye, and chicken breast are also available. Potent cocktails are poured with double shots, and lounge music plays in the background, except for Thursday nights when the music is live.

Legazpi 146, near the boatmen's cooperative. 📞 **315/107-0889.** Main courses 110–360 pesos. MC, V. Daily 11am–11pm.

Barra de Navidad After Dark

When dusk arrives, visitors and locals alike find a cool spot to sit outside, sip cocktails, and chat. Many outdoor restaurants and stores in Barra accommodate this relaxing way to end the day, adding extra tables and chairs for drop-ins. Most of the nighttime action is centered around the walking area near the church. Happy hour typically extends from 4 to 8pm. Closing times depend on the season and mood of the managers.

The colorful **Capri Sunset Bar,** facing the bay at the corner of Legazpi and Jalisco, is a favorite for sunset watching and a game of ocean-side pool or perhaps dancing. **Via Berlin Simona & Niños,** on the second floor of the Hotel Alondra, is another popular watering hole. **Piper Lover,** Legazpi 154 A (© **315/100-9194**), pumps out live blues most nights to a rough-and-tumble crowd.

A Visit to Melaque (San Patricio)

For a change of scenery, you may wander over to Melaque (aka San Patricio), 5km (3 miles) from Barra. Its pace is even more laid-back, as though it's stuck in time. A few yachts bob in the harbor, and the palm-lined beach is gorgeous. Restaurants and basic bungalows line the beach. You can walk on the beach from Barra or take one of the frequent local buses from the bus station near the main square in Barra for 5 pesos. The bus is marked MELAQUE. To return to Barra, take the bus marked CIHUATLAN. A taxi between the towns costs 50 pesos each way.

WHERE TO STAY & EAT   The best hotel in town is **Larios** (© **315/355-8058**), at Calle Av. Primavera 60, just a block from the beach. It has 10 rooms that cost between 500 and 700 pesos per night, depending on if there's a kitchen, cash only. Other motels in town are half that price but far less nice. There are a number of rustic *palapa* **restaurants** on the beach and farther along the bay at the end of the beach.

MANZANILLO

by Shane Christensen

256km (159 miles) SE of Puerto Vallarta; 267km (166 miles) SW of Guadalajara; 64km (40 miles) SE of Barra de Navidad

Manzanillo has long been known as a resort town with wide, curving beaches; legendary sportfishing; and a highly praised diversity of dive sites. Golf is also an attraction here. One reason for its popularity could be Manzanillo's enticing tropical geography—vast groves of tall palms, abundant mango trees, and successive coves graced with smooth sand beaches. To the north, mountains blanketed with palms rise alongside the shoreline. And over it all lies the veneer of perfect weather, with balmy temperatures and year-round sea breezes.

5

Manzanillo is a dichotomous place—it is both Mexico's busiest commercial seaport and a tranquil town of multicolor houses cascading down the hillsides to meet the central commercial area of simple seafood restaurants, shell shops, and salsa clubs. The activity in Manzanillo divides neatly into two zones: the downtown commercial port and the luxury Santiago Peninsula resort zone to the north. A visit to the town's waterfront *zócalo* provides a glimpse into local life. The exclusive Santiago Peninsula, home to the resorts and golf course, separates Manzanillo's two golden-sand bays.

ESSENTIALS

GETTING THERE By Plane Alaska Airlines (*©* **800/252-7522** in the U.S., 01-800/252-7522 in Mexico) offers service from Los Angeles; **Continental** (*©* **800/523-3273** in the U.S., 01-800/900-5000 in Mexico) flies from Houston; **AeroMar** (*©* **01-800/237-6627** toll-free in Mexico; www. aeromar.com.mx) flies to Mexico City; **CanJet**

Greater Manzanillo

HOTELS ■
Barceló Karmina Palace **3**
Brisas Las Hadas Golf Resort & Marina **2**
Hotel Colonial **9**
Hotel La Posada **8**

RESTAURANTS ◆
Bigotes **5**
El Fogón **4**
Juanito's **1**
La Toscana **6**
Legazpi **7**
Roca del Mar **7**

Information ⓘ

See "Downtown Manzanillo" Map

To Colima →
Libramiento
Del Trabajo
Central Ote. Minatitlán/Manzanillo 2 Ote
Madrid Hurtado
D. Hidalgo
LAS JOYAS
Train Station
Central Plaza
Laguna de Cuyutlán
LAS BRISAS
Laguna de San Pedrito
Cruise Pier
Morelos
F. Madero
Mexico
Leona Vicario
Playa Las Brisas
Playa Azul
Laguna de las Garzas
LOMAS DEL VALLE
Paseo de Las Gaviotas
Av. Elias Zamora Verduzco
Costera Miguel de la Madrid
Costera Miguel de la Madrid
SALAGUA
De Las Garzas
Bahía de Manzanillo
VIVEROS PELAYO
V. Carranza
MANTARRAYA
GOLF COURSE
Playa Salahua
Playa Las Hadas
Playa Santiago
Playa Audiencia
Península de Santiago
SANTIAGO
Laguna Peñitas
Playa Peñitas
Playa Olas Altas
MIRAMAR
Playa Miramar
Costera Miguel de la Madrid
Bahía de Santiago
Península de Juluapan
To Airport
← Barra de Navidad
Laguna de la Boquita

JALISCO
COLIMA
Manzanillo
Mexico City

1 mi
1 km

200 mi
200 km

(📞 800/809-7777 in the U.S. and Canada; www.canjet.com) flies from select Canadian destinations.

The **Playa de Oro International Airport** is 40km (25 miles) northwest of town. *Colectivo* (minivan) airport service is available from the airport; hotels arrange returns. Make reservations for return trips 1 day in advance. The fare is based on zones and runs 130 pesos to 155 pesos for most hotels. Private taxi service between the airport and downtown area is around 350 pesos. **Alamo** (📞 314/334-0124), **Budget** (📞 314/333-1445), and **Thrifty** (📞 314/334-3282) have counters in the airport open during flight arrivals; they will also deliver a car to your hotel. Daily rates run about $50 to $80. You need a car especially if you plan to explore surrounding cities and the Costa Alegre.

By Car Coastal Hwy. 200 leads from Acapulco (south) and Puerto Vallarta (north). From Guadalajara, take **Hwy. 54** through Colima into Manzanillo. Outside Colima you can switch to a toll road, which is faster but less scenic.

By Bus Buses run to Barra de Navidad (1½ hr. north), Puerto Vallarta (5 hr. north), Colima (1½ hr. east), and Guadalajara (4½ hr. north), with deluxe service and numerous daily departures. **ETN** (www.etn.com.mx) is the main bus company. Manzanillo's **Central Camionera** bus station (📞 314/336-8035) sits about 12 long blocks east of town.

VISITOR INFORMATION The **tourism office** (📞 314/333-2277; www.vivemanzanillo.com) is on the Costera Miguel de la Madrid 875-A, Km 8.5. It's open Monday through Friday from 9am to 7pm, and Saturday from 10am to 2pm.

CITY LAYOUT The town lies at one end of an 11km-long (6¾-mile) beach facing Manzanillo Bay and its commercial harbor. The beach has four sections—**Playa Las Brisas, Playa Azul, Playa Salahua,** and **Playa Las Hadas.** At the other end of the beaches is the high, rocky **Santiago Peninsula.** Santiago lies 11km (6¾ miles) from downtown; it's the site of many beautiful homes and the best hotel in the area, Las Hadas, as well as the hotel's Mantarraya Golf Course. The peninsula juts into the bay, separating Manzanillo Bay from Santiago Bay. Playa Las Hadas sits on the south side, facing Manzanillo Bay, and **Playa Audiencia** is on the north side, facing Santiago Bay. The inland town of **Santiago** extends opposite the turnoff to Las Hadas.

Activity in downtown Manzanillo centers on the *zócalo,* officially known as the Jardín Alvaro Obregón. The plaza has flowering trees, a fountain, and a view of the bay. **Avenida México,** the street leading out from the plaza's central gazebo, is the town's

Downtown Manzanillo

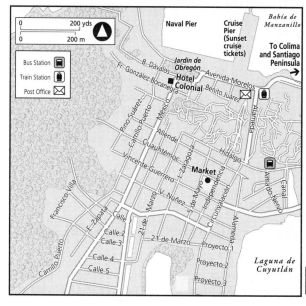

principal commercial thoroughfare. The interesting **Museo de la Perversidad** (© **314/332-5599;** www.manzanillomuseo.com) opened in mid-2009 with vivid displays of torture throughout the ages, much of it religiously motivated. The museum is located at Av. Juárez 160, just off the square, and open Monday through Friday from 11am to 8pm, and Saturday and Sunday from 11am to 9pm.

Once you leave downtown, the **Costera Miguel de la Madrid** highway (or just Costera Madrid) runs through the neighborhoods of Las Brisas, Salahua, and Santiago to the **hotel zones** on the Santiago Peninsula and at Miramar.

There are two main lagoons. **Laguna de Cuyutlán** stretches south for miles, paralleling the coast. **Laguna de San Pedrito,** north of the city, parallels the Costera Miguel de la Madrid. Both are good birding sites. There are also two bays. **Manzanillo Bay** encompasses the harbor, town, and beaches. The Santiago Peninsula separates it from the second bay, **Santiago.** Between downtown and the Santiago Peninsula lies **Las Brisas,** a flat peninsula with a long stretch of sandy golden beach, a lineup of inexpensive but run-down hotels, and a few good restaurants.

GETTING AROUND   By Taxi   Taxis in Manzanillo are plentiful. Fares are fixed by zones; rates for trips in town and to more distant points should be posted at your hotel. For example, a taxi ride from Las Hadas to the airport will cost 250 pesos. Daily rates can be negotiated for longer drives outside the Manzanillo area.

By Bus   The *camionetas* (local buses) make a circuit from downtown in front of the train station, along the Bay of Manzanillo, to the Santiago Peninsula and the Bay of Santiago to the north; the fare is 6 pesos. The ones marked LAS BRISAS go to the Las Brisas crossroads, to the Las Brisas Peninsula, and back to town; MIRAMAR, SANTIAGO, and SALAHUA buses go to outlying settlements along the bays and to most restaurants mentioned below. Buses marked LAS HADAS go to the Santiago Peninsula and pass the Las Hadas resort and the Tesoro Manzanillo and Plaza Las Glorias hotels. This is an inexpensive way to see the coast as far as Santiago and to tour the Santiago Peninsula.

[FastFACTS] MANZANILLO

Area Code   The telephone area code is **314.**

Bank   Banamex, just off the plaza on Avenida Juárez, downtown (✆ **314/332-0115**), is open Monday through Saturday from 9am to 4pm.

Hospital   Contact the **Cruz Roja (Red Cross;** ✆ **314/336-5770)** or the **General Hospital** (✆ **314/332-0029**).

Internet Access   WWW.CAFE (✆ **314/334-8004;** hours vary) is located next to Hotel Pacifico Azul at Blvd. Miguel de la Madrid 1161 and charges 25 pesos per hour.

Police   Both the general police and Tourism Police can be reached by calling ✆ **314/332-1004.**

Post Office   The *correo,* Dr. Miguel Galindo 30, opposite Farmacia de Guadalajara, downtown (✆ **314/332-0022**), is open Monday through Friday from 8:30am to 4pm, Saturday from 9am to 1pm.

WHERE TO STAY

Manzanillo's strip of coastline consists of three areas: **downtown,** with its shops, markets, and commercial activity; **Las Brisas,** the hotel-lined beach area immediately north of the city; and **Santiago,** the town and peninsula, now virtually a suburb, to the north at the end of Playa Azul. Reservations are recommended during the Easter, Christmas, and New Year's holidays.

Downtown

Hotel Colonial An old favorite, this three-story hotel sits in the central downtown district. Popular for its consistent quality, ambience, and service, it features colonial-style carved doors and windows in the lobby and traditional blue tile. Rooms provide basic comforts with one, two, or three beds, wood furniture, and small bathrooms with showers only. The hotel lies 1 block inland from the main plaza.

Av. México 100 and González Bocanegra 28, 28200 Manzanillo, Col. www.hotel colonialmanzanillo.com. ℂ **314/332-1080,** -0668, -1230. 42 units. 520 pesos double. MC, V. Underground parking. **Amenities:** Restaurant; bar. *In room:* A/C, TV, Wi-Fi.

Las Brisas

Hotel La Posada 🗝 This great value inn proudly displays a pink stucco facade leading to a broad tiled patio and beachside swimming pool. Guest rooms incorporate exposed brick walls, tile floors, and simple furnishings with Mexican decorative accents. The atmosphere is casual and informal—help yourself to beer and soft drinks; at the end of your stay, settle up with owners Juan and Lisa Martinez, who will count the bottle caps you deposited in a bowl labeled with your room number. The restaurant, which also welcomes non–hotel guests, is open daily from 8 to 10:30am and noon to 3pm. Stop by for a drink at sunset; the bar's open until 10pm year-round. The hotel lies at the end of Las Brisas Peninsula, closest to downtown.

Av. Lázaro Cárdenas 201, Las Brisas (Apdo. Postal 135), 28200 Manzanillo, Col. www.hotel-la-posada.info. ℂ/fax **314/333-1899.** 23 units. High season 900 pesos double; low season 700 pesos double. Rates include full breakfast. MC, V. Free parking. **Amenities:** Restaurant; bar; Internet kiosk; outdoor pool. *In room:* A/C (in some), ceiling fan.

Santiago

Barceló Karmina Palace ★ 😊 This is my favorite resort in Manzanillo, an all-inclusive getaway with nonstop activities, a beautiful beach and pools, quality restaurants, and an excellent spa and gym. The buildings here are designed to resemble Maya pyramids. Guests check into spacious suites featuring rich wood furnishings, recessed seating areas with pullout couches, two 27-inch TVs, and luxurious bathrooms. Most suites offer terraces or balconies with views of the ocean, overlooking the tropical gardens and swimming pools. Master suites offer spacious sun terraces with private splash pools, plus a full wet bar, refrigerator, and a large living room area. The kids' club provides a host of activities; at night live dance shows and an open-air dance club adjacent to the sea appeal to the adults. Service is not totally personalized, but this is an excellent destination for families looking for an all-inclusive resort.

Av. Vista Hermosa 13, Fracc. Península de Santiago, 28200 Manzanillo, Col. www.barcelokarminapalace.com. ☎ **314/331-1313.** Fax 314/331-1340. 324 units. $250 and up double; $430 and up 2-bedroom suite for 4. Rates are all-inclusive. Special packages and Web specials available; ask about seasonal specials. Up to 2 children 7 and younger stay free in parent's room. AE, MC, V. Free parking. **Amenities:** 4 restaurants; 5 bars; nightclub; kids' club; concierge; 9 connected pools; room service; spa w/men's and women's sauna, steam rooms, fitness center; tennis courts; nonmotorized watersports; Wi-Fi (in lobby). *In room:* A/C, TV, hair dryer, minibar.

Brisas Las Hadas Golf Resort & Marina ★ This iconic beachside resort designed in an all-white Moorish style lights up a side of the rocky Santiago peninsula. Rooms are spread over land-scaped grounds and overlook the bay; cobbled lanes lined with colorful flowers and palms connect them. The resort is large but maintains an air of seclusion. Views, room size and quality, and amenities differentiate the 10 categories of accommodations. The better rooms feature white-marble floors, sitting areas, and large, comfortably furnished balconies; 12 suites have private pools. The white colonial lobby is a splendid place for a drink in high season. A free-form pool stretches out beside the small beach in front. Pete and Roy Dye designed La Mantarraya, the hotel's 18-hole, par-71 golf course. This is the most famous resort in Manzanillo, but resembles an aging diva in need of a makeover.

Av. de los Riscos s/n, Santiago Peninsula, 28200 Manzanillo, Col. www.brisas.com.mx. ☎ **888/559-4329** in the U.S. and Canada, or 314/331-0101. Fax 314/331-0121. 232 units. High season $250 and up double; low season $180 and up double. AE, DC, MC, V. Free guarded parking. **Amenities:** 3 restaurants, including the elegant Legazpi (p. 118); 3 lounges and bars; babysitting; concierge; small exercise room; 18-hole golf course; marina; 2 outdoor pools (1 is adults only); room service; 10 lighted tennis courts; watersports equipment. *In room:* A/C, TV, hair dryer, minibar, Wi-Fi.

WHERE TO EAT
Playa Azul

La Toscana ★★ 🎁 SEAFOOD/INTERNATIONAL You're in for a treat at La Toscana, one of Manzanillo's most popular and consistently reliable restaurants, located on the beach of Playa Azul. You'll pass a decorative pool and waterfall at the entrance to the open-air dining room, where live music plays nightly. Menu items are written on boards scattered throughout the restaurant; to start I recommend the smoked salmon terrine, fresh artichoke, or escargots. Among the grilled specialties are seafood skewers, shrimp imperial wrapped in bacon, red snapper served whole with garlic and butter, sea bass with mango and ginger, and tender fresh lobster. Service is excellent.

Bulevar Miguel de la Madrid 3177. ℂ **314/333-2515.** Reservations highly recommended. Main courses 138–350 pesos. MC, V. Daily 6:30pm–midnight.

Roca del Mar SEAFOOD   Roca del Mar's menu focuses on seafood and, above all else, shrimp. Start with the tasty shrimp cocktail, shrimp prepared in lemon, or even shrimp dressed up in a coconut. The fish empanadas are a big hit, too. The best main courses include snapper grilled with a hot spice, shrimp fettuccini, and a seafood chile relleno. There's even a shrimp hamburger, unusual as this may be. This outdoor sea-view restaurant is open for breakfast, too.

Bulevar Miguel de la Madrid 2333. ℂ **314/336-9097.** Main courses 89–170 pesos. MC, V. Daily 9am–8pm.

Santiago Road

Bigotes SEAFOOD   Locals flock to this large, breezy restaurant (the name translates as "Mustaches") by the water for the good food and festive atmosphere. Strolling singers serenade diners as they eat fresh fish, shrimp cocktail, seafood soup, or shrimp prepared any number of ways—grilled with butter, garlic, spicy sauces, or simply natural. The signature "Mustache Shrimp" is a hearty portion of coconut shrimp. A lovely beach lies in front of the casual restaurant.

Puesta del Sol 3 (2nd location at Blvd. Costa M. de la Madrid 3157). ℂ **314/333-1236.** Main courses 136–288 pesos. AE, MC, V. Daily noon–10pm. From downtown, follow the Costera Madrid past the Las Brisas turnoff; the restaurant is behind the Penas Coloradas Social Club, across from the beach.

El Fogón 🎁 MEXICAN   Locals consider this to be the best Mexican restaurant in town, almost hidden in a small garden setting. The menu features a selection of unique and traditional Mexican dishes. *Molcajetes* (meat, seafood, and vegetables grilled in a stone dish) are the house specialty; options include shrimp, beef, and quail. A variety of delicious tacos and fajitas are also served. For those with a large appetite, the *plato mexicano* combines enchiladas, beef fajitas, a chile relleno, and guacamole.

Bulevar Miguel de la Madrid across from Pacifico Azul. ℂ **314/333-3094.** Main courses 67–159 pesos. MC, V. Daily 8am–midnight. From downtown, follow the Costera Madrid; the restaurant is located just before the Soriana grocery store.

Juanito's MEXICAN/BREAKFAST   It's not easy to find a good breakfast joint in Manzanillo, but this is one. The cheerful American-run eatery attracts Mexicans and tourists in equal numbers. Pancakes, waffles, and French toast are morning favorites, and customers love the fresh-fruit *licuados,* Mexico's version of smoothies. For lunch and dinner, distinctly American fare includes Texas burgers topped with bacon, cheese, and avocado, as well as chili dogs, club sandwiches, fried chicken, and barbecue ribs. Enchiladas, fajitas, and other simple Mexican dishes are also cooked to order. Diners congregate around casual wood tables; be prepared for a short wait on weekends.

Bulevar Miguel de la Madrid Km 14. ✆ **314/333-1388.** www.juanitos.com. Breakfast $3–$6; main courses $4–$11. AE, MC, V. Daily 8am–11pm.

Santiago Peninsula

Legazpi ★★ ITALIAN/INTERNATIONAL   This is a top choice in Manzanillo for elegance, service, and outstanding food. The candlelit tables are set with silver and flowers, and enormous bell-shaped windows show off the sparkling bay below. To start, consider the beef filet carpaccio or lobster bisque with a touch of caviar. Homemade pastas include ravioli stuffed with shrimp and crab, and linguine with grilled shrimp and fresh Parmesan. For main courses, the crunchy shrimp with polenta and mango chutney is delicious, as is the "veal mignon" prepared with a shitake mushroom sauce. Top off your meal with one of the decadent flambéed desserts or the Legazpi coffee with brandy, Damiana liqueur, sugar, and cream. The restaurant is open only on weekends, and piano music accompanies dinner.

In the Brisas Las Hadas hotel, Santiago Peninsula. ✆ **314/331-0101.** Main courses 250–500 pesos. AE, MC, V. Thurs–Sat 6:30–11pm.

ACTIVITIES ON & OFF THE BEACH

Activities in Manzanillo revolve around its golden-sand beaches, which sometimes accumulate a film of black mineral residue from nearby rivers. Manzanillo's public beaches provide an opportunity to see local color and scenery. They are the daytime playground for those staying at places off the beach or without pools.

BEACHES **Playa Audiencia,** on the Santiago Peninsula, offers the best swimming as well as snorkeling, but **Playa San Pedrito,** shallow for a long way out, is the most popular beach for its proximity to downtown. **Playa Las Brisas,** located south of

Santiago Peninsula as you're heading to downtown Manzanillo, offers an optimal combination of location and good swimming. **Playa Miramar,** on the Bahía de Santiago past the Santiago Peninsula, is popular with bodysurfers, windsurfers, and boogie boarders. It's accessible by local bus from town. The major part of **Playa Azul,** also south of the Santiago Peninsula, drops off sharply but is noted for its wide beach.

BIRDING   Birding is good in several lagoons along the coast. As you go from Manzanillo past Las Brisas to Santiago, you'll pass **Laguna de Las Garzas (Lagoon of the Herons),** also known as Laguna de San Pedrito, where many white pelicans and huge herons fish in the water. They nest here in December and January. Directly behind downtown is the **Laguna de Cuyutlán** (follow the signs to Cuyutlán), where you'll usually find birds in abundance; species vary between summer and winter.

DIVING   Underworld   Scuba–Scuba   Shack   ★★ (✆ **314/333-3678;** www.divemanzanillo.com), located at Blvd. M. de la Madrid Km 15, conducts professional diving expeditions and classes. Many locations are so close to shore that there's no need for a boat. Close-in dives include the jetty, and a nearby sunken frigate downed in 1959 at 8m (26 ft.). Divers can see abundant sea life, including coral reefs, sea horses, giant puffer fish, and moray eels. A two-tank boat dive costs $95 per person ($10 discount if you have your own equipment). "Discover Scuba" for beginners, which starts with instruction in a pool and continues with an ocean dive, costs $85 and lasts about 4 hours total. You can also rent weights and a tank for beach dives for $10. A three-stop snorkel trip costs $45. All guides are certified dive masters, and the shop offers PADI certification classes in intensive courses of various durations. The owner offers a 10% discount on your certification when you mention Frommer's. MasterCard and Visa are accepted.

ESCORTED TOURS   Because Manzanillo is so spread out, you might consider a city tour. **Bahías Gemelas Travel Agency** (✆ **314/333-1000**) runs half-day city tours for about $25. Other tours include the daylong Colima Colonial Tour (about $70), which stops at Colima's Archaeological Museum and principal colonial buildings, and passes the active volcano.

FISHING   Manzanillo is famous for its fishing, particularly sailfish. Marlin and sailfish are abundant year-round. Winter is best for dolphin fish and dorado (mahimahi); in summer, wahoo and rooster fish are in greater supply. The international sailfish competition is held around the November 20 Revolution Day holiday, and the national sailfish competition is in February. You can arrange fishing through travel agencies or directly at the fishermen's cooperative (✆ 314/332-1031), located downtown where the fishing boats moor. A 5-hour fishing charter costs about 3,000 pesos for up to eight people.

GOLF The 18-hole **La Mantarraya Golf Course** (✆ 314/331-0101) is open to nonguests as well as guests of Las Hadas. The compact, challenging 18-hole course designed by Roy and Pete Dye is a beauty, with banana trees, blooming bougainvillea, and coconut palms at every turn. A lush and verdant place (12 of the 18 holes are played over water), it remains a favorite. When the course was under construction, workers dug up pre-Hispanic ceramic figurines where the 14th hole now lies. It is believed to have been an important ancient burial site. The course culminates with its signature 18th hole, with a drive to the island green off El Tesoro (the treasure) beach, in front of the Karmina Palace Resort. Greens fees are 1,950 pesos for 18 holes, 1,070 pesos for 9 holes; cart rental costs 650 pesos for 18 holes and 455 pesos for 9 holes. It's open daily from 7am to 7pm.

SHOPPING Manzanillo has numerous shops that carry Mexican crafts and clothing, mainly from Guadalajara. Almost all fall on downtown streets near the central plaza. Shopping downtown is an experience—for example, you'll find a shop bordering the plaza that sells a combination of shells, religious items (including shell-framed Virgin of Guadalupe night lights), and orthopedic supplies. The Plaza Manzanillo is an American-style mall on the road to Santiago, and a traditional *tianguis* (outdoor flea market) in front of the entrance to Club Maeva sells clothes, sweets, and souvenirs from around Mexico. Most resort hotels also have boutiques or shopping arcades.

SUNSET CRUISES The *Antares* (✆ 314/333-1371; www. antaresmanzanillo.com) departs from Playa Audiencia at different times depending on the season and costs around 360 pesos; buy tickets from a travel agent or your hotel tour desk. The cruise includes drinks, music, and entertainment, and lasts 1½ to 2 hours.

MANZANILLO AFTER DARK

Nightlife in Manzanillo varies significantly depending on the season. Clubs and bars change from year to year, so check with your concierge for current hot spots. Some area clubs have a dress code prohibiting shorts or sandals, principally applying to men. For families, a fountain "show of lights" takes place at 8, 9, and 10pm nightly in front of the cruise-ship pier.

El Bar de Félix (© **314/333-9277**), at Costera Miguel de la Madrid 805, is usually open Tuesday through Sunday from 9pm to 3am and has a 100-peso minimum consumption charge. Music ranges from salsa and ranchero to rock and house—it's often the most lively place in town. Next to it, **Nautilus** is a trendy dance club open after 10pm on weekends.

GUADALAJARA

by David Baird

Guadalajara has two distinct qualities that appeal to travelers: a strong Mexican identity, and a big-city character with big-city pleasures. People who are fond of Mexico and enjoy exploring different urban scenes will love it. One of my favorite things about the city is the ease with which you can move around. Taxis are reasonably priced and numerous; you rarely have to wait more than a minute or two to find one. This eliminates the frustration of navigating a big city on your own, and obviates the need to figure out bus routes. Just grab a cab and go.

Guadalajara is a lively town with friendly locals, great food, and lots of options for entertainment. And much of what you'll find here is so very Mexican. Guadalajara is the center of mariachi culture, and, located in the tequila-producing region of Mexico, it's the center of tequila culture as well. The other things that one comes to Mexico to see are present too—colonial architecture, native craft cultures, and shopping galore. Guadalajara really has it all.

It is the second-largest city in the country, with about five million inhabitants. Its altitude (1,590m/5,200 ft.) lends it a mild climate for most of the year. It's a mildly conservative, very Catholic city, quite distinct from Mexico City. And the pace of life here is more relaxed. It's often called the biggest small town in Mexico.

While in Guadalajara, you will undoubtedly come across the word *tapatío* (or *tapatía*). In colonial times, people from the area customarily traded goods in threes, called *tapatíos*. From this practice, the locals came to be called Tapatíos as well; now *tapatío* has come to mean any person, thing, or style that comes from Guadalajara.

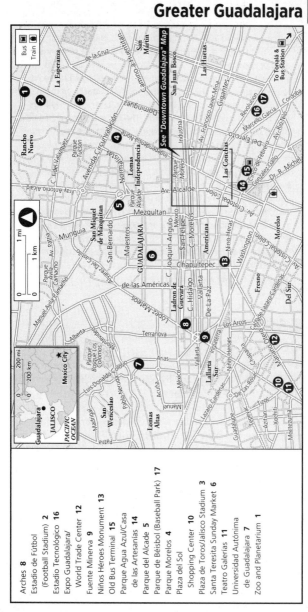

Arches **8**

Estadio de Futbol
(Football Stadium) **2**

Estadio Tecnológico **16**

Expo Guadalajara/
World Trade Center **12**

Fuente Minerva **9**

Niños Héroes Monument **13**

Old Bus Terminal **15**

Parque Agua Azul/Casa
de las Artesanías **14**

Parque del Alcalde **5**

Parque de Béisbol (Baseball Park) **17**

Parque Morelos **4**

Plaza del Sol
Shopping Center **10**

Plaza de Toros/Jalisco Stadium **3**

Santa Teresita Sunday Market **6**

Teatro Galerías **11**

Universidad Autónoma
de Guadalajara **7**

Zoo and Planetarium **1**

Public Security & Travel

In the summer of 2010, Mexican soldiers and police cornered one of Mexico's major drug figures, Ignacio Coronel, in a residential zone of Zapopan, a suburb of Guadalajara. He died in the ensuing shootout. This seemed to raise tensions in the city, and in the following month there were some shootings and attacks on the police. Then, on February 2, 2011, the police arrested two leaders of a local gang called La Resistencia. The following day, members of this gang retaliated by coordinating seven attacks in different parts of the city in a 2-hour span. The attackers used grenades, firearms, and incendiary devices, killing two people and wounding several others. A few attacks were loosely targeted, but mostly this was a show of force meant to create mayhem in the city. A couple of weeks later there was a grenade attack on a local nightclub that killed six people. These attacks have again raised tensions in Guadalajara, but they're probably isolated, and it's likely that things will return to normal. Still, before you travel to the city, check the news for more developments, and the U.S. Department of State travel page (www.travel.state.gov) to find out if there are any specific travel warnings for the city.

ESSENTIALS
Getting There

BY PLANE Guadalajara's airport (GDL) is a half-hour ride from the city. Taxi tickets, priced by zone, are for sale in front of the airport (235 pesos to downtown).

See "Airline Websites" in chapter 7 for a list of websites for international airlines serving Mexico. Major airlines serving Guadalajara are **AeroMar** (© 01-800/237-6627 in Mexico), **Aeroméxico** (© 800/237-6639 in the U.S., 01-800/021-4000 in Mexico), **Alaska** (© 800/252-7522 in the U.S., 01-800/252-7522 in Mexico), **American** (© 800/433-7300 in the U.S., 01-800/904-6000 in Mexico), **Continental** (© 800/523-3273 in the U.S., 01-800/900-5000 in Mexico), **Delta** (© 800/241-4141 in the U.S., 01-800/123-4710 in Mexico, or 33/3630-3530), and **United** (© 800/538-2929 in the U.S., 01-800/003-0777 in Mexico, or 33/3616-9489).

Of the smaller airlines, **Azteca** (© 33/3630-4615) offers service to and from Mexico City, and from there to several cities in Mexico. **Allegro** (© 33/3647-7799) operates flights to and from Oakland and Las Vegas via Tijuana.

HOTELS ■
Gran Hotel Los Reyes **19**
Holiday Inn Hotel and Suites
  Centro Histórico **10**
Hotel Cervantes **22**
Hotel de Mendoza **15**
Hotel Morales **21**
Hotel San Francisco Plaza **20**
Old Guadalajara **14**

RESTAURANTS ◆
Café Madrid **7**

El Globo **11**
La Chata Restaurant **9**
La Fonda de San Miguel **23**

ATTRACTIONS ●
Cathedral **4**
Church of San Agustín **12**
Church of Santa María
  de Gracia **16**

Instituto Cultural Cabañas **18**
Museo Regional de
  Guadalajara **3**
Palacio del Gobierno **6**
Plaza de Armas **5**
Plaza de la Liberación **8**
Plaza Guadalajara **1**
Quetzalcoatl Fountain **17**
Rotonda de los Hombres
  Illustres **2**
Teatro Degollado **13**
Universidad de Guadalajara
  Facultad de Música **12**

BY CAR Guadalajara is at the hub of several four-lane toll roads (called *cuotas* or *autopistas*), which cut travel time considerably but are expensive. From Nogales on the **U.S. border,** follow Hwy. 15 south (21 hr.). From **Tepic,** a quicker route is toll road 15D (5 hr.; 320 pesos). From **Puerto Vallarta,** go north on Hwy. 200 to Compostela; toll road 68D heads east to join the Tepic toll road. Total time is 5½ hours, and the tolls add up to 300 pesos. From **Barra de Navidad,** on the coast southeast of Puerto Vallarta, take Hwy. 80 northeast (4½ hr.). From **Manzanillo,** you might also take this road, but toll road 54D through Colima to Guadalajara (3½ hr.; 260 pesos) is faster. From **Mexico City,** take toll road 15D (7 hr.; 550 pesos).

BY BUS Two bus stations serve Guadalajara. The old one, south of downtown, is for buses to Tequila and other nearby towns; the new one, 10km (6¼ miles) southeast of downtown, is for longer trips.

The Old Bus Station   For destinations within 100km (62 miles) of town, including the Lake Chapala area, go to the old bus terminal, on Niños Héroes off Calzada Independencia Sur. For Lake Chapala, take **Transportes Guadalajara-Chapala,** which runs frequent buses and *combis* (minivans).

The New Bus Station   The **Central Camionera** is 20 to 30 minutes from downtown (125 pesos by taxi). The station has seven terminals connected by a covered walkway. Each terminal houses bus lines, offering first- and second-class service for different destinations. Buy bus tickets ahead of time from a travel agency in Guadalajara. Ask at your hotel for the closest to you. There are several major bus lines. The best service (big seats and lots of room) is provided by **ETN.**

Visitor Information

The **State of Jalisco Tourist Information Office** is at Calle Morelos 102 (© **33/3668-1600,** -1601; http://visita.jalisco.gob. mx) in the Plaza Tapatía, at Paseo Degollado and Paraje del Rincón del Diablo. It's open Monday through Friday from 9am to 7pm, and Saturday 10am to 2pm. You can come here for maps, a monthly calendar of cultural events, and good information. Of the **city tourist information booths,** one is in the **Plaza de la Liberación** (directly behind the cathedral), and another is in the **Plaza Guadalajara** (directly in front of the cathedral). These are open daily from 9am to 1pm and 3 to 7pm. Ask at either of these about free weekend walking tours.

City Layout

The **Centro Histórico (city center),** with all its plazas, churches, and museums, will obviously be of interest to the visitor. The **west side** is Guadalajara's modern, cosmopolitan district. In the northwest corner is **Zapopan,** home of Guadalajara's patron saint. On the opposite side of the city from Zapopan, in the southeast corner, are the craft centers of **Tlaquepaque** and **Tonalá.**

The main artery for traffic from downtown to the west side is **Avenida Vallarta.** It starts downtown as **Juárez.** The main arteries for returning to downtown are **México** and **Hidalgo,** both north of Vallarta. Vallarta heads due west, where it intersects another major artery, **Avenida Adolfo López Mateos,** at **Fuente Minerva** (or simply La Minerva, or Minerva Circle). Minerva Circle, a 15-minute drive from downtown, is the central point of reference for the west side. To go to Zapopan from downtown, take **Avenida Avila Camacho,** which you can pick up on Alcalde; it takes 20 minutes by car. To Tlaquepaque and Tonalá, take **Calzada Revolución.** Tlaquepaque is 8km (5 miles) from downtown and takes 15 to 20 minutes by car; Tonalá is 5 minutes farther. Another major viaduct, **Calzada Lázaro Cárdenas,** connects the west side to Tlaquepaque and Tonalá, bypassing downtown.

The Neighborhoods in Brief

Centro Histórico The heart of the city encompasses many plazas, the cathedral, and several historic buildings and museums. Here, too, are the striking murals of José Clemente Orozco, one of the great Mexican muralists. Theaters, restaurants, shops, and clubs dot the area, and an enormous market rounds out the attractions. All of this is in a space roughly 12 blocks by 12 blocks—an easy area to explore on foot, with several plazas and pedestrian-only areas. To the south is a large green space called Parque Agua Azul.

West Side This is the swanky part of town, with the fine restaurants, luxury hotels, boutiques, and galleries, as well as the American, British, and Canadian consulates. It's a large area best navigated by taxi.

Zapopan Founded in 1542, Zapopan is a suburb of Guadalajara. In its center is the 18th-century basilica, the home of Guadalajara's patron saint, the Virgin of Zapopan. The most interesting part of Zapopan is clustered around the temple and can be explored on foot. It has a growing arts and nightlife scene.

Tlaquepaque This is another suburb that for centuries was a village of artisans (especially potters). It grew into a market center, and in the last 40 years, has attracted designers and artists from across Mexico. Every major form of art and craft is for sale here: furniture, pottery, glass, jewelry, woodcarvings, leather goods, sculptures, and paintings. The shops are sophisticated, yet Tlaquepaque's center retains a small-town feel that makes door-to-door browsing enjoyable and relaxing.

Tonalá This has remained a town of artisans. Plenty of stores sell mostly local products from the town's more than 400 workshops. You'll see wrought iron, ceramics, blown glass, and papier-mâché. A busy street market operates each Thursday and Sunday.

Getting Around

BY TAXI Taxis are the easiest way to get around town. They are quite plentiful. Most have meters, and though some drivers are reluctant to use them, you can insist that they do. There are three rates: for day, night, and suburbia. Typical fares include the following: downtown to the far west side, 70 to 90 pesos; downtown or west side to Tlaquepaque, 70 to 100 pesos; downtown to the new bus station, 90 to 125 pesos; downtown to the airport, 180 to 220 pesos.

BY CAR Familiarize yourself with the main traffic arteries (see "City Layout," above) before you get behind the wheel. Several important freeway-style thoroughfares crisscross the city. **Dr. R. Michel** leads south from the town center toward Tlaquepaque. Use **González Gallo** for the return direction. **Avenida Vallarta** starts out downtown as **Juárez,** heads west past La Minerva, and eventually feeds onto **Hwy. 15,** bound for Tequila and Puerto Vallarta.

BY BUS For the visitor, the handiest route is the **TUR 706,** which runs from the Centro Histórico southeast to Tlaquepaque (10 pesos), the Central Camionera (the new bus station), and Tonalá. You can catch this bus on Avenida 16 de Septiembre. The same bus runs in the reverse direction back to the downtown area.

The **electric bus** is handy for travel between downtown and the Minerva area (5 pesos). It bears the sign PAR VIAL and runs east along Hidalgo and west along the next street to the north, Calle Independencia (not Calzada Independencia). Hidalgo passes along the north side of the cathedral. The Par Vial goes as far east as Mercado Libertad and as far west as Minerva Circle. The city also has a light rail system, **Tren Ligero,** but it doesn't serve areas that are of interest to visitors.

[FastFACTS] GUADALAJARA

Area Code   The telephone area code is **33.**

Business Hours   Store hours are Monday through Saturday from 10am to 2pm and 4 to 8pm.

Climate & Dress   Guadalajara's weather is mostly mild. From November through March, you'll need a sweater in the evening. The warmest months, April and May, are hot and dry. From June through September, the city gets afternoon and evening showers that keep the temperature a bit cooler, but it seems as though the local climate is getting warmer. Dress in Guadalajara is conservative; attention-getting sportswear (short shorts, halters, and the like) is out of place.

Consulates   The **American Consular offices** are at Progreso 175 (✆ **33/3268-2200,** -2100). Other consulates include the **Canadian Consulate,** Mariano Otero 1249, Col. Rinconada del Bosque (✆ **33/3671-4740**); the **British Consulate,** Calle Jesús Rojas 20, Col. Los Pinos (✆ **33/3343-2296**); and the **Australian Consulate,** López Cotilla 2018, Col. Arcos Vallarta (✆ **33/3615-7418**). These offices all keep roughly the same hours: Monday through Friday from 8am to 1pm.

Currency Exchange Three blocks south of the cathedral, on López Cotilla, between Corona and Degollado, are more than 20 *casas de cambio*. Almost all post their rates, which are usually better than bank rates, minus the long lines.

Elevation Guadalajara sits at 1,700m (5,576 ft.).

Emergencies The emergency phone number is ✆ **060.**

Hospitals For medical emergencies, visit the **Hospital México-Americano,** Cólomos 2110 (✆ **33/3642-7152** or 3641-3141).

Internet Access Most of the big hotels have business centers that you can use. There are many Internet cafes in the Centro Histórico.

Newspapers & Magazines Many newsstands sell the two English local papers, the *Guadalajara Reporter* and the *Guadalajara Weekly.*

Police Tourists should first try to contact the Jalisco tourist information office in Plaza Tapatía (✆ **33/3668-1600**). If you can't reach the office, call the municipal police at ✆ **33/3668-7983.**

Post Office The *correo* is at the corner of Carranza and Calle Independencia, about 4 blocks northeast of the cathedral. Standing in the plaza behind the cathedral, facing the Degollado Theater, walk to the left, and then turn left on Carranza; walk past the Hotel Mendoza, cross Calle Independencia, and look for the post office on the left. It's open Monday through Thursday from 9am to 5pm, Saturday from 10am to 2pm.

Safety Crimes against tourists and foreign students are infrequent and most often take the form of purse snatching. Criminals usually work in teams and target travelers in busy places, such as outdoor restaurants. Keep jewelry out of sight. Should anyone spill something on you, be alert to your surroundings and step away—accidental spills are a common method for distracting the victim.

WHERE TO STAY

Big hotels are apt to offer business discounts, especially if there's no convention in town. Guadalajara's hotels thrive on convention business. Most of the luxury hotels in Guadalajara are on the west side, which has the majority of the shopping malls, boutiques, fashionable restaurants, clubs, and the Expo (convention center). The Centro Histórico is also a good option because there's a lot to do, all in walking distance. And Tlaquepaque is a comfortable place to stay—it's relaxing and is perfect for shoppers; the only drawback is that almost everything shuts down by 7 or 8pm. The rates below are the standard rack rates and include the 19% tax.

Chain hotels not included below are Hilton, Marriott, Camino Real, Howard Johnson, Crowne Plaza, and Best Western. In some

Language Classes

of the cheaper, older large hotels, air-conditioning can be a bit feeble.

Very Expensive

Hotel Presidente InterContinental ★★★   This hotel offers the most comprehensive services and amenities in Guadalajara. The health club is a standout. Guest rooms are sharply designed and well appointed, with up-to-date appliances, bathroom fixtures, carpeting, furniture, and lighting. Standard rooms come as "superior" or "deluxe." Superior rooms cost only a little more and have a better view and one or two small improvements in amenities. Club rooms have discreet check-in, are on limited-access hallways, and come with extras. The extra privacy and services are good for Mexican soap opera stars or repeat guests who like having their preferences known in advance. If you're neither of these, opt for one of the other rooms. Suites are large and come with oversize bathrooms with extra fixtures. The lobby bar is popular; during the season, you'll see bullfighters relaxing here after *la corrida.*

Av. López Mateos Sur and Moctezuma (west side), 45050 Guadalajara, Jal. www. intercontinental.com. ✆ **800/327-0200** in the U.S. and Canada, or 33/3678-1234. Fax 33/3678-1222. 423 units. $215–$222 double; $229–$239 feature or club double; $330 and up suite. Promotional rates available. AE, DC, MC, V. Valet parking 55 pesos. **Amenities:** Restaurant; bar; babysitting; concierge; executive-level rooms; golf at nearby clubs; health club w/saunas, steam rooms, and whirlpools; outdoor heated pool; room service; smoke-free rooms; spa. *In room:* A/C, TV, hair dryer, minibar, MP3 docking station, Wi-Fi.

Quinta Real Guadalajara ★★★   This chain specializes in properties that are suggestive of Mexico's heritage. No glass skyscraper here—two five-story buildings made of stone, wood, plaster, and tile capture the feel of Mexican colonial architecture. Suites vary quite a bit: Eight have brick cupolas, and some have balconies. All are large, with a split-level layout and antique decorative touches. And all come with large, great bathrooms with tub/showers. The "grand-class" suites are larger and come with a few extras, such as a stereo and big bathrooms with Jacuzzi tubs. You can choose between two doubles or one king-size bed. The hotel is 2 blocks from Minerva Circle in western Guadalajara. Ask for a room that doesn't face López Mateos.

Av. México 2727 (at López Mateos, west side), 44690 Guadalajara, Jal. www. quintareal.com. © **866/621-9288** in the U.S. and Canada, or 33/3669-0600. Fax 33/3669-0601. 76 suites. $275–$300 master suite; $325–$350 grand-class suite. AE, DC, MC, V. Free secure parking. **Amenities:** Restaurant; bar; babysitting; concierge; fitness room; outdoor heated pool; room service; smoke-free rooms; discounts at local day spa. *In room:* A/C, TV, hair dryer, minibar, Wi-Fi.

Villa Ganz ★★★ This small hotel offers the most personal service in Guadalajara. You can relax and have just about any service the city offers brought to the hotel. Or the hotel can provide a car and driver to take you where you need to go. Rooms are big, well furnished, and decorated with flair. Bathrooms are large and well lit. Beds come with down comforters (hypoallergenic option available). The hotel occupies a classic old mansion with a garden and patio in the rear. Rooms facing the garden are the quietest, but those facing the street are set back from the traffic and have double-glazed windows. The common rooms and rear garden are agreeable places to relax.

A sister property, Quinta Ganz, offers furnished apartments by the week for about 1,200 pesos per night. These have mostly the same amenities as the hotel and come with a full kitchen and reduced maid service (3 times a week).

López Cotilla 1739 (btw. Bolivar and San Martín, west side), 44140 Guadalajara, Jal. www.villaganz.com. © **800/728-9098** in the U.S. and Canada, or 33/3120-1416. 10 suites. $248 junior suite; $310 master suite; $345 grand master suite. Rates include continental breakfast. Internet specials often available. AE, MC, V. Free secure parking. Pets accepted with prior notification. Children 11 and younger not accepted. **Amenities:** Bar; concierge; fitness room; golf and tennis at local club; room service. *In room:* A/C, TV, hair dryer, MP3 stereo, Wi-Fi.

Expensive

Holiday Inn Hotel and Suites Centro Histórico ★★ Of the large downtown hotels, this one has the most comfortable rooms. It is conveniently located near the area's most popular restaurants and just a few blocks from the cathedral. Guest rooms are attractive, if blandly modern with a few Mexican accents, and have comfortable mattresses and good light. The size is good, and the furniture is functional and attractive. Bathrooms in standard rooms are midsize and well equipped, with ample counter space. The suites are larger, with a few more amenities. Room rates include transportation to (but not from) the airport.

Av. Juárez 211, Centro Histórico, 44100 Guadalajara. Jal. www.holiday-inn.com. © **800/465-4329** in the U.S. and Canada, 01-800/009-9900 in Mexico, or

33/3560-1200. 90 units. $125–$170 double; $136–$180 suite; $170–$240 suite with Jacuzzi. AE, MC, V. Free secure parking. **Amenities:** Restaurant; bar; ground transportation; fitness room; room service; smoke-free rooms. *In room:* A/C, TV, hair dryer, minibar, Wi-Fi.

Hotel de Mendoza   On a quiet street next to the Degollado Theater and Plaza Tapatía, 2 blocks from the cathedral, the Mendoza has perhaps the best location of any downtown hotel. The decor would best be described as a stab at old Spanish, with wood paneling and old-world accents. Rooms face the street, an interior courtyard, or the pool. Most standard rooms are midsize, though there are a few larger ones that are split level with laminate floors and exterior windows, which go for the same price. Bed choices are one queen-size, two full, or two queens. Many of the mattresses here are pretty firm. Bathrooms are midsize, with so-so lighting. Junior suites have an additional sitting area and larger bathrooms, with the recent addition of Jacuzzi tubs.

Carranza 16, Centro Histórico, 44100 Guadalajara, Jal. www.demendoza.com.mx. ✆ **33/3942-5151.** Fax 33/3613-7310. 104 units. 1,687 pesos double; 1,947 pesos junior suite. Discounts sometimes available. AE, MC, V. Secure parking 40 pesos. **Amenities:** Restaurant; bar; fitness room; Jacuzzi; small outdoor pool; room service; smoke-free rooms. *In room:* A/C, TV, hair dryer, Wi-Fi.

Moderate

Hotel Morales ★★   A historic hotel that's attractive and comfortable, the Morales is a good downtown choice. The standard rooms are either *suite sencilla* (one queen-size bed) or *suite doble* (two double beds). The rooms are medium or large and come with laminate floors. The bathrooms are attractive, with ceramic-tile floors, good-looking countertops, and strong showers. The rooms that face the street have balconies with double-glazed windows that do a good job at screening the noise. The imperial suites offer a lot for the money, with superlarge bathrooms equipped with a two-person Jacuzzi tub and a separate shower. All rooms are set around an arcaded lobby holding an attractive bar area. There's live music on Wednesday and Friday evenings.

Av. Corona 243 (corner of Prisciliano Sánchez), Centro Histórico, 44100 Guadalajara, Jal. www.hotelmorales.com.mx. ✆ **33/3658-5232.** Fax 33/3658-5239. 64 units. 1,360 pesos double; 1,660 pesos junior suite; 2,140 pesos imperial suite. AE, MC, V. Free sheltered parking. **Amenities:** Restaurant; bar; babysitting; fitness room; room service; smoke-free rooms. *In room:* A/C, TV, hair dryer, Internet.

La Villa del Ensueño ★   This B&B in central Tlaquepaque is a convenient alternative to big-city hotels. A modern interpretation of traditional Mexican architecture, it contains small courtyards and well-tended grounds bordered by old stucco walls, with an occasional wrought-iron balcony or stone staircase. The rooms have more character than most hotel lodgings. Doubles have either two twin or two double beds. The hotel is about 8 blocks from the main plaza.

Florida 305, 45500 Tlaquepaque, Jal. www.villadelensueno.com. © **800/220-8689** in the U.S., or 33/3635-8792. Fax 818/597-0637. 20 units. 1,439 pesos double; 1,636 pesos deluxe double; 1,898 pesos junior suite. Rates include full breakfast and light laundry service. AE, MC, V. Free valet parking. **Amenities:** Bar; indoor/outdoor pool. *In room:* A/C, TV, hair dryer, Wi-Fi.

Old Guadalajara ★★

This downtown bed-and-breakfast in a colonial house is well located, quiet, and beautiful. The rooms reflect the local scene; they speak of Mexico without shouting it. They are large and airy, with high ceilings, tile floors, and comfortable bathrooms. The colonial architecture makes it possible to live without air-conditioning in the warm months, and every room is equipped with a ceiling fan. The central courtyard is cool and shaded by tall bamboo. The common rooms are open to the courtyard and are stocked with material for readers curious about the city. Paul Callahan prepares filling breakfasts for his guests using only natural ingredients.

Belén 236, Centro Histórico, 44100 Guadalajara, Jal. www.oldguadalajara.com. ©/fax **33/3613-9958.** 4 units. $110 double. Rates include full breakfast. AE, MC, V for deposit; no credit cards at B&B. Children 17 and younger not accepted. **Amenities:** Smoke-free rooms. *In room:* Hair dryer, no phone.

Quinta Don José ★★ 🏷

Good value, great location, friendly English-speaking owners—there are a lot of reasons to like this small establishment just 2 blocks from Tlaquepaque's main square. Rooms run the gamut from midsize to extra large. They are comfortable, attractive, and quiet, with some nice local touches. Most of the standard and deluxe doubles have a king-size or two double beds and an attractive, midsize bathroom. A couple of them have small private outdoor spaces. Some of the suites in back come with a full kitchen and lots of space—more than twice the size of the usual suite, with one king-size and one double bed. The breakfasts are good, and recently the owners have installed a full restaurant open for dinner. Some lodgings just have a good feel to them, and this is one of them.

Reforma 139, 45500 Tlaquepaque, Jal. www.quintadonjose.com. © **866/629-3753** in the U.S. and Canada, or 33/3635-7522. 15 units. $105 standard; $119 deluxe; $134–$180 suite. Rates include full breakfast. AE, MC, V. Free secure parking. **Amenities:** Restaurant; bar; free airport transfers; babysitting; heated outdoor pool; smoke-free rooms. *In room:* A/C, TV, hair dryer, Wi-Fi.

Inexpensive

Gran Hotel Los Reyes 💣 The rooms in this 10-story downtown hotel have good, individually controlled air-conditioning and strong showers, a rarity for budget hotels. The location is downtown near the market (7 blocks from the main square), which is central but in a somewhat decayed part of town. For entertainment, there's a modern multiplex cinema across the street that shows first-run Hollywood movies. Guest rooms are midsize; most have a king-size bed. Those on the mezzanine level are larger and often cost the same. Ask for a room facing away from the busy Calzada Independencia. The rooms on the seventh, eighth, and ninth floors have been totally remodeled and go for the higher price listed below. They are worth the extra money.

Calzada Independencia Sur 168, 44100 Guadalajara, Jal. www.granhotellosreyes. com.mx. 🕐 **33/3613-9781.** Fax 33/3614-0367. 181 units. 655–850 pesos double. AE, MC, V. Free valet parking. **Amenities:** Restaurant; outdoor heated pool; room service; smoke-free rooms. *In room:* A/C, TV, Wi-Fi.

Hotel Cervantes ★ 💣 This six-story downtown hotel offers modern amenities at a good price. The rooms are attractive and midsize. They are decorated and furnished simply and practically, without much fuss. The air-conditioning is not strong. The lower price is for one double bed; the higher price is for a king-size or two doubles. This is not a noisy hotel, but if you require absolute quiet, request an interior room. The Cervantes is 6 blocks south and 3 blocks west of the cathedral.

Prisciliano Sánchez 442 (corner of Donato Guerra), Centro Histórico, 44100 Guadalajara, Jal. www.hotelcervantes.com.mx. 🕐/fax **33/3613-6816.** 100 units. 705–745 pesos double; 1,095 pesos suite. AE, MC, V. Free secure parking. **Amenities:** Restaurant; lobby bar; small outdoor heated pool; room service. *In room:* A/C, TV, Wi-Fi.

Hotel San Francisco Plaza 💣 This colonial-style downtown hotel is both pleasant and a bargain. Most rooms are medium to large and comfortable, with attractive furnishings. All have rugs or carpeting, and most have tall ceilings. The hotel is built around four courtyards, which contain fountains and potted plants. Rooms along Prisciliano Sánchez are much quieter now that the management has installed double windows. Some units along the back wall of the rear patio have small bathrooms. Most rooms have ceramic tile flooring; some have carpeting. The San Francisco Plaza is 6 blocks south and 2 blocks east of the cathedral.

Degollado 267 (corner of Prisciliano Sánchez), Centro Histórico, 44100 Guadalajara, Jal. www.sanfranciscohotel.com.mx. 🕐 **33/3613-8954,** -8971. Fax 33/3613-3257. 76 units. 710–785 pesos double. AE, MC, V. Free parking. **Amenities:** Restaurant; room service. *In room:* A/C, TV, Wi-Fi.

WHERE TO EAT

Guadalajara has many excellent restaurants either for fine dining or for typical local fare. Good local fare can be had in the Centro Histórico, but for fine dining, head to western Guadalajara or, if it's early in the day, to Tlaquepaque. For a quick bite, there are several **Sanborn's** in the city. This is a popular national chain of restaurants known for their *enchiladas suizas* (enchiladas in cream sauce). If you're downtown and looking for baked goods and coffee, go to **El Globo** (ⓒ **33/3613-9926;** www.elglobo.com.mx), an upscale bakery at the corner of Pedro Moreno and Degollado; this chain has a couple more locations around Guadalajara. *Tip:* When taking a taxi, keep the address of the restaurant handy; taxi drivers cannot be relied upon to know where even the most popular restaurants are.

Local dishes include *birria* (goat or lamb covered in maguey leaves and roasted). It comes in a tomato broth or with the broth on the side. Another favorite is the *torta ahogada,* a sandwich with pork bathed in a tomato sauce. The most popular drink here is the *paloma,* which combines tequila, lots of lime juice, and grapefruit soda on ice.

Expensive

Adobe Fonda ★★★ NUEVA COCINA This restaurant shares space with a large store on pedestrian-only Independencia. The dining area is open and airy. Homemade bread and tostadas come to the table with an olive oil–based chile sauce, *pico de gallo,* and *requezón de epazote* (ricotta-like cheese with a Mexican herb). Among the soups are *crema de cilantro* and an interesting mushroom soup with a dark-beer broth. The main courses present some difficult decisions, with intriguing combinations of Mexican, Italian, and Argentine ingredients. The shrimp chile relleno bathed in a creamy sauce flavored with blue cheese is a good choice. Also, there's a filet mignon served in a pool of mild *chile ancho* sauce. Sample the margaritas, too.

Francisco de Miranda 27 (corner of Independencia, Tlaquepaque). ⓒ **33/3657-2792.** www.adobefonda.com. Reservations recommended on weekends. Main courses 150–230 pesos. AE, MC, V. Mon–Fri noon–7pm; Sat 9am–8pm; Sun 9am–7pm.

Chez Nené ★★★ FRENCH In a small and pleasant open-air dining room, you can enjoy a quiet and leisurely meal of delicious French food. After doing just this, I had to meet the owner to see who was behind such work. He turned out to be a French expatriate (whose Mexican wife, Nené, is the restaurant's namesake) with strong ideas about food and dining. Freshness and quality of ingredients are what matter most to him. He goes to the market every day, and from what he finds, creates a daily menu that he puts on a chalkboard. Service is excellent.

Juan Palomar y Arias 426 (continuación Rafael Sanzio, west side). ✆ **33/3673-4564.** Reservations recommended on weekends. Main courses 180–280 pesos. AE, MC, V. Tues 4–11pm; Wed–Sat 1–5:30pm and 7:30–11:30pm; Sun 1–6pm.

El Sacromonte ★★★ ALTA COCINA   The food is so exquisite that I try to dine here every time I'm in Guadalajara. El Sacromonte emphasizes artful presentation and design: Order "Queen Isabel's Crown," and you'll be served a dish of shrimp woven together in the shape of a crown and covered in divine lobster-and-orange sauce. Or try quesadillas with rose petals in a deep-colored strawberry sauce. For soup, consider *el viejo progreso* for its unlikely combination of flavors (blue cheese and chipotle chile). The menu features amusing descriptions in verse. The main dining area is a shaded, open-air patio. The restaurant isn't far from the downtown area, on the near west side. Next door is a good steakhouse operated by the same owners.

Pedro Moreno 1398 (corner of Calle Colonias, west side). ✆ **33/3825-5447** or 3827-0663. www.sacromonte.com.mx. Reservations recommended. Main courses 166–210 pesos. MC, V. Mon–Sat 1:30pm–midnight; Sun 1:30–6pm.

La Matera ★ STEAKS/PIZZA   The steaks are good, and the surroundings are inviting in this two-story open brick structure. The cuts come from the U.S. and Mexico, the lamb from New Zealand, and the wine from all over. La Matera has a decidedly Argentine influence, which of course means Italian influence. Pizzas are a popular menu item; the seafood is beautifully grilled. The bar is downstairs and most of the dining area is upstairs. In good weather it's very pleasant.

Av. México 2891 (west side). ✆ **33/3616-1626.** http://lamatera.tripod.com. Reservations recommended on weekends. Steaks 210–360 pesos; pizzas 100–140 pesos. AE, MC, V. Mon–Sat 1pm–midnight; Sun 1–6:30pm.

La Tequila ★★ MEXICAN   Contemporary and traditional Mexican cooking is on the menu in this large, popular restaurant. You'll find dishes such as a pasta stuffed with shrimp and *huitlacoche,* and a *chamorro adobado* (pork shoulder marinated in a chile sauce) wrapped in maguey leaves and cooked in the ground with a wood fire. On my last visit I tried the shrimp in a sweet-and-sour tamarind sauce, as well as tacos "plaza de toros." Both of these were excellent—the tacos were beef tips and bits of Mexican sausage on fresh tortillas served with their own sauce; the shrimp were tangy and different. The bar, too, has started making original concoctions, such as the "tequilibrio." La Tequila can get pretty lively, and the decorative touches, such as trimmed agaves, give the dining areas a regional point of reference. Indoor/outdoor dining areas and a popular upstairs bar make up most of the restaurant.

Av. México 2830 (at Napoleón, west side). ⓒ **33/3640-3440,** -3110. www. latequila.com. Reservations recommended on weekends. Main courses 135–189 pesos. AE, MC, V. Mon–Sat 1pm–midnight; Sun 1–6pm.

Moderate

Hostería del Angel ★★ TAPAS/WINE BAR   Sip wine and munch on a few tapas in this comfortable patio restaurant and wine bar just a few blocks from the basilica in Zapopan. The chef-owner cooked for years in Spain, where he became fascinated with the making of cheeses and deli meats such as Spanish *jamón serrano*. He serves a variety of tapas and popular baguette sandwiches. The menu doesn't do a good job of explaining the dishes, so don't hesitate to ask the waitstaff for explanations. Most of the tapas are under the heading "Por la noche," which also includes sandwiches and the *rotolata*—vegetables and cold cuts surrounded by a thin layer of crispy cheese, which is a house specialty. Acoustic music plays from 9 to 11pm Tuesday through Saturday. The restaurant is a half-block off the pedestrian-only *calzada,* which leads to the plaza in front of the basilica. For breakfast you can get the traditional *molletes.*

5 de Mayo 260, Zapopan (west side). ⓒ/fax **33/3656-9516.** www.hosteria delangel.com. Reservations recommended on weekends. Tapas 55–90 pesos; main courses 109–165 pesos. MC, V. Mon–Sat 9am–midnight; Sun 9am–8pm.

I Latina FUSION   Warehouse chic with a porcine motif (the owner tells me that the pig is a symbol of abundance in Thailand) is the look here. The menu is absurdly small but is supplemented with lots of daily specials. Usually there's a steak of some kind, cooked a bit differently, also some Asian fusion, including at least one noodle dish. This is a good place for people-watching—you get to see a portion of Guadalajara's hip, artsy crowd, who enjoy the antiestablishment surroundings, including the metal and plastic tables and chairs. My main problem is the noise, which at times gets to be too much. If you're looking for quiet dining, go elsewhere. Cabs have a hard time finding this place, despite the fact that it's almost right off of Minerva Circle. It's not that difficult—Inglaterra faces the railroad tracks.

Av. Inglaterra 3128 (west side). ⓒ **33/3647-7774.** www.ilatinarest.com. Reservations recommended. Main courses 99–180 pesos. MC, V. Wed–Sat 7:30pm–1am; Sun 2–6pm.

La Fonda de San Miguel 📷 MEXICAN   My favorite way to enjoy a good meal in Mexico is to have it in an elegant colonial courtyard. I love the contrast between the bright, noisy street and the cool, shaded patio. This restaurant is in the former convent of Santa Teresa de Jesús. While you enjoy the stone arches and gurgling fountain, little crisp tacos and homemade bread appear at the table. For main courses, try the shrimp *al tequila,* or perhaps the *chiles en nogada* if it's the season. Traditional *mole poblano* is also on the menu. Wednesday to Saturday, musicians perform from 3 to 5pm and 9 to 11pm.

Donato Guerra 25 (and Pedro Moreno, downtown). ✆ **33/3613-0809.** www. lafondadesanmiguel.com. Reservations recommended on weekends. Breakfast 50–80 pesos; main courses 125–170 pesos. AE, MC, V. Mon 8:30am–6pm; Tues-Sat 8:30am–midnight; Sun 8:30am–9pm.

La Trattoria Pomodoro Ristorante ★ ITALIAN   Good food, good service, and moderate prices make this restaurant perennially popular. The price of pastas and main courses includes a visit to the well-stocked salad bar. Recommendable menu items include the combination pasta plate (lasagna, fettuccini Alfredo, and spaghetti), shrimp linguine, and chicken parmigiana. The Italian owner likes to stock lots of wines from the motherland. The dining room is attractive and casual, with comfortable furniture and separate seating for smokers and nonsmokers.

Niños Héroes 3051 (west side). ✆ **33/3122-1817.** Reservations recommended, but not accepted during holidays. Pasta 80–120 pesos; main courses 95–120 pesos. AE, MC, V. Daily 1pm–midnight.

Mariscos Progreso SEAFOOD   At this outdoor restaurant in Tlaquepaque, the dining area is a rustic, open patio shaded in parts by trees or tile roofs. The tables and chairs are *equipal*—the common rustic, but comfortable, furniture of the region made with leather and rough-cut wood. The seafood cocktails are excellent and not loaded with as much ketchup as in other joints. You can order one of these or a ceviche, which I found fresh on my last visit. The menu includes all the Mexican standards—fish in toasted garlic butter *(al mojo de ajo)* or with strips of *guajillo* chile *(al ajillo).* Sometimes there's quite a bit of ambience, with mariachis adding to the commotion. At other times, the crowd thins and one can rest peacefully from the exertions of shopping with a cold drink. It's a half-block from El Parián.

Progreso 80, Tlaquepaque. ✆ **33/3639-6149.** Reservations not accepted. Main courses 118–166 pesos. MC, V. Daily 11am–7pm.

Inexpensive

Café Madrid MEXICAN   This little coffee shop is like many coffee shops used to be—a social institution where people come

You'll see multitudes of *taquerías* (taco joints) everywhere in Mexico. These are generally small places with a counter or a few tables set around the cooking area; you see exactly how they make their tacos before deciding whether to order. Most tacos come with a little chopped onion and cilantro, but not with tomato and lettuce. Find one that seems popular with the locals and where the cook performs with *brio* (a good sign of pride in the product). Sometimes a woman will be making the tortillas (or working the *masa* into *gorditas* or *sopes,* if these are also served) right there. You will never see men doing this—this is perhaps the strictest gender division in Mexican society. Men do all other cooking and kitchen tasks, and work with already-made tortillas, but will never be found working *masa.*

in, greet each other and the staff by name, and chat over breakfast or coffee and cigarettes. Change comes slowly here—the waiters still wear the white jackets with black bow ties, as they did 30 years ago. The coffee and Mexican breakfasts are good, as is the standard Mexican fare served in the afternoon. Most popular dishes include the enchiladas and the *chilaquiles.* The front room opens to the street, with a small lunch counter and another room in the back.

Juárez 264 (btw. Corona and 16 de Septiembre, downtown). ✆ **33/3614-9504.** Breakfast 35-50 pesos; main courses 55-95 pesos. No credit cards. Daily 7:30am-10pm.

La Chata Restaurant REGIONAL/MEXICAN   If you're staying downtown, don't let this place slip off your radar. It does a good job with all the Mexican classics and some regional specialties as well. Unlike most restaurants, this one has the kitchen in front and the dining area in back. For a reasonable sum, you can get a filling bowl of *pozole.* They also offer *flautas, sopes,* quesadillas, and guacamole. There's also traditional *mole* and a couple of combination plates. The chairs are comfortable, and you hang out with lots of locals.

Corona 126 (btw. Juárez and López Cotilla, downtown). ✆ **33/3613-0588.** www. lachata.com.mx. Reservations not accepted. Breakfast 40-60 pesos; main courses 65-119 pesos. MC, V. Daily 8am-midnight.

La Fonda de la Noche ★★ 🗏 MEXICAN   For a host of reasons, this is my favorite place in the city for a simple supper. The limited menu is excellent, the surroundings are comfortable and inviting, the lighting is perfect, and there's a touch of nostalgia for the Mexico of the '40s, '50s, and '60s. It's not far from downtown or the west side; take a cab to the intersection of Jesús and Reforma, and, when you get there, look for a door behind a small hedge. There's no sign. It's a house with five fun dining rooms. Only Spanish is spoken, and the menu is simple. To try a little of everything, order the *plato combinado,* a combination plate that comes with an *enchilada de medio mole,* an empanada called a *media luna,* a *tostada,* and a *sope.* The owner is Carlos Ibarra, an artist from the state of Durango. He has decorated the place with traditional Mexican pine furniture and cotton tablecloths and his personal collection of paintings, mostly the works of close friends. On weekends, La Fonda offers *chiles en nogada.*

Jesús 251 (corner with Reforma, Col. El Refugio). ⓒ **33/3827-0917.** Reservations not accepted. Main courses 75–109 pesos. MC, V. Tues–Sun 7:30pm–midnight.

Los Itacates Restaurant ★ 𝅘 MEXICAN   *Itacate* is Spanish for lunchbox, and the name implies Mexican home cooking at reasonable prices. Office workers pack the place between 2 and 4pm weekdays, and there's a good crowd on weekend nights, but at other times you'll have no problem finding a table. You can dine outdoors in a shaded sidewalk area, in one of the three dining rooms, or in the terrace in back that overlooks a small playground, which was recently installed. The rooms are brightly decorated, with traditional, painted wood furniture. Specialties include *lomo adobado* and chiles rellenos. *Pollo Itacates* is a quarter of a chicken, two cheese enchiladas, potatoes, and rice. Los Itacates is 5 blocks north of Avenida Vallarta. In the evenings, they serve tacos and other *antojitos.*

Chapultepec Norte 110 (west side). ⓒ **33/3825-1106,** -9551. Reservations accepted. Breakfast buffet 88 pesos; tacos 15 pesos; main courses 62–105 pesos. MC, V. Mon–Sat 8am–11pm; Sun 8am–7pm.

EXPLORING GUADALAJARA
Special Events

Throughout the autumn months Guadalajara hosts a succession of events. In September, when Mexicans celebrate independence from Spain, the city goes all out, with a full month of festivities. The celebrations kick off with the **Encuentro Internacional del Mariachi** (www.mariachi-jalisco.com.mx), in which mariachi bands from around the world play before knowledgeable audiences and hold sessions with other mariachis. Bands come from as far as

GUADALAJARA bus tours

Two companies are now offering bus tours of the city. One is a
local company, **Tranvías Turísticos** (no phone), which offers two
tours on small buses that look like trolley cars. Get info and buy
tickets from the kiosk in Plaza Guadalajara (in front of the
cathedral) from 10am until 7pm. There are two routes. One is a
circuit through downtown and surrounding neighborhoods. It
lasts 1 hour and 10 minutes. The second is a slightly longer tour,
going to Tlaquepaque. It lasts 1½ hours. Both cost 90 pesos. The
other company, **Tapatío Tours** (✆ 33/3613-0887; www.tapatio
tour.com), has modern, bright-red double-decker buses. Its tour
goes from downtown to western Guadalajara to Tlaquepaque.
The tour costs 100 pesos on weekdays and 120 pesos on weekends. It goes farther out, into western Guadalajara. There are 10
stops; you can get off at any one and catch the next bus when it
passes by, which is every 45 minutes to an hour. Catch the bus
in the plaza on the north side of the cathedral after 10am.

Japan and Russia. Concerts are held in several venues. In the
Degollado Theater, you can hear orchestral arrangements of classic
mariachi songs with solos by famous mariachis. You might be
acquainted with many of the classics without even knowing it. The
culmination is a parade of thousands of mariachis and *charros*
(Mexican cowboys) through downtown. It starts the first week of
September.

On **September 15,** a massive crowd assembles in front of the
Governor's Palace to await the traditional ***grito*** (shout for independence) at 11pm. The *grito* commemorates Father Miguel Hidalgo's
cry for independence in 1810. The celebration features live music
on a street stage, spontaneous dancing, fireworks, and shouts of
"¡Viva México!" and *"¡Viva Hidalgo!"* The next day is the official
Independence Day, with a traditional parade; the plazas downtown
resemble a country fair and market, with booths, games of chance,
stuffed-animal prizes, cotton candy, and candied apples. Live
entertainment stretches well into the night.

On **October 12,** a **procession** ★★ honoring Our Lady of
Zapopan celebrates the feast day of the Virgin of Zapopan. Around
dawn, her small, dark figure begins the 5-hour ride from the
Cathedral of Guadalajara to the suburban **Basílica de la Virgen
de Zapopan** (p. 145). The original icon dates from the mid-1500s;

the procession began 200 years later. Today, crowds spend the night along the route and vie for position as the Virgin approaches. She travels in a gleaming new car (virginal, in that it must never have had the ignition turned on), which her caretakers pull through the streets. During the months leading up to the feast day, the figure visits churches all over the city. You will likely see neighborhoods decorated with paper streamers and banners honoring the Virgin's visit to the local church.

The celebration has grown into a month-long event, **Fiestas de Octubre,** which kicks off with an enormous parade, usually on the first Sunday or Saturday of the month. Festivities include performing arts, *charreadas* (rodeos), bullfights, art exhibits, regional dancing, a food fair, and a Day of Nations incorporating all the consulates in Guadalajara. By the time this is over, you enter the **holiday season of November and December,** with Revolution Day (Nov 20), the Virgin of Guadalupe's feast day (Dec 12), and several other celebrations.

Downtown Guadalajara

For a map of the attractions below, see the "Downtown Guadalajara" map on p. 125.

The most easily recognized building in the city is the **cathedral** ★, around which four open plazas form the shape of a Latin cross. Extending eastwards from the plaza behind the cathedral is a long stretch of open area leading all the way to the Instituto Cultural Cabañas. This extension of open space is called **Plaza Tapatía.**

Construction on the cathedral started in 1561 and continued into the 18th century. Over such a long time, it was inevitable that some architectural alteration would be incorporated before the building was ever completed. The result is an unusual facade—an amalgam of several styles, including baroque, neoclassical, and Gothic. An earthquake destroyed the original towers in 1818; their replacements were built in the 1850s, inspired by designs said to have been on the bishop's dinner china. The colors on the towers, blue and yellow, are Guadalajara's official colors. The interior is cavernous and majestic. Items of interest include a painting in the sacristy ascribed to the 17th-century Spanish artist Bartolomé Estaban Murillo (1617–82).

On the cathedral's south side is the **Plaza de Armas,** the oldest and loveliest of the plazas. A cast-iron Art Nouveau bandstand is its dominant feature. Made in France, it was a gift to the city from the dictator Porfirio Díaz in the 1890s. The female figures on the bandstand exhibited too little clothing for conservative Guadalajarans, who clothed them. The dictator, recognizing when it's best to let the people have their way, said nothing.

Facing the plaza is the **Palacio del Gobierno ★★**, a broad, low structure built in 1774. The facade blends Spanish and Moorish elements and holds several eye-catching details. Inside the central courtyard, above the staircase to the right, is a spectacular mural of Hidalgo by the modern Mexican master José Clemente Orozco. The Father of Independence appears high overhead, bearing directly down on the viewer and looking as implacable as a force of nature. On one of the adjacent walls, Orozco painted *The Carnival of Ideologies,* a dark satire on the prevailing fanaticisms of his day. Another of his murals is inside the second-floor chamber of representatives, depicting Hidalgo again, this time in a more conventional posture, writing the proclamation to end slavery in Mexico. The *palacio* is open daily from 10am to 8pm.

In the plaza on the opposite side of the cathedral from the Plaza de Armas is the **Rotonda de los Hombres Ilustres.** Sixteen white columns, each supporting a bronze statue, stand as monuments to Guadalajara's and Jalisco's distinguished sons. Across the street from the plaza, in front of the Museo Regional, you will see a line of horse-drawn buggies. A carriage ride around the Centro Histórico lasts almost an hour and costs 200 pesos for one to four people.

Facing the east side of the rotunda is the **Museo Regional de Guadalajara,** Liceo 60 (© **33/3613-2703**). Originally a convent, it was built in 1701 in the baroque style and contains some of the region's important archaeological finds, fossils, historic objects, and art. Among the highlights are a giant reconstructed mammoth's skeleton and a meteorite weighing 772 kilograms (1,702 lb.), discovered in Zacatecas in 1792. On the first floor, there's a fascinating exhibit of pre-Hispanic pottery and some exquisite pottery and clay figures recently unearthed near Tequila during the construction of the toll road. On the second floor is a small ethnography exhibit of the contemporary dress of the state's indigenous peoples, including the Coras, Mexicaneros, Nahuas, and Tepehuanes. It's open Tuesday through Saturday from 9am to 5:30pm and Sunday from 9am to 4pm. Admission is 45 pesos.

Behind the Cathedral is the **Plaza de la Liberación,** with the **Teatro Degollado** (Deh-goh-*yah*-doh) on the opposite side. This neoclassical 19th-century opera house was named for Santos Degollado, a local patriot who fought with Juárez against Maximilian and the French. Apollo and the nine muses decorate the theater's pediment, and the interior is famous for both the acoustics and the rich decoration. It hosts a variety of performances during the year. It's open Monday through Friday from noon to 2pm and during performances. *opera house*

To the right of the theater, across the street, is the sweet little **church of Santa María de Gracia,** built in 1573 as part of a convent for Dominican nuns. On the opposite side of the Teatro Degollado is the **church of San Agustín.** The former convent is now the **University of Guadalajara School of Music.**

Keep walking east down Plaza Tapatía, and you will arrive at the Instituto Cabañas. You will first pass between a couple of low, modern office buildings. The **Tourism Information Office** is in a building on the right side.

Beyond these office buildings, the plaza opens into a large expanse, now framed by department stores and offices, and dominated by the abstract modern **Quetzalcóatl Fountain.** This fluid steel structure represents the mythical plumed serpent Quetzalcóatl, who figured so prominently in pre-Hispanic religion and culture, and exerts a presence even today.

At the far end of the plaza is the Hospicio Cabañas, formerly an orphanage and known today as the **Instituto Cultural Cabañas ★★**, Cabañas 8 (**(C) 33/3818-2800,** ext. 31009). Admission is 70 pesos. This vast structure is impressive for both its size (more than 23 courtyards) and its grandiose architecture, especially the cupola. Created by the famous Mexican architect Manuel Tolsá, it housed homeless children from 1829 to 1980. Today it's a thriving cultural center offering art shows and classes. The interior walls and ceiling of the main building display murals painted by Orozco in 1937. His *Man of Fire,* in the dome, is said to represent the spirit of humanity projecting itself toward the infinite. Other rooms hold additional Orozco works, as well as excellent contemporary art and temporary exhibits.

Just south of the Instituto Cultural Cabañas (to the left as you exit) is the **Mercado Libertad ★**, Guadalajara's gigantic covered central market, the largest in Latin America. This site has been a market plaza since the 1500s; the present buildings date from the early 1950s (see "Shopping," below).

Other Attractions

At **Parque Agua Azul (Blue Water Park),** plants, trees, shrubbery, statues, and fountains create an idyllic refuge from the bustling city. Many people come here to exercise early in the morning. The park is open daily from 7am to 6pm. Admission is 10 pesos for adults, 5 pesos for children.

Across Calzada Independencia from the park, cater-cornered from a small flower market, is the **Museo de Arqueología del Occidente de México,** Calzada Independencia at Avenida del Campesino (no phone). It houses a fine collection of pre-Hispanic pottery from Jalisco, Nayarit, and Colima. The museum is open Tuesday through Friday from 10am to 2pm and 4 to 7pm, Saturday and Sunday 10am to 2pm. There's a small admission charge.

The state-run **Instituto de la Artesanía** (✆ 33/3030-9090) is just past the park entrance at Calzada Independencia and González Gallo. It exhibits just about every kind of craft produced in the state. (There is also a store; see "Shopping," below.) Hours are Monday to Friday 10am to 4pm, Saturday and Sunday 10am to 2pm.

Also near the park is Guadalajara's rodeo arena, **Lienzo Charro de Jalisco** (✆ 33/3619-0315). Mexican cowboys, known as *charros,* are famous for their riding and lasso work, and the arena in Guadalajara is considered the big time. Shows and competitions are every Sunday at noon. The arena is at Av. Dr. R. Michel 577, between González Gallo and Las Palomas.

Basílica de la Virgen de Zapopan ★ A wide promenade several blocks long leads to a large plaza and the basilica. It dates from the 18th-century church and is a combination of baroque and *plateresque* styles. This is the religious center of Guadalajara. On the Virgin's feast day (see "Special Events," earlier in this chapter), the plaza fills with thousands of *tapatíos.* The cult of the Virgin of Zapopan practically began with the foundation of Guadalajara itself. She is much revered and the object of many pilgrimages. In the plaza are several stands selling religious figures and paraphernalia. On one side of the church is a museum and store dedicated to the betterment of the Huichol Indians. It is worth a visit. Admission to the Huichol museum is 12 pesos.

Main Plaza, Zapopan (10km/6¼ miles northwest of downtown). No phone. Free admission. Daily 7am–7pm. Museum Mon–Sat 9:30am–1:30pm and 3–6pm; Sun 10am–3pm.

Museo de la Ciudad This museum would be of interest to those curious about the city's history. It occupies the main house of an 18th-century farm. The permanent collection includes prints from the 18th and 19th centuries, artifacts of daily life from those times, antique weapons, and armor. Descriptive text is in Spanish only.

Independencia 684 (at M. Bárcenas). ✆ **33/1201-8712.** 10 pesos. Tues–Sun 10am–4pm.

Museo de las Artes de la Universidad de Guadalajara Inside the main lecture hall of this building (use entrance facing Juárez) are some more murals by Orozco. On the wall behind the stage is a bitter denunciation of corruption called *The People and Their False Leaders*. In the cupola is a more optimistic work—*The Five-fold Man*, who works to create a better society and better self. The museum (use entrance facing López Cotilla) has a permanent collection of modern art, which includes the works of many local artists.

Juárez 975. ℂ **33/3134-1664.** www.museodelasartes.udg.mx. Free admission. Tues-Fri 10am-6pm; Sat-Sun 10am-4pm.

Museo Pantaleón Panduro ★★★ This museum houses a magnificent collection of ceramic works. Collectors and connoisseurs of pottery will love it, but so will casual students of Mexican popular culture and the arts. This could be one of the great museums of Mexico, but I would change a few things to make it perfect. Every year a national competition is held in Tlaquepaque among ceramists from across Mexico. Prizes are awarded in seven categories and a best of show among these. (*Tip:* The competition is held every June, which is a good time to visit Tlaquepaque.) After the competition, many of the winning pieces become part of the museum's collection. The virtuosity manifested in some of them will take your breath away. It would be wonderful if they were organized by category, with better explanatory text. But for now, the best thing you can do is cajole someone into showing you around and explaining the pieces on display. The staff is quite knowledgeable, and at least one member speaks English. The museum occupies a third of a large complex that in colonial times housed a religious community. It's now called **Centro Cultural El Refugio,** and it's worth ambling through after you've seen the museum's collection. Some improvements have been made to lighting.

P. Sánchez 191 (at Calle Florida, Tlaquepaque). ℂ **33/3639-5656.** Free admission. Tues-Sun 10am-6pm.

SHOPPING

Many visitors to Guadalajara come specifically for the shopping in Tlaquepaque and Tonalá (see below). If you have little free time, try the government-run **Instituto de la Artesanía Jalisciense,** González Gallo 20 at Calzada Independencia (ℂ **33/3030-9090**), in Parque Agua Azul, just south of downtown. This place is perfect for one-stop shopping, with two floors of pottery, silver jewelry, dance masks, glassware, leather goods, and regional clothing from around the state and the country. As you enter, on the right are museum displays showing crafts and regional costumes from the state of Jalisco. The craft store is open Monday through Friday from 10am to 4pm, Saturday and Sunday from 10am to 2pm.

Guadalajara is known for its shoe industry; if you're in the market for a pair, try the **Galería del Calzado,** a shopping center made up exclusively of shoe stores. It's on the west side, about 6 blocks from Minerva Circle, at avenidas México and Yaquis. There is also a section of the street Esteban Alatorre, near Parque Morelos, which has practically nothing but shop after shop of women's dress shoes. It makes for very comfortable shopping.

Women's jewelry is another good that Guadalajara is known for. There are four large buildings filled with jewelry shops on the Plaza Tapatía, by the San Juan de Dios market, also known as Mercado Libertad.

Mariachis and *charros* come to Guadalajara from all over Mexico to buy highly worked belts and boots, wide-brimmed sombreros, and embroidered shirts. Several tailor shops and stores specialize in these outfits. One is **El Charro,** which has a store in the Plaza del Sol shopping center, across the street from the Hotel Presidente InterContinental, and one downtown on Juárez.

To view a good slice of what constitutes the material world for most Mexicans, try the mammoth **Mercado Libertad ★** downtown. Besides food and produce, you'll see crafts, household goods, clothing, magic potions, and more. Although it opens at 7am, the market isn't in full swing until around 10am. Come prepared to haggle.

Gonvil, a popular bookstore chain, has a branch across from Plaza de los Hombres Ilustres on Avenida Hidalgo, and another a few blocks south at Av. 16 de Septiembre 118 (Alcalde becomes 16 de Septiembre south of the cathedral). It carries few English selections. **Sanborn's,** at the corner of Juárez and 16 de Septiembre, does a good job of keeping English-language periodicals in stock, but most are specialty magazines. For the widest selection of English-language books, try **Sandi Bookstore,** Av. Tepeyac 718 (© **33/3121-0863**), in the Chapalita neighborhood on the west side.

Shopping in Tlaquepaque & Tonalá

Almost everyone who comes to Guadalajara for the shopping has Tlaquepaque (Tlah-keh-*pah*-keh) and Tonalá in mind. These two suburbs are traditional handicraft centers that produce and sell a wide variety of *artesanía* (crafts).

Packing It In

> If you need your purchases packed safely so that you can check them as extra baggage, or if you want them shipped, talk to **Margaret del Río.** She is an American who runs a large packing and shipping company at Juárez 347, Tlaquepaque (© **33/3657-5652**). Paying the excess baggage fee usually is cheaper than shipping, but it's less convenient.

TLAQUEPAQUE

Located about 20 minutes from downtown, **Tlaquepaque** ★★★ has the best shopping for handicrafts and decorative arts in all of Mexico. Over the years, it has become a fashionable place, attracting talented designers in a variety of fields. Even though it's a suburb of a large city, it has a cozy, small-town feel and is a pleasure to stroll through, popping into one shop after another. No one hassles you; no one does the hard sell. It's a relaxing, easy-going experience. There are some excellent places to eat (see "Where to Eat," earlier in this chapter), or you can grab some simple fare at **El Parián,** a building in the middle of town that houses a number of small eateries.

A taxi from downtown Guadalajara costs 100 pesos, or you can take one of the TUR 706 buses that make a fairly quick run from downtown to Tlaquepaque and Tonalá (see "Getting Around," earlier in this chapter).

The **Tlaquepaque Tourism Office** (© **33/3562-7050,** ext. 2320; turismotlaquepaque@yahoo.com.mx) has an information booth in the town's main square by El Parián. It's staffed from 10am to 8pm daily.

If you are interested in pottery and ceramics, make sure to see the **Pantaleón Panduro Museum** (p. 146). Another is the **Regional Ceramics Museum,** Independencia 237 (© **33/3635-5404**), which displays several aspects of traditional Jalisco pottery as produced in Tlaquepaque and Tonalá. The examples date back several generations and are grouped according to the technique used to produce them. Note the crosshatch design known as *petatillo* on some of the pieces; it's one of the region's oldest traditional motifs and is, like so many other motifs, a real pain to produce. Look for the wonderful old kitchen and dining room, complete with pots, utensils, and dishes. The museum is open Tuesday through Saturday from 10am to 6pm, Sunday from 10am to 3pm; admission is free.

HOTELS ■
La Villa del Ensueño **1**
Quinta Don José **6**

RESTAURANTS ◆
Adobe Fonda **4**
Mariscos Progreso **5**

ATTRACTIONS ●
Museo Pantaleón
  Panduro **2**
Regional Ceramics
  Museum **3**

The following list of Tlaquepaque shops will give you an idea of what to expect. This is just a small fraction of what you'll find; the best approach might be to just wander among the shops. The main shopping is along **Independencia,** a pedestrian-only street that starts at El Parián. It was recently resurfaced in stone and looks pretty sharp. You can go door-to-door visiting the shops until the street ends, and then work your way back on **Calle Juárez,** the next street over, south of Independencia.

Agustín Parra So you bought an old hacienda and are trying to restore its chapel—where do you go to find traditional baroque sculpture, religious art, gold-leafed objects, and even entire *retablos* (altarpieces)? Parra is famous for exactly this kind of work, and the store is lovely. It's open Monday through Saturday from 10am to 7pm. Independencia 158. ⓒ **33/3657-8530.**

Bazar Hecht One of the village's longtime favorites. Here you'll find wood objects, handmade furniture, and a few antiques. It's

tequila: **THE NAME SAYS IT ALL**

Tequila is an entertaining (and intoxicating) town, well worth a day trip from Guadalajara. Several taxi drivers charge about 700 pesos to drive you to the town, get you into a tour of a distillery, take you to a restaurant, and haul you back to Guadalajara. A few of them speak English. One recommended driver is **José Gabriel Gómez** (📞 **33/3649-0791;** jgabriel-taxi@hotmail.com); he has a new car and drives carefully. Call him in the evening. Tour companies also arrange bus trips to Tequila; ask at the ticket kiosk of Tranvías Turísticos, mentioned earlier. That company has started a weekend tour to Tequila, taking people to the Cofradía distillery.

Tequila has many distilleries, including the famous brands **Sauza** and **José Cuervo.** All the distilleries—the big, modern ones and the small, more traditional ones—offer tours.

Another approach is to take the **Tequila Express** to the town of Amatitán, home of the Herradura distillery. This excursion is more about having a good time and enjoying some of the things this area is known for than it is about sampling tequila. Serious tequila enthusiasts will be disappointed. There's a nice tour of the distillery, but most of the time is spent watching mariachis and Mexican cowboys perform. The tequila tastings are limited. Everyone has a good time and drinks a fair share, but a trip to the town proper is more informative and offers a greater opportunity for trying different tequilas.

The Tequila Express leaves from the train station on Friday and Saturday, and sometimes on Sunday during vacation and holiday season. It's well organized. You need to be there by 10am. The Guadalajara Chamber of Commerce (Cámara de Comercio), at Vallarta and Niño Obrero (📞 **33/3880-9099**), organizes this trip. Buy tickets ahead of time at the main office; at the small office in the Centro Histórico at Morelos 395; at Calle Colón (no phone); or through Ticketmaster (📞 **33/3818-3800**). Office hours are Monday through Friday from 9am to 2pm and 4 to 6pm. Tickets cost 980 pesos for adults, 500 pesos for children 6 to 12. The tour includes food and drink. It returns to Guadalajara at about 8pm. Travel time is 1¾ hours each way. For more information, see www.tequilaexpress.com.mx.

open Monday through Saturday from 10am to 2:30pm and 3:30 to 7pm. Juárez 162. 📞 **33/3657-0316.**

Sergio Bustamante   Sergio Bustamante's imaginative, original bronze, ceramic, and papier-mâché sculptures are among the most

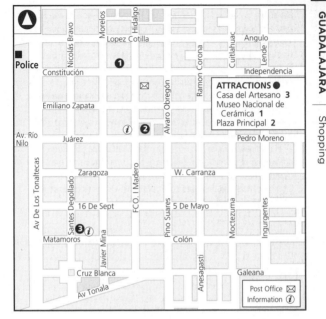

Map legend:
Police

ATTRACTIONS ●
Casa del Artesano **3**
Museo Nacional de
Cerámica **1**
Plaza Principal **2**

Post Office ⊠
Information ⓘ

sought-after in Mexico—as well as the most copied. He also designs silver jewelry. This exquisite gallery showcases his work. It's open Monday through Saturday from 10am to 7pm, Sunday from noon to 4pm. Independencia 238 at Cruz Verde. ⓒ **33/3639-5519.**

Teté Arte y Diseño Architectural decorative objects—especially hand-wrought-iron hardware for the "Old Mexico" look—are the specialty here. The store also has a large collection of wrought-iron chandeliers. It's open Monday through Saturday from 10am to 7:30pm. Juárez 173. ⓒ **33/3635-7347.**

TONALÁ: A TRADITION OF POTTERY MAKING

Tonalá ★★ is a pleasant town 10 minutes from Tlaquepaque. It is without question the largest concentration of artisans in Mexico and was a center of pottery making since pre-Hispanic times. Half of the more than 400 workshops here produce a wide variety of high- and low-temperature pottery. Other local artists work with forged iron, cantera stone, brass and copper, marble, miniatures,

China?

Mariachi & Ranchera

Mariachis, with their big sombreros, waist-length jackets and tight pants, embody the Mexican spirit. The music originated from Jalisco state's *son,* arranged for guitars, violins, string bass, and trumpets. Now heard across Mexico—Yucatecan trova music even has mariachi adaptations—and much of the American southwest, it is at its traditional best in Jalisco and its capital, Guadalajara.

The national pride, individualism, and sentimentality expressed in mariachi's kin, *ranchera,* earn it favored status as drinking music. Many Mexicans know the songs of famous composer **José Alfredo Jiménez** by heart.

Mexican-American singer/songwriter **Lila Downs** updated *ranchera* and mariachi for a modern, bicultural audience. Her debut album, *La Cantina,* explored traditional favorites, while her latest, *Shake Away,* features collaborations with famous Latin artists like Mercedes Sosa and Enrique Bunburry.

papier-mâché, textiles, blown glass, and gesso. This is a good place to look for custom work in any of these materials; you can locate a large pool of craftspeople by asking around a little.

Market days are Thursday and Sunday, when Tonalá reflects Mexico in all its chaotic glory. Expect large crowds and blocks and blocks of stalls displaying locally made pottery and glassware, cheap manufactured goods, food, and all kinds of bric-a-brac. You'll see herb men selling a rainbow selection of dried plants from wheelbarrows, magicians entertaining crowds, and craftspeople spreading their wares on the plaza's sidewalks. All kinds of crafts are for sale, most of which can be found in various parts of Mexico, but every now and then you'll come across something unique, produced by a local artisan. Visiting Tonalá on nonmarket days is easier. You can walk around more easily and find stores and workshops. Tonalá is the place for buying sets of margarita glasses, the widely seen blue-rimmed hand-blown glassware, finely painted *petatillo* ware, and the pottery typically associated with Mexico.

The **Tonalá Tourism Office** (© **33/1200-3912**) operates an information kiosk on the Plaza Principal (town square). It's open Monday to Friday from 9am to 2:30pm.

Tonalá is also the home of the **Museo Nacional de Cerámica,** Constitución 104, between Hidalgo and Morelos (© **33/3284-6000,** ext. 1523). The museum occupies most of the **Casa del Artesano,** which promotes local artisans. There is a store to the right just as you enter. You should take time to look through the store and its displays. If there's anything that interests you, ask the staff, who can tell you (in Spanish) about the different methods used to make pottery and other work and show you the difference between original methods and commercial shortcuts. If you like anything in particular they can direct you to the workshop where it was made and tell you of others that make something similar. The museum and store are open Monday through Friday from 9am to 8pm. Admission is free; the fee for using a video or still camera is 85 pesos per camera.

GUADALAJARA AFTER DARK
Mariachis

You can't go far in Guadalajara without coming across some maria-chis, but seeing really talented performers takes some effort. Try **Casa Bariachi,** Av. Vallarta 2221 (© **33/3615-0029**). In Tlaquepaque, go to **El Parián,** the building on the Plaza Principal where mariachis serenade diners under the archways.

The Club & Music Scene

Guadalajara, as you might expect, has a lot of variety in entertainment. For the most extensive listing of clubs and performances, get your hands on a copy of *Ocio,* the weekly insert of *Público*. You'll find listings in the back, categorized by type of music. For good mariachis, check out **Casa Bariachi**, mentioned above. Across the street from that club is another called **La Bodeguita del Medio** (© **33/3630-1620**), at Av. Vallarta 2320. It offers live old-school Cuban *son*. The groups come from Cuba and rotate every few months. The place is small, but people were making room to dance. Another thing to do is track down a Cuban diva named **Rosalia,** who lives in Guadalajara. She's a great talent and always has a tight band playing with her as she belts out salsa and meren-gue tunes.

FAST FACTS

FAST FACTS: MID-PACIFIC MEXICO

Area Codes **33** is the area code for Guadalajara; **322** for Puerto Vallarta; and **314** for Manzanillo.

Business Hours Most businesses in larger cities are open between 9am and 7pm; in smaller towns they may close between 2 and 4pm. Many are closed Sunday. In resort areas, stores commonly open in the mornings on Sunday, and shops stay open late, until 8 or even 10pm. Bank hours are Monday through Friday from 9 or 9:30am to anywhere between 3 and 7pm. Banks open on Saturday for at least a half-day.

Car Rental See "Getting There," p. 10.

Cellphones See "Mobile Phones," later in this section.

Crime See "Crime & Safety," p. 24.

Customs Mexican Customs inspection has been streamlined. At most points of entry, tourists are requested to press a button in front of what looks like a traffic signal, which alternates on touch between red and green. Green light and you go through without inspection; red light and your luggage or car may be inspected. If you have an unusual amount of luggage or an oversize piece, you may be subject to inspection anyway. Passengers who arrive by air will be required to put their bags through an x-ray machine, and then move to the kiosk and push a button to determine whether their luggage will be selected for any further inspection.

When you enter Mexico, Customs officials will be tolerant if you are not carrying illegal drugs or firearms. Tourists are allowed to bring in their personal effects duty-free. A laptop computer, camera equipment, and sports equipment that could feasibly be used during your stay are also allowed. The underlying guideline is: Don't bring anything that looks as if it's meant to be resold in Mexico. Those entering Mexico by air or sea can bring in gifts worth a value of up to $300 duty-free, except alcohol or tobacco products. The website for Mexican Customs (*aduanas*) is **www.aduanas.sat.gob.mx**.

Doctors Any embassy or consulate for an English-speaking country can provide a list of area doctors who speak English. If you get sick, consider asking your hotel concierge to recommend a local doctor—even his or her own. Some hotels even have in-house medical personnel. You can also try the emergency room at a local hospital or urgent care facility. Mexican doctors may not always have access to the latest technologies, and the quality of medical facilities varies, but they usually spend considerable time with patients and charge much less than their North American counterparts. Before choosing a doctor, you may want to ask for their qualifications and where they were trained.

Also see "Hospitals," below.

Drinking Laws The legal drinking age in Mexico is 18; however, being asked for ID or denied purchase happens extremely rarely. Grocery stores sell everything from beer and wine to national and imported liquors. You can buy liquor 24 hours a day, but during major elections, dry laws are often enacted as much as 72 hours in advance of the election—and they apply to tourists as well as local residents. Mexico does not have laws that apply to transporting liquor in cars, but authorities are beginning to crack down more aggressively on drunk drivers.

It's illegal to drink in the street, but many tourists do. If you are visibly drunk, you shouldn't drink in the street, because you are more likely to get stopped by the police.

Driving Rules See "Getting Around," p. 14.

Electricity The electrical system in Mexico is 110 volts AC (60 cycles), as in the United States and Canada. In reality, however, it may cycle more slowly and overheat your appliances. To compensate, select a medium or low speed on hair dryers. Many older hotels still have electrical outlets for flat two-prong plugs; you'll need an adapter for any plug with an enlarged end on one prong or with three prongs. Adapters are available in most Mexican electronics stores. Many better hotels have three-hole outlets (*trifásicos* in Spanish). Those that don't may loan adapters, but to be sure, it's always better to carry your own.

Embassies & Consulates Typical citizen services provided by country missions include passports, notaries, lists of doctors and lawyers, regulations concerning marriages in Mexico, emergency-preparedness information, and other valuable assistance. Contrary to popular belief, your embassy cannot get you out of jail, provide postal or banking services, or fly you home when you run out of money. Consular officers can provide advice on most matters and problems, however. Most countries have an embassy in Mexico City, and many have consular offices or representatives in the provinces.

It is a good idea to register with your embassy or consulate before visiting Mexico. The **Smart Traveler Enrollment Program (STEP)** is a free service provided by the U.S. Government to U.S. citizens who are traveling to, or living in, a foreign country. STEP allows travelers to enter information about their upcoming trips abroad so that the Department of State can better assist them in an emergency, and also allows Americans residing abroad to obtain routine information from the nearest U.S. embassy or consulate. Visit https://travelregistration.state.gov.

The Embassy of **Australia** in Mexico City is at Rubén Darío 55, Col. Polanco (© **55/1101-2200;** www.mexico.embassy.gov.au). It's open Monday through Thursday from 9:30am to noon.

The Embassy of **Canada** in Mexico City is at Schiller 529, in Polanco (© **55/5724-7900,** or 01-800/706-2900 for emergencies). It's open Monday through Friday from 9am to 1pm and 2 to 5pm. Visit www.dfait-maeci.gc.ca or www.canada.org.mx for addresses of consular agencies in Mexico. The **Consulate of Canada World Trade Center** in Guadalajara (© **33/3671-4730**) is in the Torre Pacifico, Av. Mariano Otero 1249, 8th Floor. The **Consular Agency of Canada** in Puerto Vallarta (© **322/293-0098**) sits in the Hotel Zone at Plaza Peninsula, Blvd. Francisco Medina Ascencio 2485.

The Embassy of **Ireland** in Mexico City is at Cda. Bl. Manuel Avila Camacho 76, 3rd Floor, Col. Lomas de Chapultepec (© **55/5520-5803;** www.irishembassy.com.mx). It's open Monday through Thursday from 8:30am to 5pm, and Friday from 8:30am to 1:30pm.

The Embassy of **New Zealand** in Mexico City is at Jaime Balmes 8, 4th Floor, Col. Los Morales, Polanco (© **55/5283-9460;** http://nzembassy.com/mexico). It's open Monday through Thursday from 8:30am to 2pm and 3 to 5:30pm, and Friday from 8:30am to 2pm.

The Embassy of the **United Kingdom** in Mexico City is at Río Lerma 71, Col. Cuauhtémoc (© **55/5207-2089** or 5242-8500; http://ukinmexico.fco.gov.uk/en). It's open Monday through Thursday from 8am to 4pm and Friday from 8am to 1:30pm.

The Embassy of the **United States** in Mexico City is at Paseo de la Reforma 305, next to the Hotel María Isabel Sheraton at the corner of Río Danubio (© **55/5080-2000;** http://mexico.us embassy.gov); hours are Monday through Friday from 8:30am to 5:30pm. The U.S. Consulate in Guadalajara (© **333/268-2100**) is located at Progreso 175. There is also a U.S. consular agent in Nuevo Vallarta (© **322/222-0069**) at Paseo de los Cocoteros 85 Sur in Paradise Plaza, Local L-7.

Emergencies   In case of emergency, dial © **066** from any phone within Mexico. Dial © **065** for the Red Cross. For police emergency numbers, turn to the "Fast Facts" sections in each of the individual chapters. The 24-hour Tourist Help Line in Mexico City is © **01-800/987-8224** in Mexico or 55/5089-7500, or you can now simply dial © **078.** The operators don't always speak English, but they are always willing to help.

Gasoline   See "Getting There," p. 10.

Hospitals   Many hospitals also have walk-in clinics for emergency cases that are not life-threatening; you may not get immediate attention, but you won't pay emergency room prices. The quality varies, but is often quite high, especially in resort towns.

See "Emergencies" and "Embassies & Consulates," above.

Insurance   While traveling in Mexico, you may have to pay all medical costs upfront and be reimbursed later. Before leaving home, find out what medical services your health insurance covers. To protect yourself, consider buying medical travel insurance.

For information on traveler's insurance, trip-cancellation insurance, and medical insurance while traveling, please visit www.frommers.com/planning.

Internet & Wi-Fi   Wi-Fi is increasingly common in Mexico's major cities and resorts. Mexico's largest airports offer Wi-Fi access, provided for a fee by Telcel's Prodigy Internet service. Most five-star hotels now offer Wi-Fi in the guest rooms for free or for a fee. Hotel lobbies often have Wi-Fi as well. To find public Wi-Fi hotspots in Mexico, go to **www.jiwire.com**; its Hotspot Finder holds the world's largest directory of public wireless hotspots.

Many large Mexican airports have Internet kiosks, and quality Mexican hotels usually have business centers with Internet access. You can also check out copy stores such as **FedEx Office** and **OfficeMax,** which offer computer stations with most standard software (as well as Wi-Fi).

Language   Spanish is the official language in Mexico. English is spoken and understood to some degree in most tourist areas. Mexicans are very accommodating toward foreigners who try to speak Spanish, even in broken sentences. See chapter 8 for a glossary of simple phrases for expressing basic needs.

Legal Aid   Embassies and consulates can often provide a list of respected lawyers in the area who speak English.

Mail   Postage for a postcard or letter varies depending on its destination; it may take anywhere from a week to over a month to arrive. The price for registered letters and packages depends on weight. The recommended way to send a package or important mail is through FedEx, DHL, UPS, or another reputable international mail service.

Medical Requirements   See "Health," p. 21.

Mobile Phones   **Telcel** is Mexico's expensive primary cellphone provider. It has upgraded its systems to GSM (Global System for Mobile Communications) and offers good coverage in much of the country, including the major cities and resorts. Most Mexicans buy their cellphones without a specific coverage plan and then pay as they go or purchase prepaid cards with set amounts of air-time credit. These cellphone cards with scratch-off PINs can be purchased in Telcel stores as well as many newspaper stands and convenience stores.

Many North American and European cellphone companies offer networks with roaming coverage in Mexico. Rates can be very high, so check with your provider before committing to making calls this way. An increasing number of Mexicans, particularly among the younger generation, prefer the less expensive rates of **Nextel** (www.nextel.com.mx), which features a range of service options. **Cellular Abroad** (www.cellularabroad.com) offers cellphone rentals and purchases as well as SIM cards for travel abroad. Whether you rent or purchase the cellphone, you need to purchase a SIM card that is specifically for Mexico.

Newspapers & Magazines   The English-language newspaper the *Miami Herald* is published in conjunction with *El Universal*. You can find it at most newsstands. *The News* is an English-language daily with Mexico-specific news, published in Mexico City. Newspaper kiosks in larger cities also carry a selection of English-language magazines.

Packing   In general, Mexico is an easy destination to pack for, as weather is consistent and predictable, and the style is casual and accepting. Check forecasts before you go and always bring something for cool nights. For more helpful information on packing for your trip, download our convenient **Travel Tools** app for your mobile device. Go to www.frommers.com/go/mobile and click on the Travel Tools icon.

Passports See "Entry Requirements," p. 8.

The following agencies can provide you with information on obtaining a passport.

Residents of Australia Contact the **Australian Passport Information Service** (© 131-232; www.passports.gov.au).

Residents of Canada Contact the **Passport Office,** Department of Foreign Affairs and International Trade, Ottawa, ON K1A 0G3 (© 800/567-6868; www.ppt.gc.ca).

Residents of Ireland Contact the **Passport Office,** Setanta Centre, Molesworth Street, Dublin 2 (© 01/671-1633; www.foreignaffairs.gov.ie).

Residents of New Zealand Contact the **Passports Office,** Department of Internal Affairs, 47 Boulcott St., Wellington, 6011 (© 0800/225-050 in New Zealand, or 04/474-8100; www.passports.govt.nz).

Residents of the United Kingdom Visit your nearest passport office, major post office, or travel agency, or contact the **Identity and Passport Service (IPS),** 89 Eccleston Square, London, SW1V 1PN (© 0300/222-0000; www.ips.gov.uk).

Residents of the United States To find your regional passport office, check the **U.S. State Department** website (travel.state.gov/passport) or call the **National Passport Information Center** (© 877/487-2778) for automated information.

Petrol Please see "Getting Around," p. 14.

Police Several Mexican cities, including Puerto Vallarta, have a special corps of English-speaking Tourist Police to assist with directions, guidance, and more. In case of emergency, dial © 060 or 066 from any phone within Mexico. For police emergency numbers, turn to "Fast Facts" in the individual chapters.

Smoking In early 2008, the Mexican president signed into law a nationwide smoking ban in workplaces, in public buildings, and on public transportation. Under this groundbreaking law, private businesses are permitted to allow smoking only in enclosed ventilated areas. Hotels may maintain up to 25% of guest rooms for smokers. Violators face stiff fines, and smokers refusing to comply could receive up to 36-hour jail sentences. The law places Mexico—where a significant percentage of the population smokes—at the forefront of efforts to curb smoking and improve public health in Latin America. So before you light up, be sure to ask about the application of local laws in public places and businesses you visit.

Taxes Mexico has a value-added tax of 16% (*Impuesto de Valor Agregado,* or IVA; pronounced "*ee*-bah") on most everything, including restaurant meals, bus tickets, and souvenirs. Hotels charge the usual 16% IVA, plus a locally administered bed tax of 3% (in most areas), for a total of 19%. The prices quoted by hotels and restaurants do not necessarily include IVA. You may find that upper-end properties (three or more stars) often quote prices without IVA included, while lower-priced hotels include IVA. Ask to see a printed price sheet, or ask if the tax is included.

Telephones Most telephone numbers have 10 digits. Every city and town that has telephone access has a two-digit area code (Mexico City, Monterrey, and Guadalajara) or three-digit area code (everywhere else). In Mexico City, Monterrey, and Guadalajara, local numbers have eight digits; elsewhere, local numbers have seven digits. To place a local call, you do not need to dial the area code. Many fax numbers are also regular phone numbers; ask whoever answers for the fax tone ("*me da tono de fax, por favor*").

The country code for Mexico is **52.**

To call Mexico:

1. Dial the international access code: **011** from the U.S. and Canada; 00 from the U.K., Ireland, or New Zealand; or **0011** from Australia.
2. Dial the country code: **52.**
3. Dial the two- or three-digit area code, then the eight- or seven-digit number. For example, if you wanted to call the U.S. consulate in Guadalajara (📞 333/268-2100), the entire number would be 011-52-333-268-2100. If you wanted to dial the U.S. embassy in Mexico City (📞 55/5080-2000), the entire number would be 011-52-55-5080-2000.

To make international calls: To make international calls from Mexico, dial **00,** then the country code (U.S. or Canada 1, U.K. 44, Ireland 353, Australia 61, New Zealand 64). Next, dial the area code and number. For example, to call the British Embassy in Washington (📞 202/588-7800), you would dial 00-1-202-588-7800.

To call a Mexican cellular number: From the same area code, dial **044** and then the number. To dial the cellular phone from anywhere else in Mexico, first dial **01,** and then the three-digit area code and the seven-digit number. To place an international call to a cellphone (for example, from the U.S.), you now must add a **1** after the country code: for example, 011-52-1 + 10-digit number.

For directory assistance: Dial 📞 **040** if you're looking for a number inside Mexico. *Note:* Listings usually appear under the owner's name, not the name of the business, and your chances of finding an English-speaking operator are slim.

For operator assistance: If you need operator assistance in making a call, dial ℭ **090** to make an international call, and ℭ **020** to call a number in Mexico.

Toll-free numbers: Numbers beginning with 800 within Mexico are toll-free, but calling a U.S. toll-free number from Mexico costs the same as an overseas call. To call an 800 number in the U.S., dial **001-880** and the last seven digits of the toll-free number. To call an 888 number in the U.S., dial **001-881** and the last seven digits of the toll-free number. For a number with an 887 prefix, dial **882;** for 866, dial **883.**

Time Central Time prevails from Manzanillo to Puerto Vallarta, while Mountain Zone extends along the coast north of Puerto Vallarta. All of Mexico observes daylight saving time.

Tipping Most service employees in Mexico count on tips for the majority of their income, and this is especially true for bellboys and waiters. Bellboys should receive the equivalent of 5 to 15 pesos per bag; waiters generally receive 10% to 15%, depending on the level of service. It is not customary to tip taxi drivers, unless they are hired by the hour or provide touring or other special services.

Toilets Public toilets are not common in Mexico, but an increasing number are available, especially at fast-food restaurants and Pemex gas stations. These facilities and restaurant and club restrooms commonly have attendants, who expect a small tip (about 5 pesos).

VAT See "Taxes" above.

Visas See "Entry Requirements," p. 8.

Visitor Information The **Mexico Tourism Board** (ℭ **800/44-MEXICO** [639-426] in the U.S.; or 01-800/006-8839 or 078 from within Mexico; www.visitmexico.com) is an excellent source for general information; you can request brochures and get answers from the exceptionally well-trained, knowledgeable staff. You can also call the Cancún location at ℭ **998/884-8073.**

The **Mexican Government Tourist Board**'s main office is in Mexico City (ℭ **55/5278-4200**). Satellite offices are in the U.S., Canada, and the U.K. In Canada: Toronto (ℭ **416/925-0704**). In the United Kingdom: London (ℭ **020/7488-9392**). In the United States: Chicago (ℭ **312/228-0517**), Houston (ℭ **713/772-2581**), Los Angeles (ℭ **213/739-6336**), Miami (ℭ **786/621-2909**), and New York (ℭ **212/308-2110**).

The **Mexican Embassy** in **Canada** is at 2055 Rue Peel, Bureau 100, Montreal, QUE, H3A 1V4 (📞 **514/288-2502**); Commerce Court West, 199 Bay St., Ste. 4440, Toronto, ON, M5L 1E9 (📞 **416/368-2875**); 411–117 W. Hastings Street, 4th Floor, Vancouver, BC, V6E2K3 (📞 **604/684-1859**); and 1500–45 O'Connor St., Ottawa, ON, K1P 1A4 (📞 **613/233-8988;** fax 613/235-9123).

The **Mexican Embassy** (Consular Section) in the **United Kingdom** is at 16 Georges St., London, W1S1FD (📞 **020/7499-8586**).

The **Mexican Embassy** in the **United States** is at 1911 Pennsylvania Ave. NW, Washington, DC 20006 (📞 **202/736-1600**).

Water   Tap water in Mexico is generally not potable, and it is safest to drink purified bottled water. Some hotels and restaurants purify their water, but you should ask rather than assume this is the case. Ice may also come from tap water and should be used with caution.

Wi-Fi   See "Internet & Wi-Fi," earlier in this section.

AIRLINE WEBSITES
MAJOR AIRLINES

Aeromexico
www.aeromexico.com

Alaska Airlines/Horizon Air
www.alaskaair.com

American Airlines
www.aa.com

British Airways
www.british-airways.com

Continental Airlines
www.continental.com

Delta Air Lines
www.delta.com

Iberia Airlines
www.iberia.com

United Airlines
www.united.com

US Airways
www.usairways.com

Virgin America
www.virginamerica.com

Virgin Atlantic Airways
www.virgin-atlantic.com

BUDGET AIRLINES

Frontier Airlines
www.frontierairlines.com

Interjet
www.interjet.com.mx

JetBlue Airways
www.jetblue.com

Volaris
www.volaris.com.mx

USEFUL TERMS & PHRASES

SURVIVAL SPANISH

Most Mexicans are very patient with foreigners who try to speak their language; it helps a lot to know a few basic phrases. Included here are simple phrases for expressing basic needs, followed by some common menu items.

ESSENTIAL PHRASES

English	Spanish	Pronunciation
Hello	**Hola**	*Oh*-lah
Good day	**Buen día**	Bwehn *dee*-ah
Good morning	**Buenos días**	*Bweh*-nohs *dee*-ahs
Good afternoon	**Buenos tardes**	*Bweh*-nohs *tahr*-dehs
Good evening	**Buenos noches**	*Bweh*-nohs *noh*-chehs
How are you?	**¿Cómo está?**	*Koh*-moh eh-*stah*
Very well	**Muy bien**	Mwee byehn
My name is . . .	**Me llamo . . .**	meh *yah*-mo
And yours?	**¿Y usted?**	ee oos-*tehd*
It's a pleasure to meet you.	**Es un placer conocerle.**	*Ehs* oon plah-*sehr* koh-noh-*sehr*-leh
Thank you	**Gracias**	*Grah*-syahs
You're welcome	**De nada**	Deh *nah*-dah
Goodbye	**Adiós**	Ah-*dyohs*
Please	**Por favor**	Pohr fah-*bohr*
Yes	**Sí**	See
No	**No**	Noh
Okay	**De acuerdo**	Deh ah-*kwehr*-doh
No problem	**No hay problema**	Noh aye proh-*bleh*-mah
Excuse me	**Perdóneme**	Pehr-*doh*-neh-meh
Give me	**Déme**	*Deh*-meh

English	Spanish	Pronunciation
Where is . . . ?	¿Dónde está . . . ?	*Dohn*-deh eh-*stah*
the station	la estación	lah eh-stah-*syohn*
a hotel	un hotel	oon oh-*tehl*
a gas station	una gasolinera	*oo*-nah gah-soh-lee-*neh*-rah
a restaurant	un restaurante	oon res-tow-*rahn*-teh
the toilet	el baño	el *bah*-nyoh
a good doctor	un buen médico	oon bwehn *meh*-dee-coh
the road to . . .	el camino a/ hacia	el cah-*mee*-noh ah/*ah*-syah
To the right	A la derecha	Ah lah deh-*reh*-chah
To the left	A la izquierda	Ah lah ees-*kyehr*-dah
Straight ahead	Derecho	Deh-*reh*-choh
I would like	Quisiera	Key-*syeh*-rah
I want . . .	Quiero	*Kyeh*-roh
to eat	comer	koh-*mehr*
a room	una habitación	*oo*-nah ah-bee-tah-*syohn*
Do you have . . . ?	¿Tiene usted . . . ?	Tyeh-neh oo-*sted*
a book	un libro	oon *lee*-broh
a dictionary	un diccionario	oon deek-syoh-*nah*-ryoh
How much is it?	¿Cuánto cuesta?	*Kwahn*-toh *kweh*-stah
When?	¿Cuándo?	*Kwahn*-doh
Who?	¿Quién? ¿Quiénes?	*Kyehn*; *Kyeh*-nehs
What?	¿Qué?	Keh
There is (Is there . . . ?)	(¿)Hay (. . . ?)	Eye
What is there?	¿Qué hay?	Keh eye
Good	Bueno	*Bweh*-noh
Bad	Malo	*Mah*-loh
Better (best)	(Lo) Mejor	(Loh) Meh-*hohr*
More	Más	Mahs
Less	Menos	*Meh*-nohs
No smoking	Se prohibe fumar	Seh proh-*ee*-beh foo-*mahr*
Postcard	Tarjeta postal	Tar-*heh*-tah poh-*stahl*
Insect repellent	Repelente contra insectos	Reh-peh-*lehn*-teh *cohn*-trah een-*sehk*-tohs
Do you speak English?	¿Habla usted inglés?	*Ah*-blah oo-*sted* een-*glehs*

English	Spanish	Pronunciation
Is there anyone here who speaks English?	**¿Hay alguien aquí que hable inglés?**	Eye *ahl*-gyehn ah-*kee* keh *ah*-bleh een-*glehs*
I speak a little Spanish.	**Hablo un poco de español.**	*Ah*-bloh oon *poh*-koh deh eh-spah-*nyohl*
I don't understand Spanish very well.	**No (lo) entiendo muy bien el español.**	Noh (loh) ehn-*tyehn*-doh mwee byehn el eh-spah-*nyohl*
I'm sorry, I don't understand.	**Lo siento, no entiendo.**	Loh *syehn*-toh no ehn-*tyehn*-doh
Do you speak any other languages?	**¿Usted habla otro idioma?**	Oos-*tehd* ah-blah *oh*-troh ee-*dyoh*-ma
I speak ____ better than Spanish.	**Yo hablo ____ mejor que español.**	Yoh *ah*-bloh ____ meh-*hohr* keh ehs-pah-*nyol*
Would you speak slower please?	**¿Puede hablar un poco más lento?**	*Pweh*-deh ah-*blahr* oon *poh*-koh mahs *lehn*-to
Would you spell that?	**¿Puede deletrear eso?**	*Pweh*-de deh-leh-treh-*ahr* eh-*so*
Would you please repeat that?	**¿Puede repetir, por favor?**	*Pweh*-deh reh-peh-*teer* pohr fah-*vohr*
May I see your menu?	**¿Puedo ver el menú (la carta)?**	*Pweh*-doh vehr el meh-*noo* (lah *car*-tah)
Do I need a reservation?	**¿Necesito una reservación?**	Neh-seh-*see*-toh oo-nah reh-sehr-vah-*syohn*
The meal is good.	**Me gusta la comida.**	Meh *goo*-stah lah koh-*mee*-dah
The check, please.	**La cuenta, por favor.**	Lah *kwehn*-tah pohr fa-*borh*
What do I owe you?	**¿Cuánto le debo?**	*Kwahn*-toh leh *deh*-boh
What did you say?	**¿Mande?** (formal) **¿Cómo?** (informal)	*Mahn*-deh *Koh*-moh
I want (to see) . . .	**Quiero (ver) . . .**	*kyeh*-roh (vehr)
a room	**un cuarto** or **una habitación**	oon *kwar*-toh, *oo*-nah ah-bee-tah-*syohn*
for two persons	**para dos personas**	*pah*-rah dohs pehr-*soh*-nahs
with (without) bathroom	**con (sin) baño**	kohn (seen) *bah*-nyoh

English	Spanish	Pronunciation
We are staying here only . . .	**Nos quedamos aquí solamente . . .**	Nohs keh-*dah*-mohs ah-*kee* soh-lah-*mehn*-teh
one night.	**una noche.**	*oo*-nah *noh*-cheh
one week.	**una semana.**	*oo*-nah seh-*mah*-nah
We are leaving . . .	**Partimos (Salimos) . . .**	Pahr-*tee*-mohs (sah-*lee*-mohs)
tomorrow.	**mañana.**	mah-*nya*-nah
Do you accept . . . ?	**¿Acepta usted . . . ?**	Ah-*sehp*-tah oo-*sted*
traveler's checks?	**cheques de via-jero?**	*cheh*-kehs deh byah-*heh*-roh

8

NUMBERS

English	Spanish	English	Spanish
1	**uno** (ooh-noh)	17	**diecisiete** (dyeh-see-syeh-teh)
2	**dos** (dohs)	18	**dieciocho** (dyeh-syoh-choh)
3	**tres** (trehs)	19	**diecinueve** (dyeh-see-nweh-beh)
4	**cuatro** (kwah-troh)	20	**veinte** (bayn-teh)
5	**cinco** (seen-koh)	30	**treinta** (trayn-tah)
6	**seis** (sayes)	40	**cuarenta** (kwah-ren-tah)
7	**siete** (syeh-teh)	50	**cincuenta** (seen-kwen-tah)
8	**ocho** (oh-choh)	60	**sesenta** (seh-sehn-tah)
9	**nueve** (nweh-beh)	70	**setenta** (seh-tehn-tah)
10	**diez** (dyehs)	80	**ochenta** (oh-chehn-tah)
11	**once** (ohn-seh)	90	**noventa** (noh-behn-tah)
12	**doce** (doh-seh)	100	**cien** (syehn)
13	**trece** (treh-seh)	200	**doscientos** (do-syehn-tohs)
14	**catorce** (kah-tohr-seh)	500	**quinientos** (kee-nyehn-tohs)
15	**quince** (keen-seh)	1,000	**mil** (meel)
16	**dieciséis** (dyeh-see-sayes)		

TIME

English	Spanish	Pronunciation
What time is it?	**¿Qué hora es?**	Keh *oh*-ra ehs
At what time?	**¿A qué hora?**	Ah *keh oh*-rah
For how long?	**¿Por cuánto tiempo?**	Pohr *kwahn*-toh *tyehm*-poh
It's one o'clock.	**Es la una en punto.**	Ehs lah *oo*-nah ehn *poon*-toh
It's two o'clock.	**Son las dos en punto.**	Sohn lahs *dohs* ehn *poon*-toh
It's two thirty.	**Son las dos y media.**	Sohn lahs *dohs* ee *meh*-dyah
It's two fifteen.	**Son las dos y cuarto.**	Sohn lahs *dohs* ee *kwahr*-toh

DAYS OF THE WEEK

English	Spanish
Sunday	**el domingo** (ehl doh-*meeng*-go)
Monday	**el lunes** (ehl *loo*-nehs)
Tuesday	**el martes** (ehl *mahr*-tehs)
Wednesday	**el miércoles** (ehl *myehr*-koh-lehs)
Thursday	**el jueves** (ehl *hweh*-vehs)
Friday	**el viernes** (ehl *vyehr*-nehs)
Saturday	**el sábado** (ehl *sah*-bah-doh)
today	**hoy** (oy)
tomorrow	**mañana** (mah-*nyah*-nah)
yesterday	**ayer** (ah-*yehr*)
the day before yesterday	**anteayer** (ahn-teh-ah-*yehr*)
one week	**una semana** (*oo*-nah seh-*mah*-nah)
next week	**la próxima semana** (lah *prohk*-see-mah seh-*mah*-nah)
last week	**la semana pasada** (lah seh-*mah*-nah pah-*sah*-dah)

MONTHS OF THE YEAR

English	Spanish
January	**enero** (eh-*neh*-roh)
February	**febrero** (feh-*breh*-roh)
March	**marzo** (*mahr*-soh)
April	**abril** (ah-*breel*)

English	Spanish
May	**mayo** (*mah*-yoh)
June	**junio** (*hoo*-nee-oh)
July	**julio** (*hoo*-lee-oh)
August	**agosto** (ah-*gohs*-toh)
Septembe	**septiembre** (sehp-*tyehm*-breh)
October	**octubre** (ohk-*too*-breh)
November	**noviembre** (noh-*vyehm*-breh)
December	**diciembre** (dee-*syehm*-breh)
next month	**el próximo mes** (ehl *prohk*-see-moh *mehs*)
last month	**el mes pasado** (ehl *mehs* pah-*sah*-doh)

TRANSPORTATION TERMS

English	Spanish	Pronunciation
airport	**Aeropuerto**	Ah-eh-roh-*pwehr*-toh
flight	**Vuelo**	*Bweh*-loh
rental-car agency	**Arrendadora de autos**	Ah-*rehn*-da-doh-rah deh *ow*-tohs
bus	**Autobús**	Ow-toh-*boos*
bus or truck	**Camión**	Ka-*myohn*
lane	**Carril**	Kah-*reel*
nonstop (bus)	**Directo**	Dee-*rehk*-toh
baggage (claim area)	**Equipajes**	Eh-kee-*pah*-hehss
intercity	**Foraneo**	Foh-rah-*neh*-oh
luggage storage area	**Guarda equipaje**	*Gwar*-dah eh-kee-*pah*-heh
arrival gates	**Llegadas**	Yeh-*gah*-dahss
originates at this station	**Local**	Loh-*kahl*
originates elsewhere	**De paso**	Deh *pah*-soh
Are seats available?	**Hay lugares disponibles?**	Eye loo-*gah*-rehs dis-pohn-*ee*-blehss
first class	**Primera**	Pree-*meh*-rah
second class	**Segunda**	Seh-*goon*-dah
nonstop (flight)	**Sin escala**	Seen ess-*kah*-lah
baggage claim area	**Recibo de equipajes**	Reh-*see*-boh deh eh-kee-*pah*-hehss
waiting room	**Sala de espera**	*Sah*-lah deh ehss-*peh*-rah
toilets	**Sanitarioss**	Sah-nee-*tah*-ryohss
ticket window	**Taquilla**	Tah-*kee*-yah

DINING TERMINOLOGY
Meals

desayuno Breakfast.

comida Main meal of the day, taken in the afternoon.

cena Supper.

Courses

botana A small serving of food that accompanies a beer or drink, usually served free of charge.

entrada Appetizer.

sopa Soup course. (Not necessarily a soup—it can be a dish of rice or noodles, called *sopa seca* [dry soup].)

ensalada Salad.

plato fuerte Main course.

postre Dessert.

comida corrida Inexpensive daily special usually consisting of three courses.

menú del día Same as *comida corrida*.

Degree of Doneness

término un cuarto Rare, literally means one-fourth.

término medio Medium rare, one-half.

término tres cuartos Medium, three-fourths.

bien cocido Well-done.

Note: Keep in mind, when ordering a steak, that *medio* does not mean "medium."

Miscellaneous Restaurant Terminology

cucharra Spoon.

cuchillo Knife.

la cuenta The bill.

plato Plate.

plato hondo Bowl.

propina Tip.

servilleta Napkin.

tenedor Fork.

vaso   Glass.

IVA   Value-added tax.

fonda   Strictly speaking, a food stall in the market or street, but now used in a loose or nostalgic sense to designate an informal restaurant.

Popular Mexican Dishes

a la tampiqueña   (Usually *bistec a la tampiqueña* or *arrachera a la tampiqueña*) A steak served with several sides, including but not limited to an enchilada, guacamole, rice, and beans.

adobo   Marinade made with chiles and tomatoes, often seen in adjectival form *adobado/adobada*.

albóndigas   Meatballs, usually cooked in a chile chipotle sauce.

antojito   Literally means "small temptation." It's a general term for tacos, tostadas, quesadillas, and the like, which are usually eaten for supper or as a snack.

arrachera   Skirt steak, fajitas.

arroz   Rice.

bistec   Steak.

bolillo   Small bread with a crust much like a baguette.

buñuelos   Fried pastry dusted with sugar. Can also mean a large, thin, crisp pancake that is dipped in boiling cane syrup.

cajeta   Thick caramel sauce made from goat's milk.

calabaza   Zucchini squash.

caldo tlalpeño   Chicken and vegetable soup, with rice, chile chipotle, avocado, and garbanzos. Its name comes from a suburban community of Mexico City, Tlalpan.

caldo xochitl   Mild chicken and rice soup served with a small plate of chopped onion, chile serrano, avocado, and limes, to be added according to individual taste.

camarones   Shrimp. For common cooking methods, see *pescado.*

carne   Meat.

carnitas   Slow-cooked pork dish from Michoacán and parts of central Mexico, served with tortillas, guacamole, and salsa or pickled jalapeños.

cebolla   Onion.

cecina   Thinly sliced pork or beef, dried or marinated, depending on the region.

ceviche Fresh raw seafood marinated in fresh lime juice and garnished with chopped tomatoes, onions, chiles, and sometimes cilantro.

chalupas poblanas Simple dish from Puebla consisting of handmade tortillas lightly fried but left soft, and topped with different chile sauces.

chayote Spiny squash boiled and served as an accompaniment to meat dishes.

chilaquiles Fried tortilla quarters softened in either a red or a green sauce and served with Mexican sour cream, onion, and sometimes chicken *(con pollo)*.

chile Any of the many hot peppers used in Mexican cooking, in fresh, dried, or smoked forms.

chile ancho A dried *chile poblano,* which serves as the base for many varieties of sauces and *moles.*

chile chilpotle (or **chipotle**) A smoked jalapeño dried or in an *adobo* sauce.

chile en nogada *Chile poblano* stuffed with a complex filling of shredded meat, nuts, and dried, candied, and fresh fruit, topped with walnut cream sauce and a sprinkling of pomegranate seeds.

chile poblano Fresh pepper that is usually dark green in color, large, and not usually spicy. Often stuffed with a variety of fillings (chile relleno).

chile relleno Stuffed pepper.

chivo Kid or goat.

cochinita pibil Yucatecan dish of pork, pit-baked in a *pibil* sauce of *achiote,* sour orange, and spices.

col Cabbage. Also called *repollo.*

consomé Clear broth, usually with rice.

cortes Steak; in full, it is *cortes finas de carne* (fine cuts of meat).

cuitlacoche Variant of *huitlacoche.*

elote Fresh corn.

empanada For most of Mexico, a turnover with a savory or sweet filling. In Oaxaca and southern Mexico, it is corn *masa* or a tortilla folded around a savory filling and roasted or fried.

empanizado Breaded.

enchilada A lightly fried tortilla, dipped in sauce and folded or rolled around a filling. It has many variations, such as *enchiladas* *suizas* (made with a cream sauce), enchiladas del portal or enchiladas placeras (made with a predominantly *chile ancho* sauce), and enchiladas verdes (in a green sauce of tomatillos, cilantro, and chiles).

enfrijoladas   Like an enchilada, but made with a bean sauce.

enmoladas   Enchiladas made with a *mole* sauce.

entomatadas   Enchiladas made with a tomato sauce.

escabeche   Vegetables pickled in a vinegary liquid.

flan   Custard.

flautas   Tortillas that are rolled up around a filling (usually chicken or shredded beef) and deep-fried; often listed on a menu as *taquitos* or *tacos fritos*.

gorditas   Thick, fried corn tortillas, slit open and stuffed with meat or cheese.

horchata   Drink made of ground rice, melon seeds, ground almonds, or coconut and cinnamon.

huazontle   A vegetable vaguely comparable to broccoli, but milder in taste.

huitlacoche   Salty and mild-tasting corn fungus that is considered a delicacy.

jitomate   Tomato.

lechuga   Lettuce.

limón   A small lime. Mexicans squeeze them on everything from soups to tacos.

lomo adobado   Pork loin cooked in an *adobo*.

masa   Soft dough made of corn that is the basis for making tortillas and tamales.

menudo   Soup made with beef tripe and hominy.

milanesa   Beef cutlet breaded and fried.

mole   Any variety of thick sauce made with dried chiles, nuts, fruit or vegetables, and spices. Variations include *mole poblano* (Puebla style, with chocolate and sesame), *mole negro* (black *mole* from Oaxaca, also with chocolate), and *m. verde* (made with herbs and/or pumpkinseeds, depending on the region).

pan   Bread. A few of the varieties include *p. dulce* (general term for a variety of sweet breads), *pan de muerto* (bread made for the Day of the Dead holidays), and *pan Bimbo* (packaged sliced white bread).

panuchos A Yucatecan dish of *masa* cakes stuffed with refried black beans and topped with shredded turkey or chicken, lettuce, and onion.

papas Potatoes.

papadzules A Yucatecan dish of tortillas stuffed with hard-boiled eggs and topped with a sauce made of pumpkinseeds.

parrillada A sampler platter of grilled meats or seafood.

pescado Fish. Common ways of cooking fish include *al mojo de ajo* (pan seared with oil and garlic), *a la veracruzana* (with tomatoes, olives, and capers), and *al ajillo* (seared with garlic and fine strips or rings of *chile guajillo*).

pibil See *cochinita pibil.* When made with chicken, it is called *pollo pibil.*

picadillo Any of several recipes using shredded beef, pork, or chicken and onions, chiles, and spices. Can also contain fruit and nuts.

pipián A thick sauce made with ground pumpkinseeds, nuts, herbs, and chiles. Can be red or green.

poc chuc A Yucatecan dish of grilled pork with onion marinated in sour orange.

pollo Chicken.

pozole Soup with chicken or pork, hominy, lettuce, and radishes, served with a small plate of other ingredients to be added according to taste (onion, pepper, lime juice, oregano). In Jalisco it's red *(p. rojo)*, in Michoacán it's clear *(p. blanco)*, and in Guerrero it's green *(p. verde)*. In the rest of Mexico, it can be any one of these.

puerco Pork.

quesadilla Corn or flour tortillas stuffed with white cheese and cooked on a hot griddle. In Mexico City, it is made with raw *masa* folded around any of a variety of fillings (often containing no cheese) and deep-fried.

queso Cheese.

res Beef.

rompope Mexican liqueur, made with eggs, vanilla, sugar, and alcohol.

salbute A Yucatecan dish like a *panucho,* but without bean paste in the middle.

sopa azteca Tortilla soup.

sopa tarasca   A blended soup from Michoacán made with beans and tomatoes.

sope   Small fried *masa* cake topped with savory meats and greens.

tacos al pastor   Small tacos made with thinly sliced pork marinated in an *adobo* and served with pineapple, onion, and cilantro.

tamal   (Not "tamale.") *Masa* mixed with lard and beaten until light and folded around a savory or sweet filling, and encased in a cornhusk or a plant leaf (usually corn or banana) and then steamed. *Tamales* is the plural form.

taquitos   See *flautas.*

tinga   Shredded meat stewed in a chile chipotle sauce.

torta   A sandwich made with a *bolillo*.

Index

See also Accommodations and
Restaurant indexes, below.

General Index

Accommodations

Restaurants